COMPUTATION INTO CRITICISM

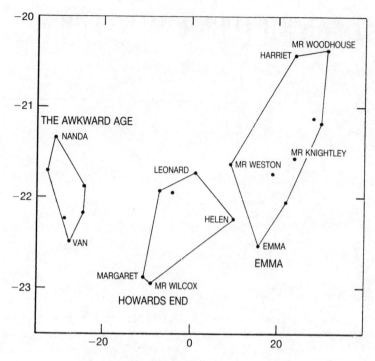

Some Major Characters of Three Novels
(Relative locations of basic idiolects)

COMPUTATION INTO CRITICISM

A *Study of Jane Austen's Novels*
and
an Experiment in Method

J. F. BURROWS

CLARENDON PRESS · OXFORD
1987

Oxford University Press, Walton Street, Oxford OX2 6DP
Oxford New York Toronto
Delhi Bombay Calcutta Madras Karachi
Petaling Jaya Singapore Hong Kong Tokyo
Nairobi Dar es Salaam Cape Town
Melbourne Auckland
and associated companies in
Beirut Berlin Ibadan Nicosia

Oxford is a trade mark of Oxford University Press

Published in the United States
by Oxford University Press, New York

British Library Cataloguing in Publication Data
Burrows, J. F.
Computation into criticism: a study of Jane
Austen's novels and an experiment in method.
1. Austen, Jane—Criticism and interpretation
I. Title
823'.7   PR4037
ISBN 0-19-812856-8

Library of Congress Cataloging in Publication Data
Burrows, John Frederick
Computation into criticism.
Includes index.
1. Austen, Jane, 1775-1817—Technique.
2. Characters and characteristics in literature.
3. Speech in literature.
4. Criticism—Data processing.
I. Title. PR4038.T4B87
1986   823'.7   86-12482
ISBN 0-19-812856-8

Phototypeset by Dobbie Typesetting Service,
Plymouth, Devon
Printed in Great Britain
at the University Printing House, Oxford
by David Stanford
Printer to the University

There's nothing you can't turn into a sum, for there's nothing but what's got number in it.

George Eliot, *Adam Bede*, Bk. II, ch. xxi

'What's the *use*? Let's show him, Josh.' And he passed the canister to the other guy, who takes out a spool of tape and fits it on to one of the machines. 'Come over here', says Dempsey, and sits me down in front of a kind of typewriter with a TV screen attached. 'With that tape,' he said, 'we can request the computer to supply us with any information we like about your idiolect.' 'Come again?' I said. 'Your own special, distinctive, unique way of using the English language. What's your favourite word?' 'My favourite word. I don't have one.' 'Oh yes you do!' he said. 'The word you use most frequently.' 'That's probably *the* or *a* or *and*,' I said. He shook his head impatiently. 'We instruct the computer to ignore what we call grammatical words — articles, prepositions, pronouns, modal verbs, which have a high frequency rating in all discourse. Then we get to the real nitty-gritty, what we call the lexical words, the words that carry a distinctive semantic content. Words like *love* or *dark* or *heart* or *God*. Let's see.' So he taps away on the keyboard and instantly my favourite word appears on the screen. What do you think it was?

David Lodge, *Small World*, Bk. III, ch. 1

ACKNOWLEDGEMENTS

Everyone who has spent the greater part of a professional lifetime in the teaching and study of literature bears more debts than he can ever recognize to his predecessors, his contemporaries, and his students. Among the more recognizable debts, for any student of Jane Austen, are those owed to R. W. Chapman, as editor and grandmaster of the documents; to Mary Lascelles, whose book-length study, published in 1939, remains unsurpassed for subtlety of mind and attunement to its subject; and to a multitude of others ranging from Richard Simpson and G. H. Lewes, authors of the best nineteenth-century writings on the subject, to those more recent scholars and critics whose growing command of the historical background and whose attention to nuances continue to enrich our understanding. Among those who have given particular emphasis to Jane Austen's language, I am especially indebted to R. W. Chapman, Howard Babb, K. C. Phillipps, Norman Page, Stuart M. Tave, and F. W. Bradbrook. But to the extent that the emphasis has almost entirely fallen upon matters of *visible* interest and importance, the present study stands some way apart from any of theirs. Even G. L. Dillon's remarkable treatment of poetic syntax, *Language Processing and the Language of Literature* (Bloomington, 1978), is focused on unusual and difficult structures and not on the common staple of the language.

In the broader field of communication-theory, however, there is the work of Gregory Bateson in *Steps to an Ecology of Mind* (London, 1972); that of George K. Zipf in *Human Behavior and the Principle of Least Effort* (Cambridge, Mass., 1949); and that of more recent scholars who have built upon the foundations laid by these and other pioneers. Work of this kind makes a capacious and appropriate framework for the argument that the commonest words of all have at least as rich and various a part to play in the conduct of ideas and the diversities of 'style', even within a single novel, as have the time-hallowed schemes of tropes and figures, or the image-clusters and the keywords elucidated by more recent scholars.

While I should hope to observe the proper courtesies as this book proceeds, the evidence is too complex to bear the weight of any more footnotes than prove strictly necessary. All those mentioned above and many others have influenced the argument that follows in one way or another. They are not to be thought responsible for errors or shortcomings of any kind.

The same *caveat* applies to those to whom I am indebted in other ways. The Council of St John's College, Cambridge, elected me as Commonwealth Fellow for 1979–80 and have harboured me on two more recent visits. The period of the Fellowship marked the effective beginning of the research-project on which the present study is based. It is a pleasure, therefore, to be writing these pages in Cambridge under the kindly aegis of the Master and Fellows and—if 'aegis' is not too narrow a word to use of the dead—of such former Fellows as G. Udney Yule, Gregory Bateson, N. F. M. Henry, and Hugh Sykes Davies. The Research Committee and the English Department of the University of Newcastle, NSW, have given considerable financial and immeasurable moral support. Without the generous funding of the Australian Research Grants Scheme, it would have been impossible to prepare a large enough set of machine-readable texts and concordances.

J. L. Dawson and the Ven. Sik K. Yeshe Zangmo, of the Literary and Linguistic Computing Centre in Cambridge University; N. M. McLaren, of the University of Cambridge Computing Service; Susan Hockey and Alan Jones, of the Oxford University Computing Service; and John Lambert of the University of Newcastle (and those whose work will be described in the Introduction) have all given more reliable help and valuable advice than anyone could reasonably expect on entering an unfamiliar field. Especially when my argument touches on questions of literary theory, David Boyd, of the University of Newcastle, has done his best to make me read and think—and read and think again. N. Collis-George, of the University of Sydney, has led me out of ignorance into any glimmer of statistical competence that emerges in these pages.

My remaining debts are to those colleagues and friends—the terms are practically synonymous—who have assisted towards the publication of parts of the work-in-progress, resolved an unexpected problem, or read and commented more generously than I have often deserved. G. A. Wilkes, J. P. Hardy, Mary Lascelles, N. R. Cattell, K. R. Dutton, D. L. Frost, A. J. Hassall, P. L. Kavanagh,

C. W. F. McKenna, D. M. Osland, and C. J. Rawson have all figured prominently in these phases of a long drawn-out affair. The graphs were drawn by B. K. Marsden. Marie Hill has acquired the art of typing pages of data of a kind that no ordinary Secretary of an English Department would wish to see on her desk. Apart from their more direct help, my wife and our three daughters have not faltered in the extraordinary belief that something worthwhile would find its way out of the muddle of words and numbers. Whether that belief is justified is for others to determine.

For permission to prepare machine-readable texts my thanks are due to the following: Oxford University Press, for the Oxford Illustrated Edition of Jane Austen's novels (ed. R. W. Chapman); Messrs William Heinemann Ltd., for *Sanditon* by Jane Austen and Another Lady (London, 1975); Messrs Booker McConnell PLC, for *Frederica* by Georgette Heyer (London, 1965); Hogarth Press, for *The Waves* by Virginia Woolf (London, 1931); Messrs Edward Arnold and Messrs Alfred A. Knopf, for *Howards End* by E. M. Forster (London, 1910); Messrs Charles Scribner's Sons, for *The Awkward Age* by Henry James (New York, 1908).

I am grateful to *The British Journal for Eighteenth-Century Studies* for permission to draw on an article of my own: '"Nothing out of the Ordinary Way": Differentiation of Character in the Twelve Most Common Words of *Northanger Abbey*, *Mansfield Park*, and *Emma*', *BJECS*, vi (1983), 17–41.

Addendum, June 1986

There is growing scholarly support for the belief that M. M. Bakhtin used the name of V. Vološinov for some of his important theoretical writings: see, for example, Michael Holquist's Introduction to *The Dialogic Imagination: Four Essays by M. M. Bakhtin* (Austin, 1981). The argument of the fourth essay, 'Discourse in the Novel', is especially congenial to the present study but I am content to stand by the reservations offered in Chapter 9, below.

CONTENTS

Appendices

LIST OF TABLES, GRAPHS, AND FIGURES

TABLES

GRAPHS

FIGURES

ABBREVIATIONS

AA Henry James, *The Awkward Age* (New York, New York Edition, 1908).

E *Emma.*

F Georgette Heyer, *Frederica* (London, 1965).

HE E. M. Forster, *Howards End* (London, 1st edn., 1910).

JA Jane Austen's Six Novels, ed. R. W. Chapman (Oxford Illustrated Edition: 3rd edn., 1932–5).

MP *Mansfield Park.*

NA *Northanger Abbey.*

P *Persuasion.*

PP *Pride and Prejudice.*

S1 'Sanditon', *Minor Works*, ed. R. W. Chapman (1st edn., 1954).

S2 *Sanditon*, by Jane Austen and Another Lady (London, 1975). (Our analysis treats only of that part of the text, much the larger part, which begins at the point where Jane Austen's manuscript breaks off.)

SS *Sense and Sensibility.*

TW Virginia Woolf, *The Waves* (London, 1st edn., 1931).

KEY TO GRAPHS AND TABLES

Dialogue
Character-tags and Distribution of Word-Tokens among Characters

D: ALL	Jane Austen's dialogue	307,360		Dialogue of other novels:	
D1:	**Northanger Abbey**	**28930**	D7:	**'Sanditon'**	**10702**
1A	CATHERINE	7040	7P	Mr Parker	3536
1B	HENRY TILNEY	6149	7S	Diana Parker	2604
1D	Isabella Thorpe	5657	7H	Lady Denham	1562
1E	John Thorpe	2928	7X	Others	3000
1C	Eleanor Tilney	1938			
1X	Others	5218	D8:	**Sanditon 2**	**30023**
			8B	'SIDNEY PARKER'	8491
D2:	**Sense and Sensibility**	**52334**	8A	'CHARLOTTE HEYWOOD'	4108
2A	ELINOR	9039	8P	'Mr Parker'	2785
2C	Marianne	6580	8G	'Reginald Catton'	2700
2K	Mrs Jennings	5659	8H	'Lady Denham'	2090
2S	Willoughby	5278	8X	Others	9849
2F	John Dashwood	4462			
2Q	Lucy Steele	3977	D9:	**Frederica**	**69355**
2H	Colonel Brandon	3700	9B	ALVERSTOKE	20598
2D	Mrs Dashwood	3560	9A	FREDERICA MERRIVILLE	20479
2B	EDWARD FERRARS	2359	9F	Jessamy Merriville	3983
2P	Anne Steele	2066	9C	Charles Trevor	3285
2X	Others	5654	9D	Harry Merriville	3037
			9K	Lady Elizabeth	2352
D3:	**Pride and Prejudice**	**55976**	9E	Charis Merriville	2141
3A	ELIZABETH	13597	9X	Others	13480
3B	DARCY	6399			
3D	Mrs Bennet	6048	D10:	**The Waves**	**72054**
3E	Jane	5203	10A	Bernard	30972
3K	Collins	4444	10C	Neville	9713
3C	Mr Bennet	3248	10B	Louis	8437
3O	Mrs Gardiner	2865	10E	Rhoda	8227
3L	Lady Catherine	2342	10D	Jinny	6143
3H	Lydia	2214	10F	Susan	5960
3J	Miss Bingley	2127	10X	'Others'	2602
3V	Wickham	2040		(i.e. words attributed to others	
3X	Others	5449		by the six speakers)	
D4:	**Mansfield Park**	**63348**	D11:	**The Awkward Age**	**75894**
4B	EDMUND	14300	11D	Mrs Brookenham	17448
4C	Mary Crawford	13030	11B	VANDERBANK	15375
4D	Henry Crawford	6735	11A	NANDA	10835
4J	Mrs Norris	6659	11M	Mitchy	10778
4A	FANNY	6117	11I	The Duchess	8440
4E	Sir Thomas Bertram	3953	11L	Mr Longdon	7980
4G	Tom Bertram	2995	11X	Others	5038
4F	Lady Bertram	2162			
4X	Others	7397	D12:	**Howards End**	**45899**
			12A	MARGARET SCHLEGEL	15563
D5:	**Emma**	**78057**	12D	Helen Schlegel	9665
5A	EMMA	21501	12B	MR WILCOX	8069
5B	MR KNIGHTLEY	10112	12L	Leonard Bast	2489
5E	Frank Churchill	8225	12G	Mrs Munt	2396
5D	Miss Bates	7624	12H	Charles Wilcox	2096
5I	Mrs Elton	6415	12X	Others	5621
5M	Harriet Smith	5274			
5P	Mr Woodhouse	4639			
5O	Mrs Weston	4144			
5N	Mr Weston	3197			
5X	Others	6926			
D6:	**Persuasion**	**28715**			
6A	ANNE	4336			
6V	Mrs Smith	3985			
6P	Mary Musgrove	3733			
6B	WENTWORTH	3386			
6D	Admiral Croft	2034			
6X	Others	11241			

Overall Distribution of Word-Tokens among Principal Components

Jane Austen's Six Novels				**709917**
D:ALL All dialogue			307360	
N:ALL All narrative			402557	
PN:ALL All pure narrative		323817		
CN:ALL All character narrative		78740		
1 Northanger Abbey				**76432**
D1 Dialogue			28930	
N1 Narrative			47502	
PN1 Pure narrative		40606		
CN1 Character narrative		6896		
1a catherine	5259			
1x others	1637			
2 Sense and Sensibility				**117641**
D2 Dialogue			52334	
N2 Narrative			65307	
PN2 Pure narrative		62299		
CN2 Character narrative		3008		
2a elinor	1976			
2x others	1032			
3 Pride and Prejudice				**119963**
D3 Dialogue			55976	
N3 Narrative			63987	
PN3 Pure narrative		57560		
CN3 Character narrative		6427		
3a elizabeth	4057			
3x others	2370			
4 Mansfield Park				**157641**
D4 Dialogue			63348	
N4 Narrative			94293	
PN4 Pure narrative		66727		
CN4 Character narrative		27566		
4a fanny	15418			
4e sir thomas	3252			
4d henry crawford	2091			
4b edmund	2006			
4x others	4799			
5 Emma				**156729**
D5 Dialogue			78057	
N5 Narrative			78672	
PN5 Pure narrative		53123		
CN5 Character narrative		25549		
5a emma	19730			
5x others	5819			
6 Persuasion				**81511**
D6 Dialogue			28715	
N6 Narrative			52796	
PN6 Pure narrative		43502		
CN6 Character narrative		9294		
6a anne	5667			
6x others	3627			
Other Novels:				
7 'Sanditon'				**22803**
D7 Dialogue			10702	
N7 Narrative			12101	
PN7 Pure narrative		10890		
CN7 Character narrative		1211		
8 Sanditon 2				**77402**
D8 Dialogue			30023	
N8 Narrative			47379	
PN8 Pure narrative		42164		
CN8 Character narrative		5215		
8a 'charlotte'	3725			
8x 'others'	1490			
9 Frederica				**131694**
D9 Dialogue			69355	
N9 Narrative			62339	
PN9 Pure narrative		53171		
CN9 Character narrative		9168		
9b alverstoke	2394			
9x others	6774			
10 The Waves				**77221**
D10 'Dialogue'			72054	
N10 'Narrative' (choric and connective)			5167	
11 The Awkward Age				**129225**
D11 Dialogue			75894	
N11 Narrative			53331	
PN11 Pure narrative		52028		
CN11 Character narrative		1303		
12 Howards End				**108127**
D12 Dialogue			45899	
N12 Narrative			62228	
PN12 Pure narrative		55907		
CN12 Character narrative		6321		
12a margaret	3213			
12x others	3108			

INTRODUCTION

I

It is a truth not generally acknowledged that, in most discussions of works of English fiction, we proceed as if a third, two-fifths, a half of our material were not really *there*. For Jane Austen, that third, two-fifths, or half comprises the twenty, thirty, or fifty most common words of her literary vocabulary. The identity of these words scarcely changes from novel to novel over the twenty years of her mature career. Eight personal pronouns, six auxiliary verb-forms, five prepositions, three conjunctions, two adverbs, the definite and indefinite articles, and four other words ('to', 'that', 'for', and 'all') each of which serves more than a single main grammatical function, almost always find their place—and usually about the same place—among the thirty most common words of each novel. All the evidence available to me suggests that much the same group of words make up approximately the same proportion of the literary vocabulary of many other English novelists since Jane Austen's day. There is no obvious reason to doubt that similar figures obtain for Jane Austen's predecessors: but firm evidence for earlier novelists is in scant supply.

For most readers and most critics, it seems, such very common words as these are to be taken as perfect specimens of the harmless drudge, performing necessary tasks but deserving no particular attention. For lexicographers, the comparatively limited semantic ranges attaching to most—not all—of them can soon be spanned. For the makers of concordances, they are fit only to be excluded as 'non-significant' words. Although some of them are used by literary statisticians in studies of attribution and chronology, that is precisely because the statisticians join in the assumption that the words chosen are unambiguous enough in meaning and stable enough in incidence to admit direct contrasts between the habits of one writer and another or between the large slow phases of a development of style. Even the passage that makes my second epigraph, taken from the work of a writer whose remarkable comic gifts are matched by his understanding of modern critical theory, presses the distinction between grammatical words and lexical words: once the grammatical words are set aside, we can get to 'the real nitty-gritty, . . . the words that carry a distinctive semantic content'. There is no indication that the opinion of the abominable Dempsey is to be distinguished, on this point, from that of his author.

These various proceedings are united by the assumption, not always made so explicit, that, within the verbal universe of any novel, the very common words constitute a largely inert medium while all the real activity emanates from more visible and more energetic bodies. The falsity of any such assumption, the inappropriateness of any such model of a verbal universe, will be established in the course of the following discussion; and the far-reaching consequences that flow from the attempt to find a better model will be seen on every side.

The neglected third, two-fifths, or half of our material has light of its own to shed on the meaning of one novel or another; on subtle relationships between narrative and dialogue, character and character; on less direct and less limited comparisons between novels and between novelists; and ultimately on the very processes of reading itself. (It seems likely, too, that the evidence of the very common words can enhance our understanding of the connections between the language of literature and the 'natural language' of more everyday discourse: I have scarcely entered upon that phase of my research and it forms no part of the present study.) The evidence of the very common words bears, at times, on questions hotly contested in the critical and scholarly controversies of recent years, reinforcing received opinion on one point or indicating its deficiencies on another. At other times, the evidence increases our understanding in areas where literary criticism has seldom found firm ground. My chief object, however, is much less to show how the evidence favours one doctrine at the expense of another than to show that exact evidence, often couched in the unfamiliar language of statistics, does have a distinct bearing on questions of importance in the territory of literary interpretation and judgement. To the extent that I am conscious of being *parti pris*, I hold to the conviction, no longer taken as axiomatic and never easily practised, that a devoted and intelligent study of the text itself is a necessary, though not all-sufficient, phase of critical activity. It is through intelligence and devotion of this kind that those who have generally been regarded as the best of our mentors and colleagues have earned their reputations: it is no accident that their ideas are often upheld by evidence to which the unassisted human mind could never gain consistent, conscious access.

Computer-based concordances, supported by statistical analysis, now make it possible to enter hitherto inaccessible regions of the language, regions where, to take an extreme case, more than 26,000 instances of 'the' in Jane Austen's novels defy the most accurate memory and the finest powers of discrimination and where there is diversity enough within a single novel to cast doubt on arguments based on supposedly typical specimens of Jane Austen's prose.

The assumption that, notwithstanding their fulfilment of certain linguistic functions, the very common words constitute an essentially inert medium amounts, in effect, to an expectation that their incidence in the speech of any character will roughly correspond to that character's share of the whole dialogue: he who speaks a fifth of all the words might be expected to employ about a fifth of all the instances of inert words like 'of' and 'the'. And yet, when each character's actual share of such words is compared with his share of the whole dialogue, there is often a gulf between the expectation and the fact. Henry Tilney and Isabella Thorpe have not dissimilar shares in the dialogue of *Northanger Abbey*—6149 and 5657 words respectively. Yet he uses the word 'the' a third more often again than she and 'of' almost twice as often as she: she, in turn, uses 'not' more than half as often again as he and more than doubles his use of 'I'. With all four words, the contrast between Henry and Catherine Morland is even more extreme. To put it more exactly, Henry uses 'the' at a rate of more than 35 in every thousand of his words, Catherine at less than 17 in every thousand of hers. As an immediate point of reference, such sharp disparities can be set beside the overall incidence of each word in the whole dialogue of *Northanger Abbey* and, again, in the whole dialogue of Jane Austen's six novels. The incidence of each of the very common words in the narrative element of the novels makes for further contrasts, to be considered much later.

TABLE 1. Differences of Incidence: Four Words in Three Idiolects

	Catherine	Henry	Isabella	Mean[1]	Mean[2]
the	16.34	35.29	25.81	24.61	26.45
of	15.91	29.92	17.32	20.71	23.69
I	56.68	24.56	52.86	43.69	38.75
not	26.99	12.69	19.62	19.12	16.14

Mean[1]: overall incidence in dialogue of *Northanger Abbey*
Mean[2]: overall incidence in dialogue of Jane Austen's six novels

Table 1, in which comparative incidences are expressed (as they will be henceforward) as rates per thousand words, may clarify what has been said so far.

However narrow the linguistic function of words like these, it is evident that if, as is indeed the case, disparities like these are typical of the language of Jane Austen's major characters, the effects must colour every speech they make and leave *some* impression in the minds of her readers. Even for the most attentive novel-reader, such an impression need not—and seldom does?—consist in a definite recognition that someone is peculiarly given, for example, to the use of 'I' and 'not' and has little recourse to 'the' or 'of'. It would ordinarily consist in an awareness, however inarticulate, of the larger implications—grammatical, semantic, psychological, social—that are marked by such peculiarities. Statistical analysis of the peculiarities of incidence makes it possible to approach the whole penumbra of 'meaning' in a new and fruitful way.

From no other evidence than a statistical analysis of the relative frequencies of the very common words, it is possible to differentiate sharply and appropriately among the idiolects of Jane Austen's characters and even to trace the ways in which an idiolect can develop in the course of a novel. The construction and interpretation of 'maps' like that offered as a frontispiece will be discussed in Part Two of this study. Graph 1 and others like it will be considered in Part Three. These specimens are offered, at this early stage, in the belief that they have something to say even to readers who are ignorant or dubious of statistical analysis; and that 'the real nitty-gritty' of the language of fiction is by no means confined to 'lexical words . . . like *love* or *dark* or *heart* or *God*'.

In the map, it is enough, for the moment, to recognize that the idiolects of each group of characters set them on a different 'island' from the characters of the other novels; that the relative sizes of the islands show the extent to which the characters of each novel differ from their fellows; that the comparatively large distance between, say, Emma and Harriet Smith is in keeping with well-recognized differences between their respective ways of speaking; and that Emma and Harriet are located much further from each other than are Emma and Helen Schlegel. Graph 1, for its part, shows that the idiolects of Emma and Mr Knightley change markedly—and appropriately—in the course of the novel. In the upper sections of the graph, eight successive stages in the 'development' of their idiolects are compared

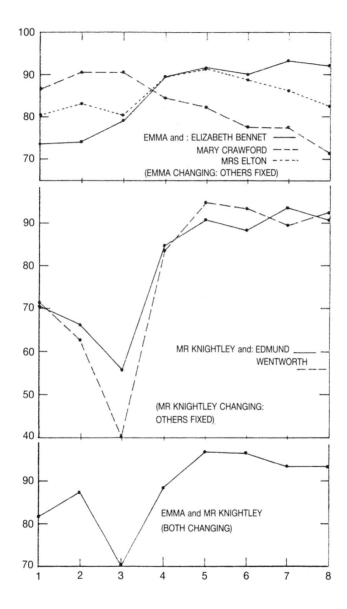

GRAPH 1. 'Development' in the Idiolects of Emma and Mr Knightley

with the idiolects of certain other characters. For the purpose of this comparison, the other idiolects are taken overall and treated as fixed 'bench-marks'. The graph shows, that is to say, how much *this* Emma or *that* resembles Elizabeth Bennet, Mary Crawford, or Mrs Elton and that she comes increasingly to resemble Elizabeth and to differ from the other two. In the bottom section of the graph, Emma and Mr Knightley are compared with each other at each successive stage, and the graph shows how much they resemble each other at first, or at the time of their worst disagreements, or in the closing chapters of the novel. The crucial point is that the configurations of the map rest entirely on the patterning of the thirty most common words, those of the graph on the twelve most common words. Only twelve and only thirty: but the twelve make up a quarter, the thirty some two-fifths of the whole dialogue of Jane Austen's novels and similar proportions of the other novels studied.

II

Before pursuing these ideas or turning from the mere tabulation of incidences to the beginnings of a proper analysis, I must take up other matters. The whole study is based upon a set of concordances, prepared in Newcastle, NSW, and Cambridge since 1979. The Oxford Concordance Package (OCP) has served as our primary computer-programme, but we have developed others as new needs have arisen. My emerging needs of this kind have been amply and effectively met by John Dawson and Sandra Britz. At the date of writing, the set comprises Jane Austen's six novels, worked into a single concordance; her manuscript fragment, 'Sanditon'; the extension of the fragment into *Sanditon*, by Jane Austen and Another Lady (1975); Georgette Heyer's *Frederica*; Virginia Woolf's *The Waves*; James's *The Awkward Age*; and Forster's *Howards End*. These other novels have been chosen with an eye to their diversity: *Sanditon 2* (as I shall call the Other Lady's additional material) as a case where no other intention than that of imitation needs to be considered; *Frederica* as representative of thoroughly competent middle-brow fiction, capable of holding a large readership without ever approaching Jane Austen's imaginative heights; *The Awkward Age* and *Howards End* as extensions of or beyond the English fiction of the nineteenth century; and *The Waves* as representative of 'high literature' in an altogether different vein from Jane Austen's. These novels are to be regarded as 'controls' in what remains essentially a study of Jane Austen. It is easy to think of other novels (in and beyond the mainstream of English fiction) that might usefully be added: but a first-hand knowledge of the work entailed is a powerful constraint.

It will not often be possible to extend the evidence by reference to such compendia of word-frequencies as Thorndike's celebrated word-count, *The Teacher's Word Book*, the first version of which appeared in 1921, and Hofland and Johansson's recent *Word Frequencies in British and American English*, based on the Lancaster–Oslo–Bergen Corpus (LOB).[1] Thorndike, unfortunately, does not treat the language of fiction as a distinct category; and, though Hofland and Johansson introduce that refinement (in their categories K–R), they offer only an introductory comment on the important distinction between narrative and dialogue. The necessity, for our rather different purposes, of incorporating these distinctions will become ever more plain as the evidence unfolds. Categories K–R in Hofland and Johansson are based on 136 samples, each of 2000 words, of recent fiction. The range of samples gives a particular value to this evidence; but the total number of words treated in these categories falls well short of the 710,000 that make up Jane Austen's six novels and the 546,000 that make up the other novels so far concorded in our own research-project.

Given their purposes, the authors of these compendia are fully justified in not separating 'homographic' words into their several constituents. But the objects of the present study could not be met if the various forms of words like 'to', 'that', and 'for' were not distinguished from each other. Chiefly through the exact and arduous work of Alexis Antonia, patiently supported by Elizabeth Lidbury and Rosemary Jurisich, our concordances make the main distinctions for all such words as seemed to warrant it. When the concordances themselves are published, the text will include Mrs Antonia's account of the bases on which the distinctions were drawn. For the present purpose, one or two comments may suffice. The distinctions are presented as a system of numerical suffixes in which 0 represents a noun form, 1 a verb form, and so on, with subsets like 5.1 and 5.2 to distinguish, say, between 'so' as an adverb of degree and the same word as an adverb of manner. The most troublesome

---

[1] Edward L. Thorndike and Irving Lorge, *The Teacher's Word Book of 30,000 Words* (New York, 1944); Knut Hofland and Stig Johansson, *Word Frequencies in British and American English* (Bergen, 1982).

of the necessary distinctions arose with words that serve variously as prepositions, adverbs, and verb particles. With the few really insoluble cases, our policy has been either to create a distinct subset or, where the number of them does not warrant that approach, to treat them as members of the largest appropriate set. On the whole, the cases that will arise in the present study — 'to', 'for', and 'by' — proved less troublesome than 'about'. The system is Jane Austen-oriented in the sense that, where *her* novels required no homographic separation, none was attempted: of the very large number of potential noun/verb homographs, like 'felt'/'felt', many are represented, in Jane Austen's novels, by one form only. Georgette Heyer, especially, presents a different picture: her more colloquial dialogue abounds in homographs of this kind and also in verb particles.

There is no unequivocal measure of the number of words in a novel. One difficulty arises from the inconsistency of authors and typesetters on questions, for example, of hyphenation. (Such inconsistencies are preserved, as they should be, by the best of modern scholarly editors — Dr Chapman among them — in their pursuit of a complete fidelity to their copy-texts.) One category may serve as example for all. The number of occasions on which 'any', 'every', 'no', and 'some' occur is affected, as is the total to which they contribute, by inconsistencies, in each of Jane Austen's novels, in the spelling of 'anybody', 'anyone', and the like. All of these words and many others are sometimes printed as one, sometimes as two, and sometimes with a hyphen. Our endeavour has been to introduce a linking asterisk, as a quasi-hyphen, on all occasions where what is sometimes combined is represented as two words. But, whenever 'any body' is represented as 'any*body', the number of words in the novel is reduced by one. (For other purposes than consistency, the asterisk is used, to like effect, in the rendering of such compound-names as 'Sir*Thomas', 'Mr*Bertram', and 'Mansfield*Park'.)

More intractable difficulties arise from the use of contracted forms like 'I'll' and 'won't', 'we'd', and 'shan't'. It is not that the habit of contraction is devoid of meaning. (Virginia Woolf and the Other Lady do not often employ contracted forms. Jane Austen uses them sparingly and, with occasional exceptions for consciously smart speakers like Tom Bertram, confines them to vulgar speakers like Mrs Jennings and the Steele sisters. Georgette Heyer's dialogue abounds in the whole range of such contractions to the extent that 'don't' ranges with 'do' among the most common words of all. The affluence of the Edwardian book-trade is registered, in the New York edition of Henry James, by the nicety of using *half* word-spaces to separate the elements of the contracted forms, which occur very freely in his dialogue and also in E. M. Forster's.) It is not that the parts cannot be separated and treated, appropriately, as instances of 'I', 'shall', 'will', 'not', and so on. It is not even that, with 'I'd' or 'we'd', traditional distinctions between 'would' and 'should' are more than ever blurred. Beyond all these, the intractable difficulty bears on the total number of words used in a given novel or in its dialogue, the number that makes the essential base for statistical analysis. So far as that total is concerned, I have followed what seems the least unsatisfactory course, that of treating each instance of these forms as one word, not two; but, when the argument requires it, the constituents have been separated.

Since computers do not recognize that the names 'Maria', 'Maria*Bertram', 'Miss*Bertram', and (the younger) 'Mrs*Rushworth' all refer to the same person but that the name 'Mrs*Rushworth' has two different referents, a system of alphabetical prefixes is used to identify the characters. Except in *The Waves*, where conventional literary roles are abandoned, the heroine of each novel is identified as A, the hero as B, the other speakers by similar prefixes, and the non-speakers by a further series beginning at ZA.

The first series of prefixes is also inserted into the texts, in the manner of a playscript, to identify the speaker of each speech. With few exceptions, the punctuation of Jane Austen's novels admits a simple, incontestable distinction between narrative and dialogue. The complex questions raised by the concept of 'character' will be considered as the argument proceeds; but only rarely can there be a sensible disagreement about which speech belongs to which character. (Even when the Bertram sisters or Mr and Mrs Musgrove speak in unison, it is made clear that they are doing so and those speeches can be classed apart: poor Mr Musgrove is left with no words whatever of his own.) While willingly conceding that it is mildly comical to 'privilege' inverted commas so highly as this policy entails, I stand by it as an *authorized* privilege. It is, moreover, a necessity for any such analysis as the present study attempts.

More serious problems of assignment, as between narrative and dialogue, arise from time to time. With General Tilney and Sir Walter Elliot, especially, Jane Austen sometimes resorts to an appropriately pompous form of quasi-indirect speech even when other characters present are conversing in the ordinary way. With Emma Woodhouse and Elizabeth Bennet, especially, she sometimes couches an unspoken thought in the form of direct speech. (On the latter point, I think it unlikely that I have maintained an entirely consistent policy throughout the five years that have gone in the preparation of the texts: but, given the amount of revision and correction that has gone on in the course of those five years, it is even more unlikely that more than an occasional lapse remains.)

Within the narrative itself, there are many occasions, well-recognized by Jane Austen's readers and critics, where the narrator resorts to the 'free indirect style', no longer speaking *of* a given character (most commonly the heroine) but speaking *for* her, rendering her ideas in a hybrid idiom recognizably akin to hers. The force of this distinction figures in much critical discussion, whether of particular points of interpretation or of such general concepts as 'point of view'. In *Emma*, for instance, it serves the essential purpose of distancing the heroine from the narrator's access to the truth. Although the exact moment of transition from one narrative-idiom to the other (from 'pure narrative' to 'character narrative', as I term them) is not always easy to mark in Jane Austen and might sometimes prove impossible in Henry James, the existence of passages of character narrative is obvious and the importance of the distinction brooks no evasion. Throughout the set of novels (except for *The Waves*), I have marked the passages of character narrative with a special symbol, followed by a lower-case version of the given character's usual tag. The upshot of a multitude of particular decisions — considered but not unquestionable judgements — about this passage or that in one or another of the novels will be seen as the analysis continues. The statistical findings certainly attest to the importance of the distinction itself and, in general, to the effectiveness with which it has been established. But, with the advantage of hindsight, I believe that, especially with *Emma* and *Howards End*, I have sometimes been too conservative in treating a doubtful passage as a comment on rather than a rendering of the heroine's ideas.

III

The methods of statistical analysis have long been applied to literary material and such eminent statisticians as G. Udney Yule were among the pioneers of an esoteric field. An assessment of the early work, which is by no means of mere antiquarian interest even now, emerges in O. S. Akhmanova *et al.*, *Exact Methods in Linguistic Research*, trans. D. G. Hays and D. V. Mohr (Berkeley & Los Angeles, 1963). The advances in computing over the last ten or fifteen years have made for an enormous range of exciting new developments among which I would single out, for their comparative proximity to my own work, the 'pattern stylistics' of Louis T. Milic and the analysis, by Karl Kroeber, of certain structures in prose fiction. Perhaps the *ALLC Journal* and the journal entitled *Computers and the Humanities*, together with the conference proceedings published by their sponsor-associations, are already the only feasible way of discovering what is going on in an expanding field of study. For the methodological bases themselves, however, Anthony Kenny's lucid little book, *The Computation of Style: An Introduction to Statistics for Students of Literature and Humanities* (Oxford, 1982) is an invaluable guide for beginners like me.

Yet Robert Louis Stevenson has many heirs in the belief that there are no exact synonyms in English and that no two instances of the same word are strictly identical in meaning. While these propositions have a strong ring of truth, they do not make as formidable an objection to statistical analysis as might at first appear. Any of us is justified in denying his own exact resemblance to anyone else who has ever lived; and it is easy to sustain the argument that I am neither my yesterday nor my tomorrow self. Yet each of us can properly be included in a wide range of demographic analyses bearing on anything from political attitudes or physiological characteristics to shoe-sizes or preferences in food: the fact that, as in any field of human inquiry, some of the work is shallow or incompetent does not affect the principle.

Now, as will appear in the opening chapter of the present study, 'we' can sometimes be used where 'I' or 'you' would more plainly signify the 'true meaning' of the statement. 'Perhaps we should be getting ready' may well imply 'You are making us late again'. But the very existence of border-disputes suggests that there are borders, and that most instances of 'we' inhabit a sufficiently distinctive territory of meaning to permit statistical analysis. And, lying far from the borderlands of 'we' are altogether foreign lands: even if 'we' has somewhere been used to mean 'however' or 'heretofore', the overwhelming majority of instances remain in their homeland, are most densely clustered in some parts of it, and behave very like their neighbours. This whole range of questions, nevertheless, is too important to be swept aside with metaphors and analogies, however apt. They will necessarily be tested as the present study develops— and tested, especially, in the extent to which there is a recognizable consonance between the statistical findings and the ideas suggested by the words themselves.[2]

---

[2] Almost all of the forms of calculation used in this study can be undertaken, at a not unacceptable speed, with such programmable calculators as the Texas TI59. But a computer, employing programmes like MINITAB (University of Pennsylvania), makes light work of it.

Part One

COMMON MEASURES

1

A Set of Pronouns

Lady Catherine de Bourgh finds a need for the pronoun 'we' on only two occasions, and matches them with two instances of 'us' and one of 'our'. Her insolence of rank (the generous condescension that Collins so much admires) is to be felt when, on learning that Elizabeth Bennet plays and sings, she rejoins, 'Oh! then—some time or other we shall be happy to hear you. Our instrument is a capital one, probably superior to—You shall try it some day' (p. 164).[1] An 'us' escapes her when she is too preoccupied to think of condescension: 'Let us sit down. You are to understand, Miss Bennet, that I came here with the determined resolution of carrying my purpose; nor will I be dissuaded from it. I have not been used to submit to any person's whims' (pp. 355–6). The other two instances, which also arise in the same attempt to bend Elizabeth to her purpose, testify to her ill-judged belief that her family shares all her narrow pride. She tries to make a weapon out of a fancy, shared long ago with her dead sister, Lady Anne Darcy: 'While in their cradles, we planned the union: and now, at the moment when the wishes of both sisters would be accomplished, in their marriage, to be prevented by a young woman of inferior birth, of no importance in the world, and wholly unallied to the family!' In that intolerable event, she resumes, 'You will be censured, slighted, and despised, by every one connected with him. Your alliance will be a disgrace; your name will never even be mentioned by any of us' (p. 355). Only the assiduous Collins, so it proves, stands loyal to these ideas— and only until he discovers that the Vicar of Bray is a wiser man than he.

Gregarious, uxorious, anecdotal as he is, Admiral Croft stands at the other pole from Lady Catherine. Whereas her 2342 words include only these five instances of the first person plural pronouns, his 2034 words need fifty:

---

[1] All such bare page-references are to the Oxford Illustrated Edition of Jane Austen's novels, edited by R. W. Chapman. Titles will be included only when clarity requires them.

There comes old Sir Archibald Drew and his grandson. Look, he sees us; he kisses his hand to you; he takes you for my wife. Ah! the peace has come too soon for that younker. Poor old Sir Archibald! How do you like Bath, Miss Elliot? It suits us very well. We are always meeting with some old friend or other; the streets full of them every morning; sure to have plenty of chat; and then we get away from them all, and shut ourselves into our lodgings, and draw in our chairs, and are as snug as if we were at Kellynch, ay, or as we used to be even at North Yarmouth and Deal. (p. 170)

Of these three pronouns, 'we' ranks thirty-ninth of all the words in Jane Austen's dialogue, 'us' beyond eightieth, and 'our' a little beyond one hundredth. They make an appropriate point of departure because they occur infrequently enough to be approached in something akin to the familiar idiom of literary analysis, yet frequently enough to illustrate some rudimentary forms of statistical analysis. Towards each end of a range of incidences bounded by Admiral Croft (24.58 per 1000 words) and Lady Catherine (2.13 per 1000 words) lie characters whose temperament and situation so plainly influence their recourse to these pronouns that we need only glance at them in passing. Mr Weston's fondness for his wife, pride in his son, and too promiscuous capacity for friendship set him sixth among Jane Austen's forty-eight major characters on this particular scale.[2] Mrs Dashwood's sense of family unity, focused on her daughters, sets her seventh. Lydia Bennet, who ranks second, and Lucy Steele, who ranks fifth, begin in an assertive but insecure claiming of association with everyone about them and end by flaunting their new claims as brides. Lucy, alas, turns most of all to 'we' in the letter she writes when she thinks she has made sure of Edward Ferrars and can thus afford to taunt Elinor more openly than before. But the same 'we', translated into 'they' in the report given by the Dashwoods' man-servant (p. 354) is manifest when she settles for Edward's foolish brother. Tom Bertram, Miss Bates, and Mrs Elton (who rank third, fourth, and tenth respectively) use this set of pronouns in ways we shall consider at more length.

Some of those characters who occupy the lower end of the same scale are there for obvious reasons. Mrs Smith, of *Persuasion*, is personally isolated by her widowhood and illness, and 'stylistically

[2] For the purposes of this study, the 'major characters' comprise the forty-seven who speak more than 2000 words apiece and Eleanor Tilney, who ranks next with 1938 words. My trial analyses have shown that, as might be expected, the smaller speaking-parts of the 'minor characters' yield striking but statistically untenable results.

isolated' by the extent to which her part in the novel consists in her account of her late husband's misguided trust in William Walter Elliot and of the more recent machinations of the latter. She ranks forty-fourth. Notwithstanding Emma's patronage, Harriet Smith (who ranks just above her namesake) finds neither friends nor peers among the Hartfield set: she is seldom so much as mentioned save in conversations where Emma has the initiative. Because of Emma's patronage, she loses touch with her earlier friends and is discouraged from speaking about them. She sometimes uses the first person plural pronouns in expressions, usually hesitant, of her association with Miss Woodhouse but only claims firm common ground when they speak openly, at last, of her belief that Mr Knightley may reciprocate her 'love' for him: 'I know we agreed never to name him . . . [but] when we talked about him, it was as clear as possible' (pp. 405–6). These pronouns come more freely from Harriet's lips when she does advert to her friendship with the Martins or to an episode at Mrs Goddard's when Mr Elton first appeared in Highbury: 'The two Abbotts and I ran into the front room and peeped through the blind when we heard he was going by, and Miss Nash came and scolded us away, and staid to look through herself; however, she called me back presently, and let me look too, which was very good-natured. And how beautiful we thought he looked!' (p. 75). To each her own: by taking Harriet up so energetically, Emma not only separates her from her friends and imperils her prospects in life but even deprives her of a highly congenial set of pronouns.

It is no surprise to find Elinor Dashwood, Mrs Jennings, and Fanny Price towards the lower end of this scale. With Fanny, indeed, the question is rather why she should rank so high as fortieth. The ideas of social comfort and mutual reliance, which are so often implicit in these pronouns, are almost entirely lacking in her idiom. Five of her twenty-one instances of 'we'—like 'the next time we come to a seat' (p. 94)—suggest little more than that she is sometimes, albeit uneasily, in the company of her fellows. Five carry the impersonal sense of the French pronoun 'on' at moments when Fanny speaks sententiously of human attitudes or human knowledge. Eight are employed, in an idiom equally characteristic of her but even less common among her fellows, as expressions of *disjunction* when she seeks to dissociate herself from Henry Crawford: 'We are so totally unlike, . . . we are so very, very different in all our inclinations and ways' (p. 348). At one point, Fanny uses 'we' to associate herself with her brother, but in such a way as to hide herself behind him: 'Oh! Mr. Crawford, we are infinitely obliged to you' (p. 300). Only twice in the whole novel and even then without much confidence in her present security does Fanny's use of 'we' evoke a straightforward sense of personal relationship: 'It is a great while since we have had any star-gazing' (p. 113); and, when Sir Thomas and his sons are to dine at Sotherton, 'We shall be quite a small party at home' (p. 199). Meanings just like these are to be found in Fanny's even rarer uses of 'our' and 'us'. Like the self-excluding sense that she attaches to 'family' until the novel is almost ended; like her persistent association of 'home' with Portsmouth — the instance in the phrase last quoted is exceptional at that stage of events; like these and many another indication of the kind, Fanny's use of pronouns in the first person plural reflects an important aspect of her 'character' and marks the wonted solitariness of her life at Mansfield Park. Were it not for the counter-effect of the sententious and the disjunctive expressions, noted above, she would lie near the very bottom of the scale.

But, though they are outnumbered overall by twenty-eight to twenty, male characters predominate in the lower ranges of this scale. Three of the last four are men; six of the last ten; twelve of the last twenty. The last ten include four of the heroes; the last twenty include all six. It is easy to infer that there are resemblances of 'character' and 'situation' to be found here. Of the twelve men who rank among the last twenty characters, only the highest ranking of them, John Dashwood, is a married man: only he, that is to say, has occasion for one very common use of the first person plural. As it proves, however, he is so fearful of committing himself and so doting a husband as to report the opinions of his wife — and his mother-in-law — more freely than he presents opinions shared by both — or all three — of them. The other eleven of these characters, neither married nor lacking in self-reliance, arrive at their own decisions and speak their own minds without often seeking corroboration or reassurance by allying themselves with others. But, though women like Lucy Steele and Mrs Elton outdo them in specious practices, most of them are capable, in varying degrees, of imposing their ideas on others through a pretence of mutual accord. Such broad inferences are supported by a study of their pronoun idioms: that study, however, also brings out individual differences which will carry our argument much further.

Darcy's customary aloofness, Edward Ferrars's wretched isolation, and Willoughby's self-imposed exile from the Dashwoods sufficiently account for their proximity to Lady Catherine at the very bottom of the scale. Frank Churchill and Henry Crawford, a little further up, are among those who repay scrutiny. They closely resemble each other in a dearth of certain common pronoun-idioms. Only when Crawford speaks of the beauties of 'our liturgy' (*Mansfield Park*, p. 340) and when Churchill covers his traces, characteristically, with the suggestion that 'we gentlemen labourers' behave differently from 'your real workmen' (*Emma*, p. 242) does either of them lean, even momentarily, in the direction of that dignified—sometimes comically dignified—impersonality which Fanny shares with Mr Knightley and Henry Tilney: she with her disquisitions on what we know of evergreens or the faculty of memory, they with their confident presuppositions about us human beings, us male creatures, or us Englishmen; she with her ardent faith in conscience, the inner light, as our best and only guide, they with their firm reliance on the powers of our reason.

Granted that neither Churchill nor Crawford has compelling family affiliations, they scarcely ever pronoun idioms in such a way as to associate themselves with their connections. Whereas Mary Crawford often includes Henry in a 'we' or an 'us', Henry only twice repays the compliment. Frank Churchill uses 'we' and 'our' to associate himself with his Churchill relatives on three occasions, his Weston relatives on two. But Frank's comment that, when his father joins him at Hartfield, 'we shall walk back [to Randalls] together' (p. 260) is a fair specimen of a set of remarks in which neither young man does much more than acknowledge the presence of a companion.

Each of them finds advantage, Churchill more frequently, in associating himself with one woman when he is preoccupied with another. Crawford is more given to reminding Julia Bertram of 'the many laughs we have had together' (p. 133) than to acknowledging that he and Maria may find more than laughs in common. Even in his final letter, when Frank Churchill confesses that 'Miss Woodhouse was my ostensible object' and that he had made 'more than an allowable use of the sort of intimacy into which we were immediately thrown', he remains willing to give more than its—admitted—deserts to the idea that 'we seemed to understand each other' (p. 438). Both men, nevertheless, have their sincerities. As even Mr Knightley concedes, it is not merely as 'the child of good fortune' (p. 448) but partly through his own rather belated endeavours that Frank Churchill is eventually able to declare, of himself and Jane, 'we are reconciled, dearer, much dearer, than ever' (p. 443). And, though Henry Crawford's resolution does not hold, he has 'moral taste enough' (p. 235) to foresee what Fanny would require of him: 'You think me unsteady. . . . But we shall see. — It is not by protestations that I shall endeavour to convince you. . . . My conduct shall speak for me' (p. 343).

For Frank Churchill, the pronoun idioms of the first person plural arise, above all, in connection with the matters touched on in the last paragraph; and well over a third of all his share in these pronouns is to be found in the admissions and forecasts of his long letter and of the final chapter of the novel. Up to a point, however, he participates in the use of those collective idioms, those idioms of the ostensible group, which play the largest part in Henry Crawford's recourse to these pronouns.

Frank Churchill is especially adept at bending the Westons and Emma to his wish that Miss Bates (and her niece) should join their company as frequently as possible: 'I think we do want a larger council. Suppose I go and invite Miss Bates to join us?' (p. 255). Emma and Mrs Weston offer polite but predictable objections. His father, however, obligingly approves and goes on to insist that, 'I shall think you a great blockhead, Frank, if you bring the aunt without the niece' (loc. cit.). From the first small dance at the Coles' to the ball at the Crown Inn, the device succeeds at each attempt: by including the others in a group-pronoun, he induces them to suppose that their motives are entirely in keeping with his own. On one occasion, it seems, he almost goes too far: Mrs Weston is puzzled by his reminder that she had promised to visit Miss Bates that morning; but she accepts his assurance, persuades him to accompany her, and hopes to console him with the thought that, 'We will go to Hartfield afterwards' (p. 234).

Whenever Henry Crawford offers himself as spokesman for the would-be improvers of Sotherton, the improvement of his opportunities with Maria Bertram is uppermost in his mind. One characteristic series of manoeuvres begins in a deferential gesture to his host: 'Mr. Rushworth, shall we summon a council on this lawn?' (p. 90). By the time they encounter Fanny near the iron gates, Crawford has only two companions. While it is Maria who first suggests passing through the gates, Crawford is quick to bolster her preference by remarking the 'knoll not half a mile off, which would give them exactly the requisite command of the house' (p. 98). After the hapless Rushworth has been induced to go off for the key, Crawford maintains a gentle pressure: 'It is undoubtedly the best thing we can do now, as we are so far from the house already' (p. 98). He soon afterwards succeeds in encouraging Maria not to wait for Rushworth and in ensuring that Fanny stays where she is: 'if we are [out of sight], Miss Price will be so good as to tell him, that he will find us near that knoll, the grove of oak on the knoll' (p. 99). Up to a point, it is true, Crawford's pronouns merely reflect his success in overcoming 'the extreme difficulty which secret Lovers must have in finding a proper spot for their stolen Interviews' (*Minor Works*, p. 427). And certainly Maria, his sister, and Edmund are his willing allies in dissolving the original large group. But his pronouns-of-the-group are not the least delicate or effective of the instruments he calls to hand.

The same pronouns serve him in essentially similar ways during the long episode of the theatricals. Although his love of novelty and his interest in acting are shown, throughout the novel, to be genuine, the Bertram sisters—which is chiefly to say, Maria—are never overlooked: '"Let us be doing something. Be it only half a play—an act—a scene; what should prevent us? Not these countenances I am sure," looking towards the Miss Bertrams, "and for a theatre, what signifies a theatre? We shall be only amusing ourselves."' (p. 123) The singling out of Maria gains force as, purporting wherever possible to speak for the collective interest and unwittingly abetted by Tom Bertram, he ensures that she, not Julia, will play Agatha to his Frederick. This point secured, he diplomatically attempts to save Julia from the minor role of Cottager's wife: 'we must not suffer her good nature to be imposed on. We must not *allow* her to accept the part' (p. 135). It is as Amelia, he urges Julia, that 'you must oblige us' (p. 135) after which he adds a more personal appeal. He might have withstood Tom Bertram's downright opposition to this part of his scheme: but Maria, less suave than himself, cannot disguise her satisfaction; and, seeing her smile, Julia withdraws to a jealous solitude broken only by the condolences of the opportunistic Mr Yates.

It is through no afflatus of plain dealing but through a simple change of object that Crawford will assure Fanny, long afterwards, that 'I should be sorry to have my powers of *planning* judged of by the day at Sotherton' (p. 245). She had previously offered a quiet but unyielding resistance to his attempt, *ex post facto*, to include her among the devotees of *Lovers' Vows* and, likewise, to his unwary assumption that her opinion of the whole enterprise must match that of the group. The suggestion that, at the time of 'our theatricals', 'we were all alive' brings only 'silent indignation' (p. 225). But, when the proposition that 'we were unlucky' in the timing of Sir Thomas's return grows into a sustained embroidering of the fancy that, 'if we had had the disposal of events', 'we would have indulged ourselves with a week's calm in the Atlantic', even Fanny is driven into an emphatic self-assertion: 'As far as *I* am concerned, sir, I would not have delayed his return for a day' (p. 225). Crawford concedes, in surprise, that 'we were getting too noisy' (p. 226); turns the conversation; and begins to take an interest in a young woman with so uncommon a capacity for resisting his discreet stratagems. The interest then established swiftly leads on to a moment of high comedy when, anticipating his married life with Fanny before he has even proposed to her, he invites Mary to become their guest: 'You must give us more than half your time . . .; I cannot admit Mrs. Grant to have an equal claim with Fanny and myself, for we shall both have a right in you. Fanny will be so truly your sister!' (p. 295).

On more than half of the few occasions on which Henry Tilney resorts to pronouns in the first person plural, he is speaking to Catherine of themselves. Of the remainder, several treat of himself and Eleanor, two introduce his brother, but most tend in the direction of the French '*on*'. Some of the implied unions of thought or action are light-hearted fancies, some serious to the point of earnestness. Some set Catherine down rather heavily while others reflect his growing admiration of her gentle nature. Almost without exception, however, these pronouns bear on his desire to lead her from ingenuousness into a better understanding. That intention is at its plainest in such an emphasis on the force of *proper* evidence as, 'During the progress of her disorder, Frederick and I (*we* were both at home) saw her repeatedly; and from our own observation can bear witness to her having received every possible attention' (p. 197); and in such expressions of incredulity as, 'Remember the country and the age in which we live. . . . Does our education prepare us for such atrocities? Do our laws connive at them?' (p. 197).

The dawning of the intention can scarcely be separated from the
dawning of his wish that 'we shall soon be acquainted' (p. 29); and
both motives underlie the dexterity with which he exploits the forms
of association implicit in the punctilio of the Rooms: 'We have
entered into a contract of mutual agreeableness for the space of an
evening, and all our agreeableness belongs solely to each other for
that time' (p. 76). There is something of the same intention even in
the undeserved reproof of, 'We were much obliged to you at any
rate for wishing us a pleasant walk after our passing you in Argyle-
street' (p. 94) and, likewise, in the well-deserved mockery of
Catherine's Gothic visions of the Abbey: 'We shall not have to explore
our way into a hall dimly lighted by the expiring embers . . .' (p. 158).
But his intention is most tactfully realized in several instances where
he speaks, ostensibly jointly, for a position that has only just come
within *her* reach:

'If the *effect* of his behaviour does not justify him with you, we had better
not seek after the cause.'
'Then you do not suppose he ever really cared about her?' (p. 219)

By this time, however, he has come to recognize that, for all her
ignorance and naivety, she has lessons to teach him: 'You feel, as
you always do, what is most to the credit of human nature' (p. 207).
  The most striking feature of Mr Knightley's use of these pronouns
lies in his turning from expressions of a relationship with Emma that
she, no Catherine Morland, regards as condescending, to more direct
expressions of the affection that he has never dared suppose she might
return.[3] Although this development can be charted more closely in
his changing use of pronouns in the first person singular, it may
suffice, for the moment, to illustrate its more extreme manifestations.
  With no intention but to comfort Emma for the loss of Miss
Taylor, Mr Knightley's first recourse to any of the plural pronouns

---

[3] I have come to accept that a number of reviewers and friends were right to
suggest that, in *Jane Austen's 'Emma'* (Sydney, 1968), I dealt more sceptically with
Mr Knightley than the novel warrants. To acknowledge this, however, is not to concede
that he stands immune, his author's 'privileged' spokesman, above the action of the
novel.
  Jane Austen herself is a useful, if not unequivocal witness: 'she did not, however,
suppose that her imaginary characters were of a higher order than are to be found
in nature; for she said, when speaking of two of her great favourites, Edmund Bertram
and Mr Knightly [sic]: "They are very far from being what I know English gentlemen
often are"' [J. E. Austen-Leigh, *A Memoir of Jane Austen* (London, 1870), p. 203].

associates her father with himself in a kindly but patronizing judgement of a well-loved child: 'It is impossible that Emma should not miss such a companion. . . . We should not like her so well as we do, sir, if we could suppose it' (p. 11). When she points out, on a later occasion and with 'a little sauciness' (p. 98), that the two of them seem better able to agree about their nephews and nieces than about Harriet Smith and Robert Martin, he answers that 'we might always think alike' (p. 99) if *she* were more often 'guided by nature' rather than 'the power of fancy and whim' (pp. 98–9). Challenged by her on the implicit assumption of superior judgement, he allows himself the truthful but less than endearing reply that, 'I have still the advantage of you by sixteen years' experience, and by not being a pretty young woman and a spoiled child. Come, my dear Emma, let us be friends and say no more about it' (p. 99). In their later disagreement about Frank Churchill, Mr Knightley ascends— without the support of any evidence available to the reader except a visit to Weymouth—to an almost royal use of the plural: 'We know . . . that he has so much of both [money and leisure], that he is glad to get rid of them at the idlest haunts in the kingdom. We hear of him for ever at some watering-place or other' (p. 146).

Jane Austen's astonishing exactitude of mind is evident here, as so often elsewhere, in her having Mr Knightley recant these idioms, almost point by point, in later conversations with Emma. He speaks of the difficulty of persuading her father of 'our having every right that equal worth can give, to be happy together' (p. 465). He goes far towards her in the matter of Harriet and Robert:

'There is one subject', he replied, 'I hope but one, on which we do not think alike. . . . I wish our opinions were the same. But in time they will. Time, you may be very sure, will make one or the other of us think differently; and, in the meanwhile, we need not talk much on the subject.' (pp. 470–1)

He makes a small joke against the supposed habits of women and the supposed pretensions of men: 'She will give you all the minute particulars, which only woman's language can make interesting. — In our communications we deal only in the great' (p. 472). And, without foregoing its use entirely, he even turns his royal plural back upon himself: 'One man's style must not be the rule of another's. We will not be severe' (p. 445).

Since they reflect the homogeneity of constant habit, the idioms of those who make most use of these pronouns assume more obvious patterns. Without a single clear exception, the basis of Mrs Elton's deployment of them is a lust for power and 'status' (as we have come to call it). When she turns to the first person plural to associate herself with the Sucklings, her idiom is not that of nostalgia but that of an ostentatious parade of her connections. When she uses it in token of her union with Elton, the hesitancies and the affection that might be expected of a bride are lost, if ever she was touched by them, in a strenuous display of the worst side of a bride's insistence on her social prerogatives; a housewife's exultation in property and possession ('one of our men, I forget his name': p. 295); and an incipient matron's still veiled desire for dominance over her *caro sposo*. Her attempted *entente* with Emma ('if *we* exert ourselves, I think we shall not be long in want of allies': p. 277) is short-lived. Mrs Weston ('we married women must begin to exert ourselves': p. 305), Knightley, and Frank Churchill prove less amenable than she would wish. And she is left to a merciless exploitation of Jane Fairfax, whether by gathering her to her bosom ('We will not allow her to do such a thing again': p. 295); by forcing her, against her express wish and her concealed best interest, upon the bosom of society ('indeed, indeed, we must begin inquiring directly': p. 300); or by excluding others from these horrid rites ('But not a word more. Let us be discreet — quite on our good behaviour': p. 454). The phrases quoted include nine of the pronouns we have been considering: the habits of mind they illustrate are to be seen in another seventy.

Relative to the size of his speaking-part, Tom Bertram ranks third highest of all users of the first person plural pronouns. Three instances are associated with his early anecdotes of himself and his friend such-and-such: at this stage of the novel, his idiom is much like that of Crawford and Churchill in its customary reliance upon self alone. For the rest, however, he turns repeatedly to these pronouns as elder son, master of the Mansfield theatricals, and chief spokesman for that short-lived demesne. Since the roles described are usually consonant with each other and since there is a widespread, though not unanimous, interest in the idea of producing a play and — the play once chosen — in carrying the production forward, he often speaks for a willing majority. But difficulties will arise: Julia's rivalry with Maria for the part of Agatha and with Mary for the part of Amelia; Edmund's abortive challenge to the whole scheme, and the proposal that he be replaced by one of the Olivers or Charles

Maddox; and Fanny's inconceivable unwillingness to help the players in a time of need. Each little crisis brings an assertion of Tom's authority. At each such moment, the voice of the elder son, speaking for the family, can be heard behind that of the theatre manager: 'I shall think our time very well spent, and so I am sure will he [my father]' (p. 126). His father's premature return brings an immediate division of his roles and supports the idea that, for a few happy days, he had envisaged himself as no mere amateur producer, much less a continental Cottager, but as the incipient English baronet. Now, alas, the producer must condole with his departing cast: 'I am sorry you are going—but as to our play, *that* is all over—entirely at an end (looking significantly at his father)' (p. 193). Worse still, the young master must resume his worn-out role as son: 'we brought home six brace between us, and might each have killed six times as many; but we respect your pheasants, sir, I assure you, as much as you could desire' (p. 181). From the time of Crawford's exit, Tom takes up a station at the edge of the stage and has nothing more to say.

As the reader may have noticed, the 'ideas of social comfort and mutual reliance', which were referred to earlier, have not figured very conspicuously in the subsequent discussion. They come into their own in the idiom of Miss Bates. The people with whom she associates herself in the first person plural pronouns are, overwhelmingly, the members of her own household. She speaks for her mother and herself (and Patty); for her niece and herself; and sometimes for all three, or four, of them. The only noteworthy range of exceptions, a handful in over a hundred, arises when she speaks for a larger group of which she and Jane are members. On most occasions, moreover, those for whom she—unlike Crawford and Churchill—speaks are evidently of one mind. Take the cases of the pleasure she and her mother share in Jane's letters, pored over by the one for the benefit of both; in the prospect of a long visit from her; or in the many little kindnesses of Mr Knightley and Mr Woodhouse, magnified by genuine but otiose gratitude. As she tells the latter, 'Oh! my dear sir, as my mother says, our friends are only too good to us. If ever there were people who, without having great wealth themselves, had every thing they could wish for, I am sure it is us. We may well say that "our lot is cast in a goodly heritage"' (p. 174). Given their present and prospective disadvantages, so eloquently described by Mr Knightley when he rebukes Emma at Box Hill (p. 375), the question arises as to whether the satisfaction Miss Bates discovers in her family's lot is a mark of mere obtuseness or the expression of a stalwart act of will.

In one important matter, certainly, she may be thought of as obtuse — but no more so than Mrs Weston or Miss Woodhouse. Like them, she notices the little oddities of behaviour that spring from the secret engagement. But, whereas Emma launches on a series of mistaken inferences, Miss Bates and Mrs Weston do not address their minds to what may be implied; and it is left to Mr Knightley, supposedly ignorant of such matters, to discern the truth. Among the symptoms registered but not diagnosed by Miss Bates are a number of small but recognizable departures from the ordinary — or erstwhile — behaviour of her seemingly close-knit group: 'I forget where we had been walking to — very likely to Randall's' (p. 346); 'Do not we often talk of Mr. Frank Churchill?' (p. 323); and, most revealingly:

Well, where shall we sit? where shall we sit? Any where, so that Jane is not in a draught. Where *I* sit is of no consequence. Oh! do you recommend this side? — Well, I am sure, Mr. Churchill — only it seems too good — but just as you please. What you direct in this house cannot be wrong. Dear Jane, how shall we ever recollect half the dishes for grandmamma? Soup too! Bless me! I should not be helped so soon. (p. 330)

While the ubiquitous presence of Mr Frank Churchill makes plainer evidence, the interplay of the pronouns in such passages suggests, at least, that the group is no longer as stable as Miss Bates supposes.

In the general conduct of their lives, however, there are much more suggestive gaps between the characteristic 'us' of Miss Bates's idiom and the 'me' that would spell the truth. Where there is a burden of decision or opinion, she usually defers to her mother in a spinster daughter's habit of 'projection' (as Freud was to call it) made poignant by the reality. ('My mother', in her idiom, also frequently means 'I'.) Where the burden is one of action, it falls even more firmly upon her shoulders. One detail, mentioned only in passing, says much of the arrangements in that household: 'I was only gone down to speak to Patty again about the pork . . . for my mother was so afraid that we had not any salting-pan large enough. So I said I would go down and see, and Jane said, "Shall I go down instead?"' (p. 173). There are signs of a disagreement, for once, between Miss Bates and Jane about Mr Knightley's much needed gift of apples: 'I could not absolutely say that we had a great many left' (p. 238). Presumably Miss Bates's own neighbourliness has much to do with the Wallises' being so 'extremely civil and obliging to us', even though 'some people say that Mrs. Wallis can be uncivil and give a very rude answer' and though 'it cannot be for the value of our custom *now*' (pp. 236–7; my italics). Faced with troubling possibilities of quite another order than any of these trifles, Miss Bates insists that 'nobody could nurse her [Jane], as we should do' (p. 161). And, faced with Jane's imminent departure, she puts her own distress aside: 'My poor mother does not know how to bear it. So then, I try to put it out of her thoughts, and say, Come ma'am, do not let us think about it any more' (p. 382). Foolish as Miss Bates can be, these are not the remarks of one who is blind to her situation.

II

The gulf in comparative incidence between the opposite extremities of the scale that underlies the foregoing discussion is a matter of demonstrable fact, to which we shall return. The differences between the actual pronoun idioms of the various characters lie in the more open ground of literary inference and interpretation. So far as literary interpretation is well-founded, they can be seen as illuminating the 'personality' and 'situation' of each character who has been discussed. This, obviously, is not to suggest that my particular interpretations have any claim to be definitive. It is rather to insist that, even with such inconspicuous words as 'we', 'our', and 'us', worthwhile interpretative possibilities arise and that, in the further matter of literary evaluation, Jane Austen's long-standing reputation for exactitude and for 'density of texture' is given fresh support.

But how much should be made of so inconspicuous a word as 'we'? Even for one whose primary interest is in literary studies, it is necessary to step back for a time from the inspection of examples and to reflect a little on the meaning of meaning. Up to a point, 'we' can serve as an appropriate test case.

It might seem reasonable, in the first place, to counter my seemingly pointillistic brand of evidence with the objection that a word like 'we' means nothing whatever until it is set in context. In answer to such an objection, a traditional grammarian would maintain that 'we', like other words, should be regarded as having incipient meaning, in a sort of Aristotelian potentiality, not realized until it is set in context. More recent authorities, following Roman

Jakobson, would maintain that, for any speaker of English, 'we' bears a certain 'context' even before it is brought into use. It is among those words that can open a sentence. It is among those words that can stand as subject to a verb. It is among those words that allude to more than one referent (the speaker being among them) without actually naming those referents. Already it is distinct from 'John', 'I', 'you', and 'us'—to say nothing of 'although' and 'purple': for none of these words conforms even to this rudimentary set of constraints on meaning. (Like most English words, moreover, it stands at an advantage over such undeniably homographic words as 'bear' and 'tear', which do not assume a definite identity until they are brought into use.) As soon as it is mentioned, even if it is the opening word of a fresh discourse, 'we' takes on a more immediate meaning by identifying its referents: the bases of identification, not always unambiguous at first, are likely to be predominantly grammatical when other utterances have led on to the 'we', predominantly social when it initiates a fresh discourse. On either traditional or more recent doctrine, 'we', taken alone, is not devoid of meaning.

Further accretions of meaning and an increasing exactness of application attach to a given instance of 'we' as its context is elaborated. On a traditional account, these processes are best understood as a syntactical development. The little set of forms 'we shall', 'we will', 'you will', and 'you shall' illustrate the reciprocal processes that begin as soon as two words are conjoined. When a main verb is added, further interactions occur. And so the development continues, back and forth, towards a sentence; a complete speech or a paragraph; a conversation or a chapter . . .

Jakobson, however, emphasizes the forward thrust of this linear development, describes it as 'syntagmatic' rather than 'syntactical', and treats it as one main 'axis' of meaning. He matches it with another, the 'semantic' or 'paradigmatic'. Instead of confining the idea of the 'semantic' to a choice among the received—or even neologistic—meanings of a particular word, Jakobson expands it to include the choice, at any given moment, from among a host of rival words: from among *all* those words, for example, that can initiate an English sentence. For him, accordingly, the full meaning of a word is to be located at the intersection of the 'syntagmatic' and 'paradigmatic' axes.

If that is a fair sketch of Jakobson's main doctrine on this point, I would argue that it is necessary to take account of a dimension of meaning which cannot be located at the intersection of the axes and which overrides the distinction between them. With each of the characters whose use of a particular set of pronouns was examined in the foregoing pages, an idiosyncratic pattern of 'meaning' emerged. It consisted partly in habitual choices of referents from among all the other characters of the novel concerned; partly in habitual idioms and devices; and, indisputably, in the sharply differing extent of each one's recourse to that particular set of words. At the moment of *each* decision to use 'we' or not to do so, to single out these referents or those, to impose a claim on them or to assume their support: at that moment, no doubt, the concept of the 'paradigmatic' affords a heavily burdened but not inappropriate explanatory framework. But scarcely any of these decisions acquires its full complement of meaning until it can be recognized as either habitual or not: and that recognition depends upon an iterative process of comprehension which (though ultimately linear in nature) seems to transcend Jakobson's concept of the 'syntagmatic' almost as completely as it transcends the traditional concept of syntactical development. The continued iteration of a single 'paradigm', that is to say, accrues a kind of meaning that cannot well be located at a single notional intersection. If anything, the traditional account has the advantage here in more readily admitting a retrospective mode of recognition.

Suppose, however, that my sketch is unfair; that the concept of the 'paradigmatic' can legitimately be extended to include every conceivable kind of 'synchronic' meaning or 'meaning-in-the-moment'; and that the 'syntagmatic' can likewise be extended to include every conceivable kind of 'diachronic' or 'linear' meaning, even an iteration repeated only at intervals of many pages and not recognized as in any way unusual until a whole discourse is almost ended. Even then, there are dimensions of meaning that cannot reasonably be explained as lying at the intersection of the axes. Of the nine characters from *Emma* who find a place in our set of forty-eight, Miss Bates is the most given, in relative terms, to using pronouns in the first person plural. (Even in absolute terms, she falls second only to Emma who has a speaking-part of 21,501 words compared to her 7624.) It should now be added that, relative to the respective frequencies of each word, she is much less given to the use of 'our' (which is Mrs Elton's special province) than to the use of 'we'; and that her use of 'us' towers above both to a point where none of those other eight characters lies remotely within reach of her. The difference appears to arise from idioms that tend to objectify the family group for which she customarily speaks and tend to acknowledge a certain passivity or submissiveness as part of its inevitable role. On which axis or at which intersection does this *relationship* of meanings rest? (It is one in which Mrs Gardiner, of *Pride and Prejudice*, and Anne Steele, of *Sense and Sensibility*, make appropriate companions for her.) As so often occurs, a binary mode of explanation like Jakobson's sounds more plausible in the abstract than it proves to be when it is applied to the complexity of actual cases.[4] Still further complexities arise from the fact that, in Miss Bates's extremely sparing use of the first person *singular* pronouns, there is a more 'normal' relationship between her 'I' and 'me' than there is between her 'we' and 'us'. Something of the comically but not unsympathetically rendered struggle between her native temperament — so to put it — and her cognizance of her situation comes into issue here: '"Why, to own the truth," cried Miss Bates, who had been trying in vain to be heard the last two minutes, "if I must speak on this subject, . . ."' (pp. 345–6).

Such subtle interactions of meaning as these give rise to larger questions which demand a first comment at this point. Can a linguistic phenomenon, however firmly its existence can be demonstrated, properly be described as 'meaningful' when a computer-assisted concordance is required to bring its full ramifications to the light of day? The beginning of an answer lies in the fact that readers clearly have the capacity to recognize emphatic uses of words that are mostly inconspicuous. 'We few, we happy few, we band of brothers' enacts its own idea through emphatic repetition. Throughout *Lord Jim*, Marlow obsessively returns to the question of whether Jim is truly 'one of us'. James Joyce discovers absurd effects in the pompous use of 'one': 'When one reads these strange pages of one long gone one feels that one is at one with one who once . . .' (*Ulysses*, i). In a breathtakingly appropriate reversal of the conventional sex-roles of the day, Jane Eyre's 'Reader, I

---

[4] There are passages where Jakobson complains that modern linguistics is limited by a tendency to treat 'the *sentence* as the highest linguistic unit': *Selected Writings* vol. ii, (The Hague, 1971), p. 280. This remark and others like it are brought together, with a searching comment, in Horst Ruthrof, *The Reader's Construction of Narrative* (London, 1981), p. 36. It does not appear, however, that Jakobson himself found any effective way of overcoming a limitation to which his own binary model is predisposed.

married him' has caught the attention of generations of readers. 'Call me Ishmael' is not only prominently placed but diverges from more conventional forms like 'My name is Ishmael' or 'Ishmael [Jones?] had come to Nantucket in the hope . . .'. And Kate Croy's sombre 'We shall never be again as we were' gathers its poignancy from all that has gone before it. But the dull note of the habitual, rather than any single moment of particular emphasis, seems to account for our being equally able to recognize what is implied in *Little Me*, as title for a book about a tinsel celebrity; for 'Just what would happen to Norm and I', as one of Dame Edna's Australianisms; or for 'He always was a bit of an "I am"', as a folk-phrase.

Sometimes such modes of expression are understood in a flash of insight, to which their own sudden obtrusiveness may contribute. (The much repeated use of 'I', by Kurtz's Intended, in the closing pages of *Heart of Darkness* is a strong example.[5]) But, even if they are never consciously recognized or never recognized in their fullness, they can presumably participate, at a subliminal level, in the establishment of meaning. To accept this possibility, it is necessary only to dismiss the naive idea that the conscious and the subconscious are entirely closed off from each other, as mutually exclusive compartments of the mind, the former untouched by deeper stirrings, the latter impenetrable by intuition or a flash of recollection. Mrs Elton's mission of demeaning others and elevating herself is well represented, as I have tried to show, in her pronoun-idioms. But her qualities display themselves in many other idioms and actions, some more plainly evident than these. To give close attention to any one habitual idiom or set of idioms is certainly to consolidate, sometimes to enrich (and sometimes, conceivably, to distort) our understanding of the Eltonian. It is not to create meaning through a computer-assisted 'Fiat lux'.

Nor, finally, is it the case that 'we' itself or the first person plural pronouns in general supply peculiarly favourable specimens of Jane Austen's differentiations among the idiolects of her characters. Of the many high-frequency words examined in my research so far, none fails to show a considerable range of incidence across the set of major characters. Certainly the range is greater among some of the more obviously energetic pronouns, 'I', 'my', 'he', 'she', and 'her' being the striking examples. But even so colourless a word as 'it' produces

[5] It was drawn to my attention by a former colleague, W. M. Maidment.

a wide range. The average incidence of 'it' in the dialogue of the six novels is 18.41 per 1000 words. Eleanor Tilney (27.86) and Catherine Morland (26.28) head the scale while Collins (11.25) and Sir Thomas Bertram (11.13) bring up the rear.

The numerical resemblance between Catherine and Eleanor in the use of 'it' makes the basis of a nice contrast, especially evident when they are speaking to each other. The crisp relationship between pronoun and antecedent that pervades Eleanor's usage, together with her habit of alluding indirectly to a definite *idea*, stands beside Catherine's slackness of connection and her emphasis on *things*. While Mrs Elton (13.72) is also interested in *things*, she is far more disposed to name them for safekeeping and to take out insurance with a 'my' or 'our'. For Eleanor, however, the only *things* that attract more than a passing instance of 'it' are the portrait of her mother and the chest in Catherine's room at the Abbey. A more thoroughgoing account of 'it' would also give proper attention to its function, uncommon among these speakers, as a syntactical indicator, a reference-point for such exactly marshalled but (for conversation) rather formal constructions as Mr Knightley's 'it is fair to suppose that . . .' (p. 66); 'it is not to be conceived that . . .' (p. 146); and 'it may be hoped' (p. 448). But, as he himself might say, it may be felt that it is time to turn to matters of another kind.

2

The Chi-squared Test as a
Register of Significant Differences

Table 2 sets out the incidences, for each major character, of 'we', 'our', 'us', and also for these three words treated as a set. Enough attention has been given to the extreme ends of the scales: but it is worth noting how consistently Emma Woodhouse, Elizabeth Bennet, and Anne Elliot remain near the middle of each scale. While this might be taken, with Emma (who has 21,501 words all told) and with Elizabeth (13,597), as a mere averaging-out over a very large word-field, that line of argument is challenged by Anne (4336), who has the smallest speaking-part of any of the heroines. As the analysis continues, these three—and often Elinor Dashwood (9039)—will be found close to the mean-incidence in many other common features of vocabulary. Catherine Morland (7040) and Fanny Price (6117) are less often of their company than within reach of each other.

If the average frequencies of the three words are compared, it is evident that the shape of the total set is over-influenced by 'we'. There are less 'loaded' ways of examining such combinations. Before turning to them, however, we should consider how a statistician might test the figures to establish whether they show differences 'significant' enough to be taken seriously.

The chi-squared test of probability is a powerful but unwieldy instrument for examining questions of this kind. Its function is to establish whether a discrepancy of a given size, in a field of a given size, is too large to be dismissed as a likely chance effect. Since statistical analysis can never exclude the possibility of a freak case, the results are expressed not as truths but as degrees of probability. At the beginning of an electoral count, the first five hundred votes might show a 'swing' of massive proportions in one direction or another: but no one would regard this as a 'significant' indication of the eventual result. By the end of the evening, with three-quarters of the votes counted, a much smaller swing would justifiably be regarded as very significant indeed. And yet, even then, the probable result might be overset by a freakishly strong trend in the uncounted

TABLE 2. Comparative Incidences of Three Personal Pronouns for Jane Austen's Major Characters

ALL		we		our		us	
Admiral Croft	24.58	Admiral Croft	16.22	Admiral Croft	4.92	Anne Steele	4.84
Lydia Bennet	19.42	Lydia Bennet	14.45	Mrs Dashwood	3.93	Miss Bates	4.72
Tom Bertram	19.37	Tom Bertram	12.69	Lucy Steele	3.27	Lydia Bennet	4.52
Miss Bates	13.90	Mr Weston	8.45	Tom Bertram	3.24	Mrs Gardiner	4.19
Lucy Steele	13.33	Miss Bates	7.48	Mrs Elton	2.96	Lucy Steele	3.52
Mr Weston	12.82	John Thorpe	7.17	Collins	2.93	Jane Bennet	3.46
Mrs Dashwood	11.80	Lady Bertram	6.94	Mr Bennet	2.46	Admiral Croft	3.44
Jane Bennet	11.72	Mary Musgrove	6.70	Sir Thomas	2.28	Mr Weston	3.44
Mary Musgrove	11.25	Marianne	6.69	Mary Musgrove	2.14	Mr Bennet	3.39
Mrs Elton	11.22	Lucy Steele	6.54	Mrs Gardiner	2.09	Tom Bertram	3.34
Anne Steele	11.13	Jane Bennet	6.34	Marianne	1.98	Lady Bertram	3.24
Lady Bertram	10.74	Anne Steele	6.29	Jane Bennet	1.92	Mrs Weston	3.14
Marianne	10.33	Miss Bingley	6.11	HENRY TILNEY	1.79	Eleanor Tilney	3.10
Mrs Weston	10.14	Mrs Elton	6.08	Miss Bates	1.71	Isab. Thorpe	3.01
Sir Thomas	9.61	Mrs Weston	5.55	EDWARD FERRARS	1.70	Sir Thomas	2.78
Isab. Thorpe	9.55	Mrs Dashwood	5.34	John Dashwood	1.57	Mr Woodhouse	2.59
Miss Bingley	9.40	ANNE	5.30	Mr Woodhouse	1.51	Mrs Dashwood	2.53
Mr Bennet	9.24	ELIZABETH	5.15	Wickham	1.47	Collins	2.48
Collins	9.23	Isab. Thorpe	5.13	Mrs Weston	1.45	Mary Musgrove	2.41
John Thorpe	9.22	Mrs Norris	4.96	Isab. Thorpe	1.41	Miss Bingley	2.35
Mrs Gardiner	9.08	Wickham	4.90	ANNE	1.38	Mrs Elton	2.18
ANNE	8.53	Mary Crawford	4.76	Col. Brandon	1.35	Mrs Bennet	2.15
Eleanor Tilney	8.26	Sir Thomas	4.55	EMMA	1.30	Mrs Norris	2.10
Mr Woodhouse	8.19	Mrs Bennet	4.46	Mary Crawford	1.23	EDMUND	2.03
Mrs Norris	7.51	Eleanor Tilney	4.13	EDMUND	1.19	EMMA	1.95
Mrs Bennet	7.44	Mr Woodhouse	4.10	WENTWORTH	1.18	ANNE	1.85
ELIZABETH	7.43	Mrs Jennings	4.06	ELINOR	1.11	Marianne	1.67
EMMA	7.21	John Dashwood	4.03	ELIZABETH	1.03	ELINOR	1.66
John Dashwood	7.17	EMMA	3.95	Eleanor Tilney	1.03	John Dashwood	1.57
EDMUND	7.13	EDMUND	3.92	John Thorpe	1.02	CATHERINE	1.42
Mary Crawford	6.98	Churchill	3.89	CATHERINE	0.99	HENRY TILNEY	1.30
Wickham	6.86	Crawford	3.86	Mr Weston	0.94	ELIZABETH	1.25
CATHERINE	6.11	Collins	3.83	Miss Bingley	0.94	Mrs Jennings	1.06
HENRY TILNEY	6.02	CATHERINE	3.69	Mrs Bennet	0.83	Crawford	1.04
ELINOR	5.64	FANNY	3.43	FANNY	0.82	John Thorpe	1.02
Churchill	5.35	Mr Bennet	3.39	KNIGHTLEY	0.79	Mary Crawford	1.00
Crawford	5.35	WENTWORTH	2.95	DARCY	0.78	Churchill	0.85
Mrs Jennings	5.30	HENRY TILNEY	2.93	Willoughby	0.76	Lady Catherine	0.85
WENTWORTH	4.73	ELINOR	2.88	Mrs Smith	0.75	WENTWORTH	0.59
FANNY	4.41	Mrs Gardiner	2.79	Churchill	0.61	Willoughby	0.57
KNIGHTLEY	3.76	Harriet Smith	2.65	Lady Bertram	0.46	Col. Brandon	0.54
Col. Brandon	3.51	KNIGHTLEY	2.47	Mrs Norris	0.45	Mrs Smith	0.50
Harriet Smith	3.03	Col. Brandon	1.62	Lydia Bennet	0.45	KNIGHTLEY	0.49
Mrs Smith	2.76	Mrs Smith	1.51	Crawford	0.45	Wickham	0.49
DARCY	2.66	DARCY	1.41	Lady Catherine	0.43	DARCY	0.47
EDWARD FERRARS	2.54	Willoughby	1.14	Harriet Smith	0.19	Harriet Smith	0.19
Willoughby	2.46	EDWARD FERRARS	0.85	Mrs Jennings	0.18	FANNY	0.16
Lady Catherine	2.13	Lady Catherine	0.85	Anne Steele	0.00	EDWARD FERRARS	0.00

votes. (The coin-tossing episode, at the beginning of Stoppard's *Rosencrantz and Guildenstern are Dead*, enters exuberantly into the relationships between the possible and the probable.) To repeat, the chi-squared test measures the degree of probability attaching to a sustained tendency of any given size in a whole field of any given size. When the proper conditions are observed, the test applies as well to the distribution of words or the germination of seeds as to coin-tossing or the distribution of votes at an election.

The formula and the method of calculation can be found in any introductory work on statistical analysis. (While the present study does not purport to be a manual of that kind, some detail is offered in Appendix B.) The basis, however, lies in postulating and testing a 'null hypothesis' in which an actual result is compared with what might have been expected: the hypothesis is upheld when the expectation is satisfied. For the purposes of this study, the null hypothesis (which was introduced, without being given its technical name, in the Introduction) is that, where a given word is as 'inert' as the very common words are customarily treated as being, it will be distributed among the speakers in proportion to the size of their speaking-parts. No one would expect this distribution to be numerically exact: the function of the chi-squared test is precisely to allow adequate leeway for small departures into the 'more or less' that characterizes the behaviour of most phenomena, and to distinguish them from those larger departures that cannot reasonably be ignored.

Since the results do not express totalities but degrees of relationship between actuality and expectation, they tend—no matter what the original size of the field—to emerge as values of about the same order. A resultant value of 3.83 or less is usually dismissed as being over-susceptible to the intrusion of chance and is described as 'non-significant'. A resultant value between 3.84 and 6.62 indicates a 'significant' result with only a 5 per cent likelihood that it comes about by chance. A resultant value between 6.63 and 10.82 indicates a 'highly significant' result with only a 1 per cent likelihood that it comes about by chance. When the values rise above 10.83, they are regarded as 'very highly significant', at the 0.1 per cent level, with only one chance in a thousand or more that they come about by chance.[1]

---

[1] The values named pertain to the 'first degree of freedom', which is appropriate to the results described in this chapter. When the context requires it, the positive and negative ranges of significance are distinguished by the single, double, or treble use of the + and − signs. See, for example, Table 5.

In the less exact of the sciences, a 'significant' result might arise two or three times in twenty calculations: so long as the proportion of one in twenty (5 per cent) is exceeded, the results are to be taken seriously. In the analysis of the distribution of Jane Austen's most common words among her major characters, 'significant' results are commonplace and results that soar far beyond the threshold of 'very high significance' are by no means rare. Some grammatical classes, especially the most common personal pronouns and the non-modal auxiliary verbs, produce particularly spectacular results; but scarcely any of the common words that I have tested fails to produce 'significant' results for several major characters. Among all the words that occur more than a hundred times in the dialogue of the six novels, the average proportion of 'significant' results is about one in every five calculations; and the proportion of highly significant and (especially) very highly significant results far exceeds the thresholds of one in a hundred and one in a thousand respectively.

But there are proper conditions to be observed. The expectation itself must be legitimate. As we have seen, the word 'we' comes altogether more freely to the uxorious Admiral Croft than to the widowed Lady Catherine. Is it legitimate to mount an argument on the almost inevitable failure of the hypothesis that, as between these two characters, 'we' might conceivably be distributed in proportion to the sizes of their speaking-parts? Perhaps not: it depends upon the sort of argument that is mounted. He who cheerfully ignores the role of such words in the shaping of literary characters may not be the worse for a vivid reminder of the fact that they are continually at work. He who would hold that such a demonstration of the difference between the vocabulary of widowhood and that of happy marriage is a trivial display of the self-evident might consider where Jane Austen's various widows lie in Table 2. In the 'we' column, for example, they range from Mrs Dashwood (5.34) to Lady Catherine (0.85): even if young brides are excluded, the married women span a wide and partly overlapping range from Lady Bertram (6.94) to Mrs Gardiner (2.79). The various differences in both groups depend, of course, upon differences of temperament and situation, along such lines as were developed in the previous chapter. By the time all that was properly understood, a recognition of the power and the diversity of 'we' might well have replaced the notion that the word serves only self-evident purposes; and the statistical evidence might have been recognized as a useful point of departure.

TABLE 3. The Overall Differentiation of Three Common Words

	we	of	very
Very highly significant	6	9	6
Highly significant	5	5	8
Significant	5	4	8
Non-significant	32	30	26
Total	48	48	48

Suppose, however, that it were argued that 'we' carries too many semantic possibilities to belong among the grammatical words and should not, therefore, be regarded, even hypothetically, as inert. That position would be more persuasive if it were not the beginning of an irresistible slide. When the chi-squared test is applied to 'we', 'of', and 'very', the first yields the *least* striking range of significant differentiations among the forty-eight characters. (See Table 3.)

On the basis of evidence which will be unfolded in the following chapters, but of which this remarkable comparison is a fair specimen, I no longer believe that the null hypothesis, in the form proposed above, is beyond refinement. The proportion of significant results and the frequency with which very high values appear are too marked for that. And yet the majority of the non-significant results hold so very close to 0.00 that the hypothesis cannot be put aside as disreputable. In its present form, it serves, certainly, to emphasize how little room there is for chance effects even in the least visible regions of Jane Austen's dialogue. And, by supplying a common ground for the testing of all high-frequency words alike, it serves the twin purposes of revealing their enormous energy and destroying the crude distinction between 'lexical' and 'grammatical' words. It will not be time to discard this particular version of the null hypothesis until discussions of literary works cease to proceed as if it were tenable. And, when that time comes, it will still be better to refine it than to discard it—to frame it, that is to say, as a test of more reasonable expectations than those upon which so much discussion of literature tacitly, if unwittingly, relies. Much has been made, in critical discussion, of Jane Austen's 'little bit (two Inches wide) of Ivory'. We still have a great deal to learn about the precision with which ('after much labour') 'so fine a Brush' produces its effects (*Letters*, ed. R. W. Chapman, p. 469).

For its straightforward operation, the chi-squared test also requires that the observed phenomena should be pretty uniformly spread throughout the whole field and not gathered into clusters in one part or another. When a pronounced clustering occurs, it is obviously unreasonable to offer propositions that imply uniformity—such propositions as that Emma uses 'we' at a rate of 3.95 per 1000 words. The possibility that significant clustering-effects are present can be tested by extracting a different set of chi-squared values, in which one half of a given field is set against the other: the comparison reflects any marked difference between the first and second halves of a given speaking-part. (In this operation, a non-significant value is the mark of uniformity; and the more significant the value, the more striking the departure from uniformity.) Since characters come and go in the course of a novel—since Frank Churchill does not make his first appearance until the second volume of *Emma* is well advanced and since even Mrs Norris's tongue is almost stilled by the middle of *Mansfield Park*—this set of calculations can only be based on the point at which each character arrives at his particular halfway mark.

All in all, the evidence of stable *differentiation* between character and character, idiolect and idiolect, is far more pronounced than the evidence of *variation* within any one idiolect. Even with the commonest words of all, in the largest speaking-parts, 'significant' variation (as registered by this application of the chi-squared test) is comparatively uncommon. But closer inspection of the evidence shows that what began as a routine check against random breaches of uniformity needs to be pursued more rigorously as a test of meaningful character-development. No one who is well acquainted with *Emma* will fail to recognize why, without ever becoming very much given to the use of 'I', both Emma and Mr Knightley should find more occasion for it in the last part of the novel, where they talk increasingly of themselves in a manner very different from that of their earlier disputes about Harriet Smith and Frank Churchill. Edmund Bertram's preoccupation with himself and Mary, fully voiced at last in letters to and conversations with Fanny in the closing stages of *Mansfield Park*, coincides with an increased recourse to 'I'. Catherine Morland uses 'I' much less often as she learns to eschew such nervous makeweight phrases as 'I am sure'. What should Frank Churchill do but turn from 'it' to 'her' when it becomes possible, at last, for him to speak openly of 'her' whose secret he has flirted with but never quite betrayed and, also, of 'her' whom he has used so assiduously as a decoy? What should Fanny do but turn from the impersonalities of 'the' and more than ever towards 'I' when she is threatened with Henry's suit? The implication of most of the departures from uniformity is not that statistical analysis should be abandoned but that the departures themselves should be tested more exactly. With the assurance that the results of such testing enrich, not destroy, the argument of Parts One and Two, I propose to reserve these subtler questions for Part Three of this study.

Two smaller matters should next be recognized. Statistical analysis becomes increasingly inappropriate as field-sizes diminish. Except in special circumstances, chi-squared values are regarded as invalid when the *expected* frequency is less than five. In treating of major characters and very common words, we shall not often encounter that difficulty. When it does arise, as in Tables 4 and 5, the affected instances have been treated as incalculable (and marked 'INC'). With a plethora of valid results to consider, there is no occasion for pleading special cases.

The laws of chance have a corollary that is sometimes overlooked. If there is only one chance in a hundred that a given phenomenon will occur, we are inclined to remember the nine-and-ninety and to forget that the hundredth case must, in due course, occur. And yet the statistical tests that assure us that it will occur do little to identify it. Some of these twentieth, one hundredth, and one thousandth cases are undoubtedly buried, often beyond recovery, among the multitude of 'significant' values. Others, perhaps, are recognizable as departures from the general pattern. Only the vocabulary of Collins and that of Miss Bates yield significant values for the preposition 'with', which—from its very multiplicity of meanings—emerges as one of the most 'inert' words of all. Yet the highly significant positive value attaching to his use of the word and the significant negative value attaching to hers are in keeping with the whole pattern of their uses of the major prepositions. It is even easier to find meaning in the significant positive values attaching to 'at' for Frank Churchill, Mrs Elton, and Admiral Croft: at Enscombe, Weymouth, and Richmond; at Maple Grove, Maple Grove, and Maple Grove; in living comfortably at North Yarmouth or making do at Kellynch, in gazing scornfully at a picture of a boat or in wintering at sea. But neither the shape of his sentences nor the substance of his idiom suggests—to me at least—why Edmund Bertram should produce a significant negative value for 'at' when all those whom he usually resembles lie quiet in non-significance. It seems likely that a chance effect has carried him across the borderline into a spurious significance. And yet, while it is interesting to try to identify them, the existence, here and there, of statistical 'wild cards' scarcely affects the main thrust of an argument based on an average of one significant value in every five calculations.

A last major problem of method stems from the fact that statistical comparisons are meaningful only to the extent that they rest upon an appropriate common base. As will appear later, calculations based upon the whole vocabulary of Jane Austen's novels serve only to emphasize the overwhelming and all-pervasive differences between the language of narrative and that of dialogue. The nicer distinctions between novel and novel, character and character are engulfed by that one contrast.

Any useful comparisons between one of Jane Austen's narratives and another (or between her narratives and those of other novelists) need therefore to be based upon the vocabulary of narrative. They will be considered in due course. Comparisons within the dialogue of the characters can usefully take either of two forms. The line of argument pursued in the foregoing pages has treated of forty-eight major characters as if they inhabited a single linguistic neighbour-hood—rather in the manner of E. M. Forster's vision of all the great English novelists working, side by side, in the Reading Room of the British Museum. This approach, which takes the whole dialogue of the six novels as its base, is of value in bringing out differences and resemblances among particular characters and sets of characters across the whole range: resemblances, for example, between Henry Crawford and Frank Churchill (sometimes accompanied by Wickham or Willoughby); among Isabella Thorpe, Lydia Bennet, and Lucy Steele (though the last is the most assiduously genteel); among most of the heroes and several of the heroines; and, closest of all, between Elizabeth Bennet and Emma Woodhouse. If the approach is extended to comparisons of groups—between the generations, the sexes, or the 'classes'—some larger questions can be tested with an uncommon degree of exactitude. This whole approach would be invalidated if Jane Austen's apportionment of the commonest words of dialogue had changed very markedly over the course of her literary career. But, while there are some recognizable changes in the vocabulary of dialogue, few of the

Common Measures

TABLE 4. Chi-squared Values for the Differentiation of Three Pronouns in Six Novels (The chi-squared values are calculated for the whole dialogue of the six novels.)

ALL (we, our, us)		we (1470)		our (424)		us (567)	
Admiral Croft	67.7	Admiral Croft	53.3	Admiral Croft	INC	Anne Steele	INC
Lydia Bennet	34.7	Lydia Bennet	41.3	Mrs Dashwood	15.0	Miss Bates	32.7
Tom Bertram	46.9	Tom Bertram	37.5	Lucy Steele	9.0	Lydia Bennet	INC
Miss Bates	32.4	Mr Weston	8.2	Tom Bertram	INC	Mrs Gardiner	7.3
Lucy Steele	13.4	Miss Bates	11.0	Mrs Elton	10.5	Lucy Steele	5.2
Mr Weston	8.7	John Thorpe	3.0	Collins	6.6	Jane Bennet	6.5
Mrs Dashwood	5.9	Lady Bertram	1.7	Mr Bennet	INC	Admiral Croft	INC
Jane Bennet	8.5	Mary Musgrove	2.5	Sir Thomas	1.7	Mr Weston	3.6
Mary Musgrove	4.5	Marianne	4.6	Mary Musgrove	1.1	Mr Bennet	3.4
Mrs Elton	7.9	Lucy Steele	2.6	Mrs Gardiner	INC	Tom Bertram	2.9
Anne Steele	2.2	Jane Bennet	2.3	Marianne	1.3	Lady Bertram	INC
Lady Bertram	1.6	Anne Steele	0.7	Jane Bennet	0.8	Mrs Weston	3.1
Marianne	4.2	Miss Bingley	0.5	HENRY TILNEY	0.5	Eleanor Tilney	INC
Mrs Weston	2.1	Mrs Elton	2.0	Miss Bates	0.4	Isab. Thorpe	3.5
Sir Thomas	1.1	Mrs Weston	0.4	EDWARD FERRARS	INC	Sir Thomas	1.4
Isab. Thorpe	1.5	Mrs Dashwood	0.1	John Dashwood	0.0	Mr Woodhouse	1.0
Miss Bingley	0.4	ANNE	0.2	Mr Woodhouse	0.0	Mrs Dashwood	0.6
Mr Bennet	0.5	ELIZABETH	0.3	Wickham	INC	Collins	0.7
Collins	0.7	Isab. Thorpe	0.1	Mrs Weston	0.0	Mary Musgrove	0.4
John Thorpe	0.4	Mrs Norris	0.0	Isab. Thorpe	0.0	Miss Bingley	INC
Mrs Gardiner	0.3	Wickham	0.0	ANNE	0.0	Mrs Elton	0.2
ANNE	0.1	Mary Crawford	0.0	Col. Brandon	0.0	Mrs Bennet	0.2
Eleanor Tilney	0.0	Sir Thomas	0.0	EMMA	0.1	Mrs Norris	0.1
Mr Woodhouse	0.0	Mrs Bennet	0.1	Mary Crawford	0.1	EDMUND	0.2
Mrs Norris	0.2	Eleanor Tilney	0.1	EDMUND	0.3	EMMA	0.1
Mrs Bennet	0.2	Mr Woodhouse	0.3	WENTWORTH	0.0	ANNE	0.0
ELIZABETH	0.5	Mrs Jennings	0.5	ELINOR	0.3	Marianne	0.0
EMMA	1.6	John Dashwood	0.4	ELIZABETH	1.0	ELINOR	0.1
John Dashwood	0.3	EMMA	2.9	Eleanor Tilney	INC	John Dashwood	0.1
EDMUND	1.3	EDMUND	2.0	John Thorpe	INC	CATHERINE	0.5
Mary Crawford	1.6	Churchill	1.2	CATHERINE	0.5	HENRY TILNEY	0.7
Wickham	0.2	Crawford	1.0	Mr Weston	INC	ELIZABETH	2.3
CATHERINE	2.9	Collins	0.7	Miss Bingley	INC	Mrs Jennings	1.5
HENRY TILNEY	2.8	CATHERINE	1.5	Mrs Bennet	1.0	Crawford	2.0
ELINOR	6.0	FANNY	2.1	FANNY	1.0	John Thorpe	0.7
Churchill	6.9	Mr Bennet	1.1	KNIGHTLEY	2.1	Mary Crawford	4.6
Crawford	5.6	WENTWORTH	2.0	DARCY	1.3	Churchill	3.9
Mrs Jennings	4.8	HENRY TILNEY	4.1	Willoughby	1.1	Lady Catherine	INC
WENTWORTH	4.2	ELINOR	6.5	Mrs Smith	0.7	WENTWORTH	2.3
FANNY	9.4	Mrs Gardiner	2.0	Churchill	3.0	Willoughby	4.0
KNIGHTLEY	22.3	Harriet Smith	4.6	Lady Bertram	INC	Col. Brandon	2.7
Col. Brandon	8.8	KNIGHTLEY	10.8	Mrs Norris	3.5	Mrs Smith	3.2
Harriet Smith	15.7	Col. Brandon	7.1	Lydia Bennet	INC	KNIGHTLEY	9.3
Mrs Smith	13.1	Mrs Smith	8.3	Crawford	3.6	Wickham	INC
DARCY	22.2	DARCY	14.6	Lady Catherine	INC	DARCY	5.8
EDWARD FERRARS	8.1	Willoughby	13.9	Harriet Smith	4.6	Harriet Smith	7.0
Willoughby	19.6	EDWARD FERRARS	6.8	Mrs Jennings	5.1	FANNY	8.5
Lady Catherine	9.4	Lady Catherine	6.8	Anne Steele	INC	EDWARD FERRARS	INC

Note. In order to emphasize the difference between simple incidences and the chi-squared values, the characters are listed in the same sequence as in Table 2. The threshold values for significance, high significance, and very high significance are 3.84, 6.63, and 10.83.

TABLE 5. Chi-squared Values for the Differentiation of Three Pronouns within each Novel
(The chi-squared values are calculated separately for each novel, with its dialogue as base.)

		ALL	we	our	us
Northanger Abbey	(28930)				
1A	CATHERINE (7040)	5.7–	3.5	0.6	1.0
1B	HENRY (6149)	5.3–	6.5–	0.4	1.3
1D	Isabella Thorpe (5657)	0.2	0.0	0.0	2.1
1E	John Thorpe (2928)	0.0	1.4	INC	1.0
1C	Eleanor Tilney (1938)	0.0	0.4	INC	INC
	(Others 5218)				
Sense and Sensibility	(52334)				
2A	ELINOR (9039)	3.0	3.1	0.4	0.0
2C	Marianne (6580)	8.1++	9.8++	1.1	0.0
2K	Mrs Jennings (5659)	2.7	0.0	5.3–	1.1
2S	Willoughby (5278)	16.1–––	10.7––	1.2	3.4
2F	John Dashwood (4462)	0.0	0.0	0.0	0.0
2Q	Lucy Steele (3977)	19.3+++	5.0+	8.4++	6.5+
2H	Colonel Brandon (3700)	6.7––	5.0–	0.0	2.4
2D	Mrs Dashwood (3560)	9.5++	1.0	14.2+++	1.0
2B	EDWARD FERRARS (2359)	6.6–	5.4–	INC	INC
2P	Anne Steele (2066)	3.8	1.9	INC	INC
	(Others 5654)				
Pride and Prejudice	(55976)				
3A	ELIZABETH (13597)	0.6	1.0	0.7	5.0–
3B	DARCY (6399)	22.4–––	13.2–––	1.0	7.8––
3D	Mrs Bennet (6048)	0.2	0.0	0.8	0.0
3E	Jane (5203)	8.3++	3.4	1.0	3.4
3K	Collins (4444)	0.6	0.4	7.5++	0.1
3C	Mr Bennet (3248)	0.4	0.7	INC	1.7
3O	Mrs Gardiner (2865)	0.3	1.6	INC	4.4+
3L	Lady Catherine (2342)	9.4––	6.2–	INC	1.3
3H	Lydia (2214)	34.3+++	45.8+++	INC	4.5+
3J	Miss Bingley (2127)	0.3	0.8	INC	0.0
3V	Wickham (2040)	0.2	0.0	INC	INC
	(Others 5449)				
Mansfield Park	(63348)				
4B	EDMUND (14300)	1.8	5.1–	0.0	1.0
4C	Mary Crawford (13030)	2.1	0.7	0.0	0.0
4D	Henry Crawford (6735)	6.3–	2.5	2.5	1.2
4J	Mrs Norris (6659)	0.3	0.1	2.4	0.6
4A	FANNY (6117)	10.2––	3.8	0.4	7.4––
4E	Sir Thomas (3953)	0.8	0.3	3.1	2.4
4G	Tom Bertram (2995)	44.5+++	29.0+++	INC	4.1+
4F	Lady Bertram (2162)	1.3	0.8	INC	INC
	(Others 7397)				
Emma	(78057)				
5A	EMMA (21501)	0.6	1.5	0.0	0.0
5B	MR KNIGHTLEY (10112)	19.7–––	9.1––	1.5	9.4––
5E	Frank Churchill (8225)	5.5–	0.6	2.3	4.0–
5D	Miss Bates (7624)	37.8+++	13.7+++	0.8	32.2+++
5I	Mrs Elton (6415)	10.1++	3.0	13.2+++	0.2
5M	Harriet Smith (5274)	14.2–––	3.8	4.0–	7.0––
5P	Mr Woodhouse (4639)	0.1	0.1	0.1	1.0
5O	Mrs Weston (4144)	3.0	0.7	0.0	3.0
5N	Mr Weston (3197)	10.4++	9.8++	INC	3.5
	(Others 6926)				
Persuasion	(28715)				
6A	ANNE (4336)	0.1	0.0	0.8	0.0
6V	Mrs Smith (3985)	16.5–––	10.0––	2.9	2.4
6P	Mary Musgrove (3733)	1.9	1.2	0.0	1.1
6B	WENTWORTH (3386)	6.4–	3.0	1.0	1.6
6D	Admiral Croft (2034)	53.4+++	44.5+++	INC	INC
	(Others 11241)				

common words show a clear line of development and most tend rather to distinguish their main owners than to mark the 'note' of one novel as against another. (When whole sets of different words are united, however, there is some evidence of change. This will be considered in Chapter 7.)

To compare the characters of a single novel, with the whole dialogue of that novel as the base for calculation, is to shed light on questions of another kind. This approach, of course, bears more directly on what we ordinarily experience as we read a novel— attuned, say, to the passing resemblances and the fundamental differences between Catherine and Isabella in the earlier part of *Northanger Abbey* and (even if our knowledge extends there) not much occupied, for the time, in reflecting that Isabella has sisters beneath the skin in Jane Austen's other early novels. This second approach makes for more tenable comparisons between some aspects of Jane Austen's dialogue and that of other novelists. To demonstrate—as I shall—that the range of differentiation among the major characters of a novel by Georgette Heyer is narrower than Jane Austen's range, it is only reasonable to limit the comparison to what Jane Austen accomplishes in a single novel and not to allow her the plenitude of all six. This second approach also brings out a further dimension in Jane Austen's dialogue, more revealing than any simple change in the mere identity of the words she gives her speakers. In the earlier novels, culminating in *Pride and Prejudice*, both the frequency and the degree of 'significant' differentiations are higher than in the Chawton novels of her resumed career. In the Chawton novels, these effects are generally more subdued (though possibly more pervasive); there are more complex relationships between the spoken language of the heroines and the 'character narrative' that renders their thoughts; and there is clear evidence that these heroines, less stable 'linguistic entities', change more significantly in their language from relationship to relationship and also in the larger course of their dramatized careers. While both Georgette Heyer and the 'Other Lady' of *Sanditon 2* show a certain capacity for effects like those of Jane Austen's earlier novels, these later effects seem to lie beyond their reach.

As the examples offered in Tables 4 and 5 might suggest, the chi-squared values derived by taking the dialogue of one of Jane Austen's novels as the base do not often differ greatly, for the characters in question, from the values derived by taking the whole dialogue of the six novels as the base. The exceptions are mostly straightforward: since the major characters of *Northanger Abbey* talk more directly *at* each other (and rather less freely about each other) than is usual in the other novels, 'I' and 'you' are more prominent than usual while the third person pronouns are less so. Such differences are not often pronounced enough to cause the major characters of one of the novels to lie huddled together in one part of a scale. And yet, to take full advantage of the different virtues of these two approaches to the analysis of dialogue, it is necessary to remember that they *are* intrinsically different.

The unwieldiness of the chi-squared test, which was mentioned at the beginning of this chapter, is a defect of its power. In the use of 'us', the comparative incidences for Jane Bennet, Mr Weston, and Admiral Croft are 3.46, 3.44 and 3.44 per 1000 words: but, when the whole dialogue of the six novels is taken as the base, Jane attracts a 'significant' chi-squared value of 6.5, Mr Weston falls just below the level of significance at 3.6, and no valid calculation is possible for Admiral Croft. That is as it should be: their speaking-parts amount, respectively, to 5203, 3197, and 2034 words; and the whole force of the chi-squared test is to give more weight to a discrepancy sustained in a larger field than in a smaller. But, while it is as it should be and while it protects us against frivolous games played with depleted numbers, it does not make for simplicity of comparison. With such consistently sustained tendencies as typify Jane Austen's differentiation of her characters, the effect of laying all the weight of analysis upon chi-squared values would be to highlight comparatively small differences among the half-dozen or so central characters and to cloud over what goes on among those other major characters whose speaking-parts are somewhat smaller. For purposes of comparison, therefore, we should turn to other statistical methods without forgetting the enormous protective benefits afforded by the fact that the data has been 'screened' by being subjected to the chi-squared test.

3

Normal Distribution as a Method of Comparison

In statistical analysis, as in most forms of inquiry, the limitations of one approach can usually be made good by adopting another — which, in turn, has limitations of its own. The 'standard normal curve' and the 'z-scores' of which it is composed make for altogether more direct comparisons than chi-squared values afford. But a sizeable number of individual scores is required to give proper substance to the curve. (The problems arising here will be considered a little later.) And, since z-scores can be derived from small numbers as readily as from large, they can give a deceptive weight to disparities for which no valid chi-squared values could be offered. The number of incalculable values for 'our', in Tables 4 and 5, serve as warning that no normal curve should be offered even for a word that occurs around four hundred times in the dialogue of the six novels. Five hundred seems to be an acceptable working minimum, but much larger numbers are preferable.

The idea that any large group of comparable scores is likely to fall into the pattern of a bell-shaped curve, with a majority lying near the average and a dwindling minority ranging out towards either extremity, is widely recognized — whether in measuring the heights of fifteen-year olds or in assessing the proportion of manufactured articles that exactly conform to specification. (A Chad Newsome of our time would undoubtedly bring statisticians to Woollett to work on 'quality control'. It is to be hoped that the secret of the firm's 'product identity' would not be betrayed.) Such possibilities as that, under particular conditions, the peak of the curve will be steeper, flatter, or skewed to either side and that the extremities of the curve will be extended or truncated — these possibilities are scarcely less familiar. It is less commonly understood that, through processes of standardization that change the notation along the base-line of a curve without altering its shape in any way, a diversity of curves can be brought into exact comparison.

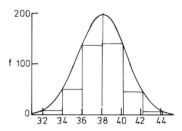

Figure 1. The Normal Distribution Curve
Waist-sizes of adult males

A bell-shaped curve is derived from a histogram in which the frequency with which each score occurs is set out in a series of columns. (See Figure 1.) To transform this mere description into a useful measure, it is necessary first to establish the mean-value of all the scores. The degree to which any one score deviates from the mean can then be derived, by a complex formula of which modern calculators make light work, from an assessment of the extent to which all the scores so deviate. The basic unit of deviation is called a 'standard deviation' and is expressed as 'sigma'. When the bell-shaped curve is roughly normal in character, as in Figure 1, its peak will lie at or near the mean-score; and a range of three units of standard deviation in either direction will cover almost all the cases.

Suppose, however, that the scale along the bottom axis were registered in other terms. If the mean, whatever its arithmetical size, were replaced by 0 and the arithmetical scores by units of standard deviation (1, 2, and 3 and − 1, − 2, and − 3), nothing would be altered except the names of these base-units. Instead of saying that

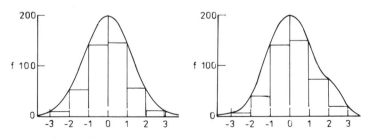

Figure 2. Two Distribution Curves
Waist-sizes of adult males (*left*)
Waist-sizes of adult females (*right*)

a waist-size of 39 for adult males and 30 for adult females both represent 0.63 of a standard deviation above the mean — the figures given are merely speculative — we can now say that each has a z-score of 0.63. The obvious advantage is that of an international currency-exchange whose rates were always stable. But the statistical advantages of the conversion go much further. It is now possible to compare the shape of any actual histogram with that of the 'standard normal curve', the theoretic model of a perfect distribution; and it is also possible to assess the 'normality' of the frequencies attaching to any given z-score by reference to a table, that of the 'Area of the Standard Normal Distribution', which is derived from the standard normal curve. For any given z-score, the table indicates precisely what proportion of a standard normal curve lies above and what below it. On this basis, it is easy to establish how far the peak of a given histogram is skewed; whether its extremities are abnormally extended or truncated; and whether any aberrations in the histogram need to be regarded as 'significant'. In the examples given in Figure 2, the aberration in the histogram for adult females would undoubtedly prove 'significant': but it would chiefly signify the investigator's lack of forethought in not allowing for the incidence of pregnancy.

The use of this method of analysis for the vocabulary of Jane Austen's major characters soon reveals that a set of forty-eight scores is too small to admit the more sophisticated forms of comparison based on the 'Area of the Standard Normal Distribution'. Forty-eight is not too few to give each curve a rough shape. Nor is it too few to suggest how markedly the pattern of incidences departs from the shape of the standard normal curve: the departures evident in each of the following graphs can be matched for almost every one of the very common words. At all events, forty-eight must suffice. If the working-definition of 'major character' is extended to include the sixty-two characters who speak more than a thousand words apiece, the additional fourteen characters do *not* make for a normalizing of the curves. Most of them are strong caricatures, including General Tilney and Mrs Allen; Mrs Palmer and Fanny Dashwood; Maria Bertram; Mr Elton and the John Knightleys; and Sir Walter Elliot. Each of these contributes, more often than not, to the extreme ends of the ranges of incidence, far outweighing the tempering effects usual (though not universal) among the remaining five — Mr Gardiner, Charles Bingley, Mrs Grant, Jane Fairfax, and Tom Musgrove. On

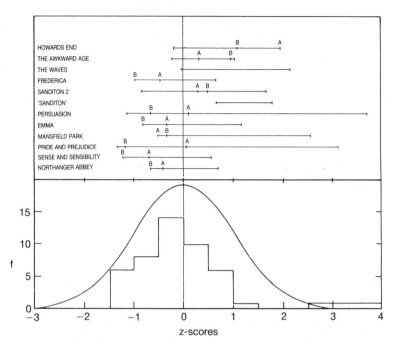

GRAPH 2. Distribution of 'we' among Jane Austen's Major Characters

a looser definition still, the pompous absurdity of Sir Edward Denham, in Jane Austen's 'Sanditon', produces no fewer than 46 instances of 'of' in his total of 739 words, an extraordinary incidence of 62 per 1000.

In the lower part of each of Graphs 2, 3, and 4 a histogram of incidences for a particular word can be compared with the superimposed standard normal curve. It is evident that (except with 'of') the histograms are much truncated in the negative range. In the positive range, however, they extend well beyond the effective limit of the standard normal curve. Only with 'of' does the peak approximate to normality: and even that peak is surrounded by abnormally low frequencies. The 'notch' of no scores at all between the main group and the outliers in these histograms appears in all but a few of the many such histograms I have examined: with only forty-eight scores available, the notch is better regarded as a 'stretch-mark'—a concomitant of the abnormal number of very high scores—than as an absolute peculiarity in its own right.

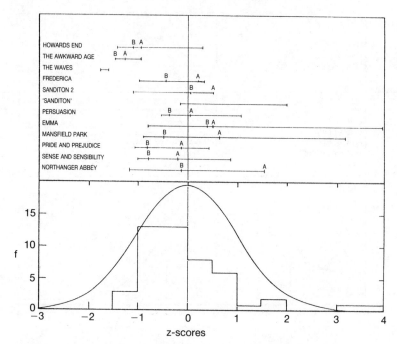

GRAPH 3. Distribution of 'very' among Jane Austen's Major Characters

Up to a point, indeed, all the unusual characteristics of these and many other such histograms for Jane Austen's common words can be associated with the same abnormality, the large number of very high scores. The manner in which standard deviations are derived is sensitive to the influence of such marked aberrations; and these particular aberrations serve to raise the mean-scores and to increase the size of the z-score units. If the extremely high scores were left out of account, the resulting lower means and smaller z-score units would produce histograms in which the peaks for 'we' and 'very' were less skewed and the truncation in the negative range for 'we' was less marked. But the contrast between the positive and negative ranges for 'very' would then be even more extreme; the peak for 'of' would be more skewed than it is; and the shape of all three histograms would remain intractably abnormal. Instead of trying to normalize the abnormal, let us accept its force and try to understand it.

The set of bar graphs above each of the histograms firmly rebuts the possibility that the aberrations stem from a misguided attempt,

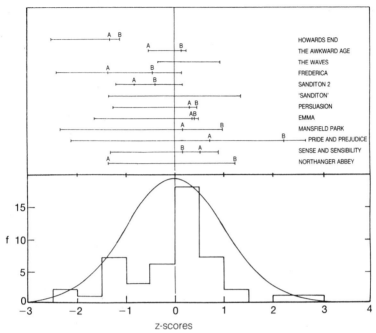

GRAPH 4. Distribution of 'of' among Jane Austen's Major Characters

on my part, to unite the disparate vocabularies of six essentially different novels. For, as the bar graphs show, each of these words (in common with most others) behaves in rather a similar fashion not only across the range of Jane Austen's novels but also, broadly speaking, in the other novels studied.

For each word so treated, the bar graphs distinguish the contribution of each of Jane Austen's novels to the overall histogram beneath. They are arranged on the same scale as the histogram with the vertical centre-line indicating the overall mean. The z-score for each major character is indicated by the appropriate marker-point along each bar with the location of the heroines and the heroes identified by the As and Bs. The major characters of the other novelists are disposed in the same fashion to afford a broader ground of comparison. But these others do *not* contribute to the histogram itself or to the calculation of its mean or z-scores. The fact that they conform so closely to a scale in whose construction they play no part is a point of considerable importance.

The length of each bar reflects the degree of differentiation, for the given word, among the major characters of the novel in question. The disposition of the marker-points indicates whether the characters are widely spread, closely grouped, or (as with 'we' in *Pride and Prejudice*, *Mansfield Park*, and *Persuasion*) fairly closely grouped save for a striking exception. The relative locations of the As and Bs cast light on resemblances and differences among the heroines and heroes as compared to each other or to the secondary characters. With 'very', for example, the heroines are less close to each other than are the heroes: but every one of the heroines stands higher, in the incidence of this word, than the hero of her novel. Precisely the same relationship obtains with the other major intensifiers—'quite', 'so', and 'too' as adverbs of degree—save only that Anne Elliot stands a trifle below Wentworth near the bottom of the range for 'quite'.

The highest scores in Jane Austen's dialogue are not confined to a few major characters or to any one or two novels. With 'of', the range for *Pride and Prejudice* is stretched beyond the rest by the very high scores for Collins and Darcy and the very low score for Lydia Bennet. This is consistent with the fact that most major prepositions, the relative pronouns, and some conjunctions all contribute strongly to the especially marked *syntactical* differentiations among the characters of that novel. With 'very', four characters from three different novels stand out above the rest: Mr Woodhouse, Lady Bertram, Harriet Smith, and Catherine Morland; but, except for Mr Weston, all the major characters of *Emma* lie above the mean. Some of Jane Austen's major characters have very little use for any of the emphatic forms of speech. Among those who have, 'very' provides a mild but highly addictive substitute for the 'vastlys', 'amazinglys', and 'perfectlys' in which certain others regularly indulge. With 'we', enough has been said of the extreme cases. All in all, the exceptionally high scores are widely disseminated; and, if they are momentarily shut out of mind, the six bar graphs for each word balance nicely about the overall mean while continuing to register marked differentiations among the remaining characters.

The incidence-levels for the other novelists studied resemble those for Jane Austen more closely than might be expected and presumably attest to broader 'generic' incidence-levels for the dialogue of fiction or even those of the spoken language at large. On closer inspection, however, revealing contrasts emerge. Much the most striking arises with the use of 'very' in *The Waves*. None of the six characters of that novel is much given to the use of any of the common intensifiers. (In the extreme case, Bernard uses 'quite' only five times in his 30,972 words, Neville only once in 9713, and the other four not at all in speaking-parts ranging from 5960 to 8437 words. At the opposite extreme, in the genteel vocabulary of Mrs Elton, it is called for thirty-seven times in 6415 words.) More innocent intensifiers, like 'very', do not lie under so complete a prohibition in *The Waves*: but it is still not easy to fit them inside the lower boundary of a graphic scale that easily accommodates Jane Austen and the other four novelists.

Virginia Woolf's interest in developing new and less obviously individualized embodiments of 'character' than those of earlier novelists is well attested. That may have more to do with the dearth of outward and visible distinctions between idiolects (like those supplied by the major intensifiers) than it has to do with any Bloomsburyish distaste for (mere) hyperbole. However that may be, such less visible forms of character-differentiation as are effected through the modal verbs and the major connectives testify to an underlying linguistic energy. While Bernard's exceptionally large speaking-part—larger by half than even Emma Woodhouse's—produces the highest chi-squared values, all six of Virginia Woolf's characters take their turn at the extremities of those scales where noteworthy differentiations occur.

The bar graphs for *Frederica* and *Sanditon 2* suggest what further analysis will confirm: that both novelists, especially Georgette Heyer, are capable of differentiating among their characters even in the idioms associated with the very common words; but that this capacity is more evident in the more conspicuous idioms; and that, far more than for Jane Austen, it is the same characters who tend to lie at the extreme ends of most word-ranges.

In *Sanditon 2*, the most frequently differentiated major character is a young man named Catton, who has no original in Jane Austen's fragment. His chief role is to report what has been going on and he is given to a sort of telegraphese, reminiscent of Mr Jingle in *Pickwick Papers*. For both reasons, his idiolect is unlike the rest. The more conventional idiolects of the other major characters are much less clearly differentiated from each other: the Other Lady, it seems, is more capable of vigorous devices than of subtle ones. So far as accuracy of imitation is concerned, only Mr Parker has more than two thousand words in both versions of 'Sanditon'; but if 1500 words is accepted as sufficient for a 'major character' in the manuscript, it is possible to make direct comparisons between two Mr Parkers and two Lady Denhams. The chief outcome of these comparisons is that the Other Lady's Mr Parker is the more recognizable imitation; but—more important—that, when the idiolects of the Other Lady's characters deviate from those of their originals, it is almost always in the direction of the mean-incidence for the word in question. The Other Lady's imitation, that is to say, though by no means a discreditable attempt at a difficult exercise, is rarely exact *except* when Jane Austen's version of a particular character lies quietly near the middle of a range and is 'found' there by his pastiche equivalent.

In *Frederica*,[1] only two of the seven major characters are often found at the extremities of the word-ranges. Like Mrs Smith in *Persuasion*, the hero's gentleman-secretary has a small and laconic role until the closing chapters when he assumes the 'historian's style' to recount how he intervened to prevent a runaway marriage. The heroine's beautiful but simple-minded sister is also located at one or other end of many bar graphs: in those offered, she stands easily first for 'very' and 'we' but falls far behind for 'of'. This portrait loses its impression of individuality when it is recognized that (as these bar graphs do not show) her idiolect is frequently indistinguishable from those of her schoolboy-brothers. Save for the 'stylistic isolation' of the secretary, Charles Trevor, Georgette Heyer's character-differentiation, that is to say, tends to dissolve into a single grand differentiation between adults, on the one side, and real or virtual children on the other.

On the whole, the characters of *The Awkward Age* and *Howards End* are less sharply differentiated from each other than are those of Jane Austen's novels. For Forster (as for Jane Austen), it is secondary characters—'flat' characters like Leonard Bast, Mrs Munt, and Charles Wilcox—who are most often to be found at the extremities of the bar graphs. (Leonard's incidence for 'I' runs to more than 80 in the thousand, one word in every twelve he speaks: even Catherine Morland needs 'I' only once in every eighteen words and is regularly able, therefore, to produce whole sentences in which 'I' does not appear.) For James, however, the pattern is quite unlike

---

[1] Seven examples of the contracted forms in which 'we' participates have been included: they are distributed indiscriminately among the characters. Jane Austen's only instance, 'we'd', is given to Anne Steele. There are no instances at all in *Sanditon 2* or *The Waves*. There are 110 instances in *The Awkward Age* and 45 in *Howards End*, widely distributed in both.

that of Forster or Jane Austen. Mrs Brookenham's charmed circle, 'one beautiful intelligence' (*The Awkward Age*, p. 297), has an argot of its own; and woe to him who departs from it enough to let his feelings show: '"Mitchy's silent, Mitchy's altered, Mitchy's queer!" Mrs. Brook proclaimed . . . to a pleasant talkative ring in which the subject of their companion's demonstration, on a low ottoman and glaring in his odd way in almost all directions at once, formed the conspicuous attractive centre' (ibid., pp. 423–4). Apart from so eccentric a bystander as the Duchess, it is Nanda herself and Mr Longdon, therefore, who are least like the rest. And, concentrated as it is in episodes of particular intensity for one or another of them, the differentiation of Vanderbank, Mitchy, and the ineffable Mrs Brook will call for subtler forms of analysis than single-word bar graphs.

In the last two or three pages, the argument has run a little ahead of the evidence so far available to the reader. That is because histograms and bar graphs, though admirable instruments of inquiry, take up too much space to be printed out at all lavishly. But, from the figures tabulated in Appendix C, the reader can easily construct further bar graphs and, not much less easily, convert the various base-scales into z-scores.[2]

Even on the evidence already made available, however, certain lines of argument can now be laid to rest. The patterns displayed are too many, too various, and altogether too suggestive to countenance arguments favouring either the random or the essentially inert distribution of the very common words. Assuming that—as is the case—I have offered fair specimens of the evidence at large, the close correspondences of mean incidence, for almost every common word, across the range of Jane Austen's novels and (with some marked exceptions, chiefly in *The Waves*) in the work of other novelists make it reasonable to dismiss the possibility that the peculiarities observed are due to my yoking together of disparate vocabularies. The other novelists, let me repeat, are not even included

---

[2] It should be noted that, whereas chi-squared values rest on the whole population of a given field—all dialogue, all narrative, and the like—histograms and bar graphs rest on the whole vocabulary of those included in them: for the latter calculations, the dialogue of the 'minor characters' is set aside. The influence of the minor characters does not often affect the overall mean-score to any marked extent. (The chorus of middle-aged spectators in *Northanger Abbey*, all of them much given to the use of the first person plural pronouns, is among the exceptions.) But this difference between the two forms of analysis should not be overlooked.

in the calculation of the mean-incidences to which they so closely and frequently conform.

Certain more plausible lines of thought, which will help to shape the later argument of this study, should now be sketched. Some might attribute the whole range of phenomena so far observed to the energies of *'la langue'* itself, to what would formerly have been described as 'the genius of the language': and the overall conformities of incidence would support them. Others might look behind the empirical patterns that I have sketched to 'generic codes' in the language of fiction or 'societal codes' in the language of everyday: the signs of kinship already glimpsed, especially among the heroes, would support either a literary or a social line of argument. Others again might stand by a doctrine of creative genius, emphasizing the evidence of a greater linguistic energy in Jane Austen than in the modern heiresses of 'that sort of fiction'; in James's subtle modulations; and in Virginia Woolf's pursuit of other possibilities.

When such ideas are so loosely formulated as this, there can be no serious choosing among them. But, with further evidence brought forward and with further progress in its analysis, it should be possible to see more clearly what each of them means, what each of them entails, and whether they should be so rigidly distinguished from each other as some contemporary manifestoes would insist. In assessing a different approach to statistical analysis, we can take another step or two in these directions.

4

Linear Regression as a
Test of Relationships

In an extensive set of trials like those illustrated earlier, the chi-squared test makes it clear that, among the very common words of dialogue, the differences of incidence from character to character are too pronounced to be ignored. The normal distribution methods reinforce that conclusion and allow more straightforward comparisons between the patterns of incidence for different words. To consider what those patterns may 'mean', however, it is desirable to study their interrelationships and to turn, accordingly, to the statistics of correlation. For those who are sceptical of the premises that govern some forms of statistical analysis, correlation-measures have the further merit of taking the evidence on its own terms instead of trying it against a hypothetical expectation or an implicit norm.

Measures of this kind are based on interrelationships of rank-order. If every candidate at an examination achieved precisely the same place in class for French as for Physics, there would be a perfect positive correlation between the two sets of results. This would be expressed as a correlation-coefficient of 1.00. If the rank-order for Physics were an exact inversion of that for French, the perfect negative correlation would be expressed as -1.00. If there were no correspondence between the two rank-orders, the complete lack of correlation would be expressed as 0.00.

In reality, of course, exactly concomitant relationships (positive or negative) between two sizeable rank-orders are as rare as an absolute lack of relationship. The 'perfect results' (1.00 and -1.00) are usually confined to situations where some kind of tautology is at work: the greater the number of heroic couplets, the more lines of five iambic feet; the higher the altitude, the lower the boiling-point of water. By the same token, the zero-result is usually confined to situations where some form of mutual exclusion prohibits any direct relationship.

There are occasions when the relationships among such rankings (which are correlated by Spearman's 'rank-order' formula) do not tell as much of the story as may be desired. It might, additionally, be useful to incorporate the facts that the top student in French had no close rival whereas, in Physics, several members of the class were hard on the heels of the top place-getter; that the middle ranges of the class were more tightly clustered in French than in Physics; and that a handful of determined non-scientists fell far behind the rest in Physics. That additional information can be incorporated in the correlation by replacing Spearman's formula by Pearson's 'product-moment' formula and working not from rank-orders but from the actual marks gained by the students. Both the places in class and the marks themselves, that is to say, arrange the students in the same hierarchical order; but the marks also incorporate the sizes of the gaps between one student and those on either side of him.

Pearson's method is clearly more germane to our purposes. It is something to take account of the fact that a given word is used most by Smith and least by Jones. But the value of the results is enhanced when they also take account of the fact that Smith's relative frequency is *far* higher than that of any other character or that Jones, though lowest, is only a little below the majority. As the histograms of the last chapter illustrated, the comparative size of the various frequency-gaps, especially the large gaps between the extreme cases and the upper ranges of comparative 'normality', is a prominent feature of the distribution-pattern for many of Jane Austen's common words.

In the use of Pearson's formula, a further nicety should be recognized. So far as the eventual results are concerned, it hardly matters whether the frequency-hierarchies to which the formula is applied are expressed as percentages, incidences per thousand, or raw frequencies: the sequences of the different scores and the *proportionate differences* between scores will scarcely be affected. It would not even matter if the French teacher insisted on listing his results as scores out of 107 while the Physics teacher used percentages.

Commensurate lists, expressed in the same terms as each other, are at an advantage only when the relationships between the two sets of scores are to be set out in 'linear-regression graphs' like those to be employed in the present chapter and at the beginning of the next. For the sake of those graphs, the scores will be reckoned as incidences per thousand and correlated on that basis. After that, however, we shall be leaving linear-regression graphs behind and it will be possible to work from the raw frequency-hierarchies themselves. The purpose of making that change, as soon as it becomes practicable, is to satisfy the statistician's justifiable preference for data that has not been tampered with in any way.

If the incidence for each of our forty-eight characters in the use of 'we' is matched with the corresponding set of incidences for 'us', the resulting correlation-coefficient is 0.620—a 'very highly significant' result for forty-eight pairs. For 'of' and 'in', it is 0.627. For 'very' and 'quite', the coefficient falls to 0.316 but (having been obtained from the correlation of so many pairs) still indicates a statistically significant relationship.

Before considering what these figures import for the grammatical and/or semantic relationships between one word and another in each of these three pairs, we should do two things. The first is to recall that correlation and causation are not synonymous. Although it is plainly imprudent to ignore the evidence of a powerful correlation between cigarette-smoking and the incidence of lung-cancer, no direct causal relationship can be derived from such numerical relationships. From experience in the field and close study of the evidence, an informed interpretation can nevertheless be advanced and subjected to further analysis. The second is to recall the important distinction between descriptive—or 'reconstructive'—and predictive statistics. While evidence about the other heroes might be employed as an indication of the probable idiolect of Sidney Parker, the hero-apparent of 'Sanditon' (who is overheard speaking his first thirty-eight words shortly before the manuscript breaks off), the present study is confined to the descriptive analysis of the texts we have. This limitation, I believe, is proper to a comparatively novel line of inquiry and it avoids the technical complexities of statistical prediction.

Let us look, then, behind the bare correlation-coefficients for these three pairs of words. In the straightforward type of correlation known as 'linear regression', the scores for two continuous variables—in the present case, two ranges of incidence—are plotted on an ordinary biaxial graph. The mean-line for each range is marked in, and a 'line of best fit' is calculated from the pattern of the data. (The latter is the line to which the array of plotted points most closely conforms. When, as in the following examples, it runs upward from left to right, there is a positive relationship between the two variables: the more of y, the more of x. When it slopes downward, it indicates a negative relationship: the more of y, the less of x.) If most of the

TABLE 6. Incidence of Six Common words in the Dialogue of Major Characters

		we (1470)	us (567)	very (2170)	quite (541)	of (7281)	in (4115)
Northanger Abbey							
1A	CATHERINE	3.69	1.42	12.50	1.42	15.91	10.65
1B	HENRY	2.93	1.30	5.85	0.16	29.92	18.05
1D	Isabella Thorpe	5.13	3.01	4.60	3.76	17.32	13.08
1E	John Thorpe	7.17	1.02	2.39	0.34	22.54	10.59
1C	Eleanor Tilney	4.13	3.10	5.16	0.52	24.25	14.45
Sense and Sensibility							
2A	ELINOR	2.88	1.66	5.97	0.55	26.00	13.72
2C	Marianne	6.69	1.67	4.41	0.15	25.38	13.07
2K	Mrs Jennings	4.06	1.06	7.60	2.12	17.49	11.66
2S	Willoughby	1.14	0.57	3.03	0.19	28.04	18.76
2F	John Dashwood	4.03	1.57	9.86	1.79	25.32	14.34
2Q	Lucy Steele	6.54	3.52	5.78	2.51	19.11	12.57
2H	Colonel Brandon	1.62	0.54	4.05	0.54	25.14	15.41
2D	Mrs Dashwood	5.34	2.53	3.37	1.40	25.56	15.17
2B	EDWARD	0.85	0.00	3.82	0.00	24.16	19.50
2P	Anne Steele	6.29	4.84	5.32	4.36	15.49	9.68
Pride and Prejudice							
3A	ELIZABETH	5.15	1.25	5.00	0.59	27.21	15.30
3B	DARCY	1.41	0.47	3.75	0.31	35.16	17.19
3D	Mrs Bennet	4.46	2.15	7.77	2.31	16.53	10.25
3E	Jane	6.34	3.46	5.57	2.11	19.60	12.68
3K	Collins	3.83	2.48	3.38	0.23	37.58	15.75
3C	Mr Bennet	3.39	3.39	4.31	1.23	28.63	10.47
3O	Mrs Gardiner	2.79	4.19	6.28	1.40	23.39	11.52
3L	Lady Catherine	0.85	0.85	5.55	0.85	30.74	12.38
3H	Lydia	14.45	4.52	3.16	2.71	11.74	10.84
3J	Miss Bingley	6.11	2.35	2.82	1.88	23.51	19.28
3V	Wickham	4.90	0.49	8.33	0.49	26.47	13.73
Mansfield Park							
4B	EDMUND	3.92	2.03	4.97	1.12	28.60	13.50
4C	Mary Crawford	4.76	1.00	5.83	1.53	23.87	15.50
4D	Crawford	3.86	1.04	3.41	1.78	25.39	14.70
4J	Mrs Norris	4.96	2.10	7.96	3.00	22.53	11.56
4A	FANNY	3.43	0.16	9.15	2.62	24.03	12.10
4E	Sir Thomas	4.55	2.78	5.06	1.01	28.33	14.93
4G	Tom Bertram	12.69	3.34	5.34	0.67	22.37	14.36
4F	Lady Bertram	6.94	3.24	18.50	1.85	10.64	9.71
Emma							
5A	EMMA	3.95	1.95	8.60	1.63	25.21	13.72
5B	MR KNIGHTLEY	2.47	0.49	8.21	1.09	25.42	12.36
5E	Churchill	3.89	0.85	7.54	1.58	25.90	12.16
5D	Miss Bates	7.48	4.72	9.97	5.25	15.35	9.44
5I	Mrs Elton	6.08	2.18	8.73	5.77	22.92	14.03
5M	Harriet Smith	2.65	0.19	13.08	3.98	14.41	8.34
5P	Mr Woodhouse	4.10	2.59	21.34	1.72	18.54	5.82
5O	Mrs Weston	5.55	3.14	9.41	1.45	25.10	11.34
5N	Mr Weston	8.45	3.44	3.75	1.56	22.21	14.08

TABLE 6: continued

	we (1470)	us (567)	very (2170)	quite (541)	of (7281)	in (4115)
Persuasion						
6A ANNE	5.30	1.85	6.92	0.69	25.60	17.76
6V Mrs Smith	1.51	0.50	4.77	0.75	25.60	15.06
6P Mary Musgrove	6.70	2.41	10.72	2.95	16.34	6.70
6B WENTWORTH	2.95	0.59	5.32	1.18	24.81	15.06
6D Admiral Croft	16.22	3.44	9.34	0.98	21.14	10.32
'Sandlton'						
7P Mr Parker	10.46	4.81	6.22	1.13	30.54	19.23
7S Diana Parker	9.98	3.46	6.14	1.92	23.43	13.06
7H Lady Denham	7.04	2.56	14.08	1.28	16.01	8.96
Sandlton 2						
8B SIDNEY PARKER	6.48	2.83	6.83	2.00	21.20	16.25
8A CHARLOTTE	5.84	2.68	8.76	3.41	18.74	15.82
8P Mr Parker	10.05	5.03	3.23	1.44	24.06	16.16
8G Catton	4.81	0.37	2.59	0.74	16.67	14.81
8H Lady Denham	2.39	0.48	3.83	1.44	20.10	13.88
Frederica						
9B ALVERSTOKE	1.94	1.02	5.05	1.65	20.83	10.73
9A FREDERICA	3.56	3.08	7.47	2.10	15.87	9.72
9F Jessamy	4.27	1.76	7.03	0.50	14.31	7.53
9C Charles Trevor	2.44	1.22	3.04	1.52	14.61	11.57
9D Harry	2.63	0.66	1.22	0.61	24.04	12.18
9K Lady Elizabeth	3.83	1.70	3.83	2.13	19.98	10.63
9E Charis	7.01	6.54	7.94	2.80	10.28	7.94
The Waves						
10A Bernard	9.04	2.49	0.71	0.16	28.32	17.05
10C Neville	11.53	3.60	0.10	0.10	21.83	16.99
10B Louis	8.77	3.79	0.59	0.00	25.36	17.78
10E Rhoda	7.41	2.67	0.61	0.00	23.95	13.61
10D Jinny	8.30	4.23	0.65	0.00	22.63	19.86
10F Susan	4.87	1.34	0.17	0.00	21.48	23.15
The Awkward Age						
11D Mrs Brookenham	8.02	3.78	1.78	1.83	22.35	13.18
11B VANDERBANK	7.80	2.15	1.37	2.60	23.93	14.89
11A NANDA	5.91	1.66	2.12	2.03	20.40	9.23
11M Mitchy	6.77	2.60	1.39	1.95	24.40	12.71
11I The Duchess	4.27	1.66	2.49	2.61	23.22	11.49
11L Mr Longdon	4.51	1.00	3.26	2.13	24.31	11.90
Howards End						
12A MARGARET	10.92	2.83	3.21	1.16	15.94	10.60
12D Helen	9.31	1.97	2.79	0.52	13.24	9.93
12B MR WILCOX	8.18	1.36	2.73	1.12	16.85	14.00
12L Leonard Bast	4.42	1.61	1.61	2.01	14.46	8.84
12G Mrs Munt	5.84	2.09	7.93	1.25	9.60	12.10
12H Charles Wilcox	7.16	1.43	2.86	0.48	13.36	12.40

Note. The total frequency given at the head of the column for each word bears on the whole dialogue of Jane Austen's novels, including minor characters. It amounts, all told, to 307,360 'word-tokens'.

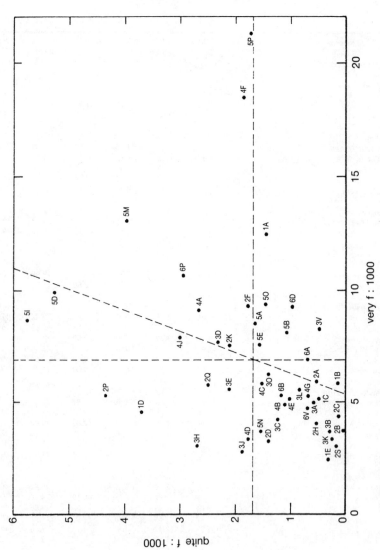

GRAPH 5. Comparative Incidences for 'quite' and 'very' in Jane Austen's Dialogue

plotted points lie in close proximity to one of the mean-lines, it is evident that there is little differentiation among the scores for that variable. If most of them lie along the line of best fit, it is evident that (whatever its empirical meaning) there is a distinct concomitance between the two variables. But, if the plotted points are scattered more or less indiscriminately throughout the graph, it is evident that the two variables have little in common: a very low (positive *or* negative) correlation-coefficient is an obvious corollary.

From the information set out in the relevant columns of Table 6, the relationships of incidence for 'very' and 'quite' among Jane Austen's major characters are plotted on Graph 5. With an incidence of 21.34 per 1000 words for 'very' and only 1.72 for 'quite', Mr Woodhouse (5P) lies near the right-hand margin of the graph with only Lady Bertram (4F) as a near neighbour. With an incidence of 8.73 for 'very' and 5.77 for 'quite', Mrs Elton (5I) has only Miss Bates (5D) near her at the top margin of the graph. Catherine Morland (1A) has one of the highest incidences for 'very' but is below the mean for 'quite': the opposite is true of Anne Steele (2P) and Isabella Thorpe (1D). Of the remainder, Harriet Smith (5M) and Mary Musgrove (6P) have the highest incidences for *both* words.

With twenty-one of forty-eight characters located there and three others just beyond its boundaries, the lower left-hand quadrant of the graph is easily the most densely populated. Five of the six heroes and two of the heroines are located there while Anne Elliot (6A) is just beyond the boundary. The inhabitants of this quadrant are, of course, those who make least use of either 'very' or 'quite'. While the majority of their neighbours—including Sir Thomas Bertram, Colonel Brandon, Eleanor Tilney, and Mr Bennet—resemble them in eschewing these and most other forms of emphasis, a higher emotional temperature is introduced by Marianne Dashwood. The 'lively minds' of the Crawfords set them, respectively, near and just beyond the fringe. And the general peace is shattered by John Thorpe. For him, especially, a comparative dearth in the use of 'very' and 'quite' points not to a customary avoidance of emphasis but to a recourse to stronger expressions than these.

In the inner part of the lower right-hand quadrant, to turn there next, four characters from *Emma* are closely grouped. They are not infrequent companions in other sorts of idiom but they are usually to be found with the main group of heroes and heroines. Once this little displacement is noticed, it is easily seen that, of all the major characters in *Emma*, only Mr Weston lies beneath the overall mean for 'very'. The narrative of *Emma* also shows a higher than narrative-average incidence for 'very'; and the word emerges as one of the few to show such a marked overall tendency in a single novel. In the milieu of Hartfield, it is an appropriate tendency. As a mild and 'proper' form of emphasis, it says something of the Woodhouses and their immediate circle. In its marked 'over-use', it says still more. At the extremity of the range are Mr Woodhouse, whose whole idiolect is limited and repetitive, and Lady Bertram, who observes the proper forms in most respects but is too indolent to look for synonyms. Next after them, still markedly above the rest, Catherine Morland and Harriet Smith stand in contrast to each other. For all her breathless overemphases, Catherine remains below the mean for 'quite': but Harriet is isolated in a part of the upper right-hand quadrant reserved for those who make strong use of both words.

A pronounced recourse to 'quite' is one of the marks of Jane Austen's vulgarians, especially the women who predominate among them. The word itself has a reputable history in emphasizing the absolute. In uses of that kind, the *OED* traces it from the fourteenth to the nineteenth century; and it continues, though less commonly, to be used so to the present day. Characters like Darcy and Mr Knightley generally turn to these senses when they use the word at all. 'You have sung quite enough for one evening' (p. 229), Mr Knightley thinks aloud when Jane Fairfax is being pressed onward by Frank Churchill. 'My interference was quite as likely to do harm as good' (p. 462), he generously concedes to Emma. 'I am quite sure', he answers, 'speaking very distinctly' (p. 474), when Emma smilingly—though by no means jokingly—challenges his report that Robert Martin is to marry Harriet after all.

From about the middle of the eighteenth century, however, the word began to decay in much the same fashion as others like 'perfectly', 'literally', and 'really' were to do. From false or dubious absolutes to mere expressions of emphasis is no great journey. Richardson (1742) and Fielding (1749) provide the *OED* with its earliest instances of the change. If Fielding's, 'The widow, quite charmed with her new lodger' retains something of the older sense, it is quite extinct in Southey's 'quite a comfortable dwelling' (1799). Although the examples abound in the closing years of the century, 'quite' continues, at that time, to mean a little more than 'rather'. And there is no sign of its later uses—some of them more familiar in Australian English? — for dry understatements and even drier inversions of meaning.[1]

Especially in the idiolects of Mrs Elton, Anne Steele, Isabella Thorpe, and Harriet Smith, Jane Austen catches the then current stage of this process of decay. Harriet, as usual, is less fashionable than muddled: 'I have now quite determined, and really almost made up my mind' (p. 53). 'I really am quite wild with impatience' (p. 70) and 'I declare positively it is quite shocking' (p. 75) are typical of Isabella's contributions. Anne Steele's are set apart by her lucubrations on who is or is not 'quite a beau'. Most of Mrs Elton's are redundant emphases of the already absolute like 'quite independent' and 'quite unnecessary', which both appear twice. She puts Emma's 'quite the gentleman' to a service Emma does not much care for when she applies it to her new friend, Knightley, and, in modified versions, to each of the Westons. And, with 'quite odious' and four instances of 'quite a horror', she slips easily into the idiom of Isabella Thorpe.

Miss Bates is more disposed to emphasize the ameliorative. She encounters 'quite delightful' experiences and is 'quite blessed' in her friends and neighbours. In her 'quite thick shoes', she is 'quite ready' when the carriage calls to take her and Jane to the Crown Inn, where she finds herself 'quite in fairyland', where good Mrs Elton is 'quite the queen of the evening', and where she herself is 'quite roasted' by the noble fire. On one occasion, she loses her epithet but keeps a firm grip on her intensifier: 'Well! that is quite — I suppose there never was a piece of news more generally interesting' (p. 173). As Miss Bates's location high on the line of best fit in Graph 5 might suggest, 'quite', in her idiolect, is almost a synonym for 'very', devoid of its semantic freight and serving as an overworked token of good-hearted but ineffectual emphasis.

Little more need be said of those who occupy the upper half of Graph 5, especially those, more given to 'quite' than to 'very', who occupy the upper left-hand quadrant. But the location of Fanny Price is worth a moment's pause. Her sixteen instances of 'quite' and fifty-six of 'very' carry her above the mean-incidence for both words and leave her among companions more outspoken than she. With Fanny, however, these words are neither idle nor interchangeable. 'Quite'

---

[1] *The Collins English Dictionary* (1979) gives 'to a noticeable or partial extent; somewhat' second place among the senses of 'quite'.

sometimes reflects her solemn little exactitudes. 'No. Not quite a month. — It is only four weeks' (p. 410) goes further and shows how painfully she counts the days at Portsmouth. It sometimes reflects her caustic (and never disinterested) emphasis on Mary Crawford's failings: 'I was quite astonished' (p. 63); 'she is quite as likely to have led *them* astray' (p. 424); and, by way of epitaph on Mary's hopes, 'Cruel! . . . quite cruel!' (p. 456). Almost half the instances, however, emphasize her hostility to Henry Crawford's overtures and her growing dismay that those about her take his part: 'I told him without disguise that it was very disagreeable to me, and quite out of my power to return his good opinion' (p. 314); 'I consider it as quite impossible that we should ever be tolerably happy together' (p. 348); and, in a desperate burst of vehemence, '"You are mistaken, Sir," cried Fanny, forced by the anxiety of the moment even to tell her uncle that he was wrong — "You are quite mistaken. How could Mr. Crawford say such a thing?"' (p. 315).

To attempt a conspectus, the line of best fit in Graph 5 traces a sufficient number of concomitant pairs and of small departures from concomitance to account for a correlation-coefficient as high as 0.316. From those, lying near its foot, who eschew emphatic forms in general or these particular forms of emphasis, it ranges upward past Mrs Jennings, Mrs Bennet, and Mrs Norris to Miss Bates. Besides drawing attention to those whose particular habits of emphasis are most pronounced, it singles out those whose marked recourse to both words suggests that, for them, the rhetoric of emphasis counts for more than the semantic niceties observed by others. This 'line of best fit', nevertheless, does not fit very well. The correlation-coefficient of only 0.316 and the wide scattering of entries throughout the graph unite with the examples offered in the last two or three pages to suggest that some strong cross-currents are flowing in this apparent backwater of Jane Austen's literary vocabulary.

With the other novelists, the cross-currents are less turbulent. In Graph 6, the major characters of the other novelists and those of Jane Austen's 'Sanditon' are entered in the same fashion and graphed to the same scale as that of Graph 5. It is significant, therefore, that Graph 6 is considerably more compact than Graph 5. As with many other words, the general level of incidences is not unlike Jane Austen's (save that, in *The Waves*, both 'very' and 'quite' are only

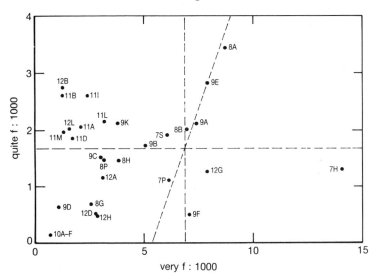

GRAPH 6. Comparative Incidences for 'quite' and 'very' in Other Dialogue

rarely used).[2] Only Jane Austen's Lady Denham stands in marked isolation (at the same extremity as that occupied by Mr Woodhouse and Lady Bertram in Graph 5). Both Georgette Heyer and the Other Lady show a capacity to distinguish between emphatic and unemphatic speakers but less capacity to distinguish appropriately among individual speakers in the two forms of emphasis. It is only fair to acknowledge that so few characters of each novelist can hardly be expected to span so wide a range as Jane Austen's forty-eight. But it should also be recognized that these are comparatively 'visible'

---

[2] For words like these where incidences in narrative and dialogue differ greatly, it is regrettable that the best contemporary evidence treats only an undifferentiated 'vocabulary of fiction'. When the incidences for 'very' and 'quite' offered in the LOB corpus (K–R) are compared with those for our novels *as whole novels*, both words prove to be less freely used in that sample of contemporary fiction than in Jane Austen's novels or in 'modern Regency' novels like *Sanditon 2* and *Frederica*. The incidences of *The Waves*, however, are lower still. Forster's incidences for both words and James's incidence for 'very' are in keeping with the LOB figures: but James outranks all others in the incidence of 'quite'.

	JA	S2	F	TW	AA	HE	LOB
very	5.31	4.73	3.78	0.53	1.49	1.91	1.461
quite	1.23	1.81	1.31	0.08	1.91	0.72	0.667

For the LOB figures, see Hofland and Johansson, pp. 433, 463.

words, in which sharper differentiations might be expected among characters whose supposed individuality is pressed on the reader by the narrators' descriptions and 'stage directions'. (The characterization of *The Waves* is quite another matter.) The more strenuous test afforded, in Graphs 7 and 8, by the correlation of a pair of prepositions will reinforce the argument.

James's characters are all closely grouped in the quadrant reserved for those who, by Jane Austen's standards, make more than average use of 'quite' and less than average use of 'very'. While those averages, as such, have no 'normative' value, it should be noted that, of eighty-one characters created by six different writers, only four or five stand in the immediate vicinity of the *habitués* of Mrs Brook's salon. 'Very', perhaps, is too shy a plant to flourish in the hothouse of *The Awkward Age*. But 'quite', at the stage its degeneration had reached by the end of the last century, is not out of place beside such artificial blooms as the 'beautiful' and 'splendid' in which some of James's characters rejoice and behind which others of them shelter. Forster's characters, however, are more sharply and more variously differentiated than those of any other of our 'other novelists'. The Schlegel sisters (and Charles Wilcox) stand in the lower left-hand quadrant, along with Jane Austen's less emphatic speakers. Mrs Munt's polite effusiveness is marked by her mild recourse to 'very' while Mr Wilcox and Leonard Bast find different paths towards a comparative preference for 'quite'.

It would be possible to speak acceptable English without ever using 'quite' or 'very': from a grammatical or a syntactical point of view they are not necessary words; and, though Jane Austen takes full advantage of their potentialities, they are limited words from a semantic point of view.[3] Their chief value resides in the *rhetoric* of dialogue, whether as words to eschew, words to enforce a genuine need for emphasis, or words to devalue in an emphasis so unremitting that it becomes no emphasis at all. Thus, while 'quite' occurs more frequently than other fashionable intensifiers of Jane Austen's day, it belongs essentially with words like 'vastly', 'excessively', and 'amazingly', most of which gradually descend the social scale from

---

[3] The original sense of 'very' as 'possessing the true character of' and 'properly so called' (*OED*) has long been outweighed by its use as a pure intensifier. But it occasionally appears, as when Emma indulges her fancy about what 'had happened to the very person, and at the very hour, when the other very person was chancing to pass by to rescue her' (p. 335).

Restoration comedy and enter the vulgar-genteel vocabulary of the late eighteenth-century and Regency parvenu, a species more discriminatingly observed by Jane Austen than by Fanny Burney. 'Amazingly', for example, occurs freely among Fanny Burney's women characters and her effete beaux alike. It occurs sixteen times in *Northanger Abbey* and then almost disappears from Jane Austen's literary vocabulary. (Lucy Steele, Mr Rushworth, and Sir Walter Elliot have one instance each and Miss Bates has two.) Of the sixteen, no fewer than thirteen belong to Isabella Thorpe and another is attributed to her in 'character narrative'. The remaining instances arise when Catherine rashly borrows the word and is promptly checked by Henry:

'But I really thought before, young men despised novels amazingly.'

'It is *amazingly*; it may well suggest *amazement* if they do — for they read nearly as many as women.' (p. 107)

As a result of recent advances in computing, it is much easier than it has ever been to bring a word like 'quite' within the ambit of rhetorical analysis. When that is done, its repertoire proves wider and more flexible than that of a more visible word like 'amazingly'. But, though that point might be pressed, a more important point remains. It is not through words like 'quite' but through still less visible words, of which 'of' and 'in' will be taken as initial specimens, that literary criticism can be drawn into territory where the maps are less well worn.

In that territory, statistical analysis is no longer an ancillary but a necessary guide. Jane Austen's dialogue includes 7281 instances of 'of' and 4115 instances of 'in'. (For the novels as wholes, the corresponding totals are 21,160 and 11,135.) Although this huge aggregate encourages the interpretation of patterns rather than a detailed examination of instances, the patterns themselves are entrenched by sheer weight of numbers. And the patterns indicate that, even here, the idiolects of many of Jane Austen's major characters are firmly and appropriately differentiated.[4]

---

[4] Unlike 'quite' and 'very', 'of' and 'in' are among those common words that no speaker of English can well avoid. (As Graph 7 shows, none of Jane Austen's major characters falls below an incidence of 10 per 1000 words for 'of' or 5 for 'in'. With the other novelists, as Graph 8 shows, the minimum incidences in dialogue are mostly even higher.) To speak of patterning and differentiation with such obligatory words as 'of' and 'in', therefore, is not to propose that a certain character's 'of'/'in' idioms are *entirely* of a particular kind. With those who range markedly above their fellows,

(Cont. on page 70)

Not all of them. The most prominent feature of Graph 7 is the large, roughly circular cluster of entries whose centre lies a little above the intersection of the mean-lines at about the point where Eleanor Tilney (1C) is located. Its members, including three heroines and two heroes, are those who use *both* prepositions to an extent 'normal' for Jane Austen's dialogue. (The small discrepancy between this conceptual 'normality' and the actual intersection of the mean-lines reflects the influence of a number of extremely low incidences for both words.) They are, without exception, a homogeneous group of articulate—though not all admirable—characters. Given that the small differences among them have no statistical significance, any attempt to distinguish among their prepositional idioms would entail an extremely close study of their uses of the words themselves.

Except for those who lie within this rough circle, the upper left and lower right-hand quadrants of Graph 7 are almost void. No single character rises markedly above the mean for 'in' without also rising above the mean for 'of'; and only Mr Bennet (3C) and Lady Catherine (3L) do the opposite. Most of those characters who lie beyond the circle, that is to say, run above the mean-incidence for both words or fall below for both. By the same token, far more of the characters lie along the line of best fit than in Graph 5, and so contribute to the correlation-coefficient of 0.627. This concomitance of incidence for both prepositions is a testimony to the grammatical force of 'prepositionality': the weight of evidence of this kind shows that, contrary to what an anti-grammarian might claim, such concepts as 'prepositionality', 'modality', and 'connection' are not abstract impositions on the living body of the language but broadly valid ways of categorizing some of its sustained modes of operation.

But concomitance is not identity. The gulf between Lydia Bennet and Lady Bertram, at the foot of the line of best fit, and Darcy and Collins, at its head, is largely due to characteristic differences of syntax; and, in due measure, this is also true of those who lie between them. These syntactical differences, however, have more to do with sentence-shape than with mere sentence-length. Suffice it to say, for the moment, that, while average sentence-lengths have something

---

it is to propose that they are especially given—like Collins—to prepositional constructions generally or—like Miss Bingley—to particular constructions. With those like Lady Bertram, who fall markedly below their fellows, it is usually to propose that their characteristic syntax is not of a prepositional cast. But even they will necessarily make some use of words like these.

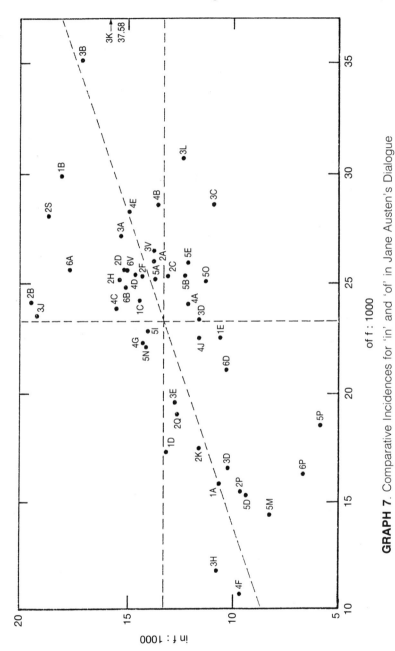

GRAPH 7. Comparative Incidences for 'in' and 'of' in Jane Austen's Dialogue

to do with characteristic sentence-shapes, there is a wide variety of relationships. Collins, who makes most use of most of the prepositions and who is also strongly given to the use of certain major connectives, has by far the highest average sentence-length. At 29.05 words per sentence, it is almost double the general mean for Jane Austen's major characters; and even the next highest, Lucy Steele and Colonel Brandon, have averages of less than 23. At the other extreme, Catherine Morland has an average sentence-length of 11.18 and Lady Catherine 11.31. If even these few averages are compared with the locations of their owners in Graph 7, it will be seen that sentence-length does not correspond very closely with the incidence of the two most common English prepositions. For Collins, the two factors correspond. For Catherine Morland, towards the foot of the line of best fit, there is a rough correspondence between the two. For Lucy Steele and Colonel Brandon, there is little or no correspondence. And Lady Catherine manages to rank third highest in the use of 'of', a little below the mean in the use of 'in', but second lowest in average sentence-length. More detail is offered in Appendix A.

In their semantic aspect, 'of' and 'in' present complexities that match their great frequency. With 'of', the *OED* arranges more than sixty distinct prepositional senses in fifteen classes and introduces the whole array with justifiably despondent comments: 'the sense-history is exceedingly complicated'; and, in many of its uses, the word expresses 'the vaguest and most intangible of relations'. With 'in', forty prepositional senses are arranged in seven classes and the editors comment, more confidently if not much more straightforwardly, that the preposition expresses 'the relation of inclusion, situation, position, or action, within limits of space, time, condition, circumstances, etc.'.

A thorough study of the semantics of these words, as exemplified in the usage of Jane Austen's characters, might well repay the work entailed. It will not be undertaken here. The striking disparities that drive a number of major characters into the outskirts of Graph 7 are sufficient evidence of semantic pressures as powerful as any we have seen so far. On the whole, the outlying groups unite appropriate companions. Mr Woodhouse, Mary Musgrove, and Harriet Smith are well below the mean-incidence for both words, but especially so for 'in': in the managing of ideas they have much in common with each other and with their next-neighbours, Miss Bates and Anne

Steele. While none of them is incapable of blundering about among 'the vaguest and most intangible of relations', they are none of them clear-headed enough to deal with 'the relation of inclusion' when ideas like 'condition', 'circumstances', or 'etc.' are involved. Only those characters who find special pleasure in what Jane Austen describes as 'too many particulars of right hand & left' (*Letters*, p. 401) are markedly given to those prepositional phrases which treat prosaically of time and place. It is a capacity for more general ideas and for a firm marshalling of syntax that unites those who range across the top edge of the graph.

At first thought Miss Bingley is not quite at home among them. But she is brought there by her generalized, though unintelligent, preoccupation with—dare one say?—the semiotics of 'manner': with her brother's writing 'in the most careless way imaginable' (p. 48); with Wickham's treating Darcy—she has it on hearsay—'in a most infamous manner' (p. 94); with 'a certain something in her air and manner of walking, the tone of her voice, her address and expression' (p. 39) that transcends the more obvious accomplishments of the truly accomplished woman; and with Elizabeth's contemptible short-comings in these respects. Poor Elizabeth is a great deal wanting 'in her air altogether'—in her beauty, in her supposedly fine eyes, and even in the lines of a nose that wants character (p. 271). Miss Bingley may be a trifle more impartial when she wishes that balls 'were carried on in a different manner'—'there is something insufferably tedious in the usual process' (p. 55). Such a ball as she envisages, her brother concedes, would indeed be 'much more rational', but 'not near so much like a ball' (p. 56).

As the weight of evidence increases, Miss Bingley will often be seen as a caricature of Elizabeth, as Collins is of Darcy. In the incidence of the prepositions treated in Graph 7, the latter pair, especially, are close neighbours. With that line of thought held in reserve, there is no need to say much at present of the rather formal, generalizing idiolects of those others—Edward Ferrars, Anne Elliot, Willoughby, and Henry Tilney—who lie at the top edge of the graph. As they range across—for there is a marked range—intellectual seriousness turns into the fine phrase-making of the man of sentiment, the youthful pedantries of Henry, and the aloof impersonalities of Darcy's earlier manner, only to topple over into the absurd pomposities of Collins. For Collins, the 'in' that governs vague abstractions figures, on average, in every second sentence that he

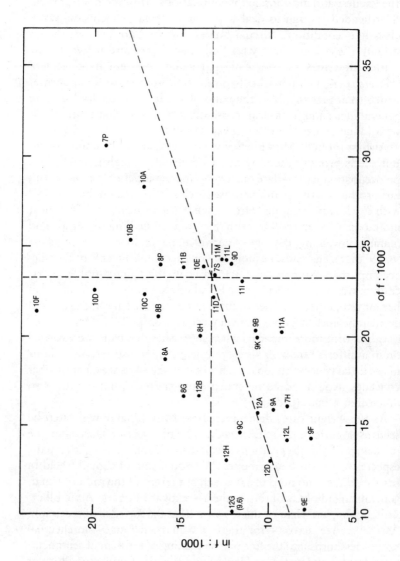

GRAPH 8. Comparative Incidences for 'in' and 'of' in Other Dialogue

speaks. And 'of', chiefly used for the 'post-modification' of his cherished abstract nouns, figures in almost every sentence: '"I am by no means of opinion, I assure you," said he, "that a ball of this kind, given by a young man of character, to respectable people, can have any evil tendency"' (p. 87).

Graph 8 indicates that with the other novelists, except for Virginia Woolf, degrees of 'prepositionality' count for more than nice semantic differentiations. The broad 'syntactical' kind of differentiation is at its most pronounced in Georgette Heyer, whose characters range furthest along Jane Austen's line of best fit. Only the characters of Virginia Woolf diverge strongly from that line. In this remote area of prose style, the individuality of her characters is more pronounced than in many more accessible areas. For them, the only feasible line of best fit would run almost vertically, showing that 'in' varies almost independently of 'of'. The chi-squared test registers two 'significant' and two 'very highly significant' results in twelve calculations. The evidence, in short, is of marked semantic differentiation through which Bernard and Susan are set particularly far apart.

The most prominent feature of Graph 10 — to take it first of the pair that bring 'we' and 'us' together — is the displacement of the entries to the right. This is accompanied by a lesser displacement upwards. On the whole, therefore, the characters of the other novelists turn more freely to these pronouns than do Jane Austen's characters, a tendency least pronounced in Georgette Heyer and the Other Lady. For each of the five novelists, the pattern of entries shows clear and appropriate distinctions between characters who turn most often and least often to the first person plural. In *The Awkward Age*, Mrs Brook turns there most and Mr Longdon least. In *The Waves*, it is Jinny and Susan respectively. In both versions of 'Sanditon', Mr Parker runs very high: as self-appointed advocate of what 'we' should do for the 'improvement' of Sanditon, he could hardly do otherwise. The 'Lady Denham' of *Sanditon 2*, a strong-willed widow more akin to Lady Catherine de Bourgh than to Jane Austen's Lady Denham, stands with the independent-minded Mr Catton at the bottom of the graph. Georgette Heyer's Charis shows much the highest incidence for 'we' in her own novel and the highest incidence for 'us' on either graph. Associating herself at first with her own family and afterwards with her beloved Endymion Dauntry, she does not often speak for herself and can hardly be said to have a mind of her own. Only in her sister Frederica, finally, does Graph 10

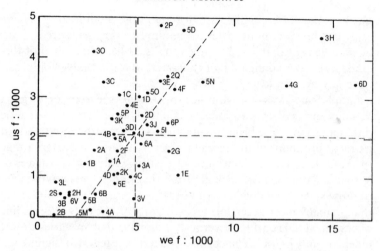

GRAPH 9. Comparative Incidences for 'we' and 'us' in Jane Austen's Dialogue

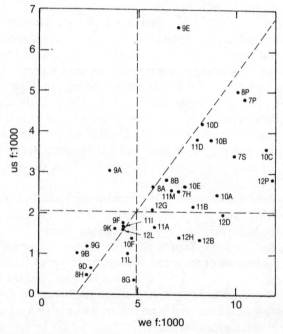

GRAPH 10. Comparative Incidences for 'we' and 'us' in Other Dialogue

show any sign of Jane Austen's 'supra-grammatical' distinctions between 'we' and 'us'. As foster-mother to a tribe of little brothers, Frederica turns to 'I' whenever she is free to take an initiative of her own and to the submissive 'us' when, as is more usual, she is caught up in theirs.

Among Jane Austen's major characters, as Graph 9 indicates, some half-dozen diverge widely from the line of best fit. Lydia Bennet, Tom Bertram, and Admiral Croft lie remote from the rest in the top right-hand corner. As was shown in Tables 4 and 5, Admiral Croft's frequency for 'us' is too low to permit a valid chi-squared calculation. He is nevertheless well placed in the vicinity of two others who, in their own ways, seize the conversational initiative and make more of what 'we' might do than of what might happen to 'us'. At a far lower incidence-level, in the lower right-hand quadrant, Marianne Dashwood and John Thorpe observe a similar distinction between the two words. Marianne is especially interesting in that she turns to the first person plural pronouns at a recognizable time and discovers a marked preference for 'we'. Her recourse to the words is associated with the grand new schemes she devises for her family as she comes to recognize her former selfishness and folly. For the first time, she overtly unites herself with them—but still on terms of her own choosing:

'When the weather is settled, and I have recovered my strength,' said she, 'we will take long walks together every day. We will walk to the farm at the edge of the down . . .; we will walk to Sir John's new plantations . . .; and we will often go to the old ruins of the Priory . . . I know we shall be happy.' (p. 343)

If a distinct leaning towards 'we' reflects a strain of dominance among these characters, the fact that Mrs Gardiner, Anne Steele, and Miss Bates lean towards 'us' is easily understood. Essentially similar distinctions, though not always with these very characters, can be drawn between 'I' and 'me' and likewise—*mutatis mutandis*—between 'you' and 'you'.

In more straightforward matters, Graph 9 reflects the sorts of differentiation between character and character, situation and situation, that were extensively illustrated in Chapter 1. It would be idle to rehearse that discussion. But something more general can now be said. A graph or a table may be a poor substitute for a well-informed analysis of detail and is certainly no substitute for a great novel. And yet, to the extent that it can clarify things that we dimly sense in the novel, it has its virtues — virtues which are especially serviceable at times when literary theorizing grows narcissistic and loses sight of the literature itself. To the extent that it draws attention to things that we had not sensed, it can take us back to the novel with a fresh awareness of its subtleties. The few specimens offered so far give only glimpses of the wealth that flows from a study of more complex interrelationships.

Part Two

NICER MEASURES

5

Correlation-matrices and the Interrelationship of Characters

Even as an examination tests its candidates, the overall 'shape' of their performances tests its effectiveness as a measure. As tests of prepositionality, 'of' and 'in' work in closer harmony than do 'very' and 'quite' as tests of emphasis; and the obvious difference between the correlation-coefficients for these two pairs makes a concise way of expressing what is illustrated by the foregoing linear-regression graphs.

But what of the candidates themselves? Just as the opportunities and constraints afforded by a given pair of words for the portrayal of forty-eight different characters can be intelligibly summarized in graphs and coefficients, so can the comparative recourse of a given pair of characters to many different words. The necessary data is of precisely the same form as that set out in Table 6, early in Chapter 4: but, instead of measuring correlations down the vertical columns, we now measure them across the horizontal rows; and, whereas Table 6 treats of only six common word-types, it is obviously desirable to bring a much larger number of word-types into the reckoning.[1]

In linear-regression graphs of this new kind, the line of best fit calculated from the particular data has not been included. A true diagonal, along which the various word-types would be arrayed if each character registered the same incidences as the other, is better suited for showing each character's conformities and divergences. The mean-lines are omitted: to know that the average incidence of the first thirty words is about 13 per 1000 serves no purpose of which I am aware. To know the aggregate of the incidences, however, is

---

[1] The received distinction between word-types and word-tokens is useful here: as a single word-type, 'and' is the aggregate of its many separate appearances as a word-token.

To avoid the repeated tabulation of an increasing body of data, the incidences, for each major character, of the most common word-types in Jane Austen's dialogue are set out, along with other material of that sort, in Appendix C.

to be reminded of the pervasiveness of the very common words. The thirty most common word-types in Jane Austen's dialogue encompass 40.06 per cent of the whole dialogue of her characters. Most major characters lie between 39 per cent and 41 per cent, with Edward Ferrars (41.97 per cent) a little above his immediate neighbours at the upper end of the range and Admiral Croft (36.19 per cent) distinctly isolated at the lower end.[2]

In Jane Austen's dialogue, taken as a whole, the thirty most common word-types differ somewhat, in both identity and sequence, from those of her novels taken as wholes. Those for dialogue are set out below with their respective mean-incidences shown, as usual, as rates per 1000 words:

38.75 I	16.14 not	9.39 as	7.06 very
26.45 the	14.92 be	8.87 he	7.00 she
24.97 you	14.85 is	8.10 her	6.82 will (vb)
24.64 and	13.39 in	7.60 that (conj)	6.51 do
23.69 of	12.20 have	7.45 for (prep)	6.32 your
20.34 to (inf)	11.19 to (prep)	7.41 me	6.22 with
18.54 a	10.35 my	7.18 was	5.88 at
18.41 it	9.99 but		

Graphs 11 and 12 treat of interrelationships in the use of these thirty words between two pairs of characters from *Pride and Prejudice*. At 0.930, the correlation between Darcy and Elizabeth, illustrated in Graph 11, is closer than most but, even within this novel, not the closest of all. Few of the thirty words lie far from the diagonal line that represents parity of incidence. Among those lying to the right of the line (those for which Darcy's incidence is higher than Elizabeth's), 'was' offers the most marked divergence. Darcy's particular recourse to that word, offset by his comparatively sparing recourse to 'is', is associated with the past tense of epistolary style in his long letter of explanation. As a group, the commonest prepositions tend to Darcy's side but only 'of' is strongly differentiated.

---

[2] Although the separation of homographic words into their main constituents serves the present argument better than it serves his, the sort of data offered in this paragraph and in the next few pages is broadly in keeping with George Zipf's famous 'straight line' of frequency-ranking. But the fact that many idiolects have their own 'straight lines' shows that Jane Austen's novels are stylistically more diverse than the prose treatises and long poems to which Zipf's researches were chiefly addressed. See his *Human Behavior and the Principle of Least Effort* (Cambridge, Mass., 1949), *passim*, but esp. Part I.

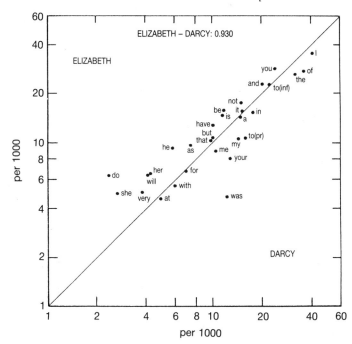

GRAPH 11. Elizabeth and Darcy: Correlation of Word-types 1-30

No one pronoun runs strongly either way: but those of the first person all lie on Darcy's side, those of the third person on Elizabeth's. On the other side of the diagonal, Elizabeth has significantly more recourse to the weakly emphatic verb-form, 'do'. But, all in all, Graph 11 illustrates a suitably close resemblance between the idiolects of two strong-minded, intelligent, and essentially well-mannered characters whose disputes are conducted on even terms and whose eventual *rapprochement* is entirely credible.

The grounds of the correlation of only 0.598 between Collins and Lydia Bennet are evident in Graph 12. It is the third lowest correlation between any of the pairs of major characters in *Pride and Prejudice*. (Mrs Gardiner participates in both of the lower correlations: her unusual combination of the submissive, the mildly hortatory, and the epistolary makes hers the most isolated idiolect of the whole forty-eight in the use of these most common words of all. Appropriately enough, her closest correlation — still only 0.829 — is with Mrs Smith of *Persuasion*.) When they are set out in

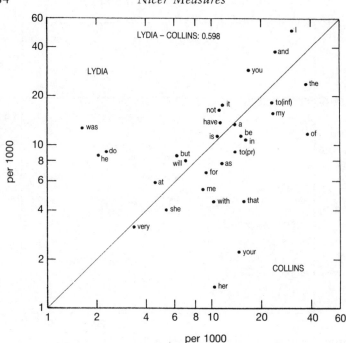

GRAPH 12. Lydia and Collins: Correlation of Word-types 1–30

this way, the sharp disparities that are scattered about the upper part of Graph 12—Lydia's 'I' and 'and', Collins's 'of' and 'the'—can be left to speak for themselves. Some even more marked differentiations can be found in the lower part of the graph.[3] Chiefly in self-gratifying anecdotes, Lydia uses 'was' at eight times as high a rate as Collins. With his honoured patroness ever foremost in his talk, if not quite foremost in his mind, Collins uses 'her' at almost eight times as high a rate as Lydia, who has little attention to spare for the remainder of the female population. With a tribe of plump sentences to support, he even uses the conjunction 'that' at more than three times the rate she requires for her syntactic starvelings. The prosaic 'at', the refutatory 'but', and the merely accumulative 'and' are the only words of a connective function to fall on her side of the

[3] The 'log–log' graphic scale has been employed to allow adequate space in the lower range: the corollary, of course, is a compression in the upper range. Although the unequal intervals of a logarithmic scale give an unfamiliar impression at first sight, the advantage in clarity soon compensates for that.

diagonal line. (In the usage of some more formal speakers, it should be noted, 'and' is not always 'merely accumulative'.) To compare Graphs 11 and 12 is, in short, to see a strong contrast between an essentially similar and a rather dissimilar pair of idiolects and to realize the immense difference between 0.930 and 0.598 as correlation-coefficients.

Such graphs might easily be multiplied to show the resemblances and differences between each and every pair of major characters in *Pride and Prejudice* or to draw comparisons and contrasts between characters from different novels. (The highest coefficient of all brings Elizabeth Bennet and Emma Woodhouse together at 0.973. The lowest of all — 0.408 — is between Collins and Harriet Smith.) To interconnect the various coefficients, however, is not only a more concise but a more generally illuminating alternative. The three lowest coefficients in this novel illustrate the striking differences of idiolect between Collins and Lydia (0.598), Lady Catherine and Mrs Gardiner (0.595), and Collins and Mrs Gardiner (0.520). But this does *not* imply a close resemblance between Lydia and Mrs Gardiner: for that pair, the coefficient is still only 0.618. At 56 and 60 miles respectively, Oxford and Cambridge are almost equidistant from London. Yet this information tells no more of the distance between Oxford and Cambridge than that it must lie between 4 and 116 miles. If only in its proportions — perhaps the proportions should suffice — the triangle on which they actually lie is not unlike that on which Lydia, Mrs Gardiner, and Collins lie. And, just as other places lie within and beyond the one triangle, in a complex network of greater and lesser distances, so there is a complex network of resemblances and differences among the correlation-coefficients for Jane Austen's major characters. (It need only be noted, for the moment, that the concept of multi-dimensionality is a more potent force in 'correlation-mapping' than in mapping the earth's surface.)

For *Pride and Prejudice*, the whole matrix of correlation-coefficients is set out in Table 7. That novel makes the best starting-point because it includes the largest number of major characters and so displays the greatest complexity of interrelationships. The most prominent general feature is the overall differentiation between the Bennet ladies (excluding Mrs Gardiner) on the one hand and Darcy's circle (including Lady Catherine and Collins) on the other. Mrs Bennet's idiolect resembles that of every member of her own family more closely than it resembles that of any member of the other set.

Nicer Measures

TABLE 7. Correlation of the Relative Frequencies of the Thirty Most Common Word in Jane Austen's Dialogue

Pride and Prejudice

		ALL	3A	3B	3D	3E	3K	3C	3O	3L	3H	3J	3
3A	ELIZABETH	0.971	**3A**										
3B	DARCY	0.910	0.930	**3B**									
3D	Mrs Bennet	0.909	0.853	0.724	**3D**								
3E	Jane	0.883	0.874	0.790	0.888	**3E**							
3K	Collins	0.779	0.818	0.889	0.600	0.651	**3K**						
3C	Mr Bennet	0.921	0.938	0.848	0.835	0.764	0.754	**3C**					
3O	Mrs Gardiner	0.730	0.726	0.702	0.618	0.715	0.520	0.611	**3O**				
3L	Lady Catherine	0.890	0.926	0.886	0.730	0.690	0.776	0.945	0.595	**3L**			
3H	Lydia	0.898	0.837	0.762	0.913	0.841	0.598	0.789	0.618	0.727	**3H**		
3J	Miss Bingley	0.916	0.897	0.869	0.809	0.750	0.834	0.847	0.637	0.838	0.765	**3**	
3V	Wickham	0.900	0.860	0.855	0.774	0.843	0.768	0.736	0.774	0.725	0.802	0.82	

Mansfield Park

		ALL	4B	4C	4D	4J	4A	4E	4G
4B	EDMUND	0.967	**4B**						
4C	Mary Crawford	0.974	0.954	**4C**					
4D	Henry Crawford	0.961	0.957	0.939	**4D**				
4J	Mrs Norris	0.957	0.954	0.957	0.936	**4J**			
4A	FANNY	0.940	0.872	0.868	0.908	0.853	**4A**		
4E	Sir Thomas	0.889	0.898	0.906	0.844	0.869	0.748	**4E**	
4G	Tom Bertram	0.882	0.894	0.924	0.887	0.938	0.775	0.809	**4G**
4F	Lady Bertram	0.834	0.760	0.746	0.770	0.782	0.846	0.652	0.648

Emma

		ALL	5A	5B	5E	5D	5I	5M	5P	5O
5A	EMMA	0.984	**5A**							
5B	MR KNIGHTLEY	0.950	0.958	**5B**						
5E	Churchill	0.942	0.890	0.870	**5E**					
5D	Miss Bates	0.891	0.866	0.864	0.853	**5D**				
5I	Mrs Elton	0.964	0.945	0.894	0.939	0.855	**5I**			
5M	Harriet Smith	0.842	0.809	0.796	0.812	0.864	0.802	**5M**		
5P	Mr Woodhouse	0.860	0.868	0.830	0.762	0.875	0.849	0.798	**5P**	
5O	Mrs Weston	0.935	0.923	0.942	0.909	0.848	0.884	0.812	0.806	**5O**
5N	Mr Weston	0.894	0.901	0.873	0.788	0.862	0.846	0.730	0.838	0.872

Sense and Sensibility

		ALL	2A	2C	2K	2S	2F	2Q	2H	2D	2B
2A	ELINOR	0.931	**2A**								
2C	Marianne	0.957	0.906	**2C**							
2K	Mrs Jennings	0.933	0.801	0.868	**2K**						
2S	Willoughby	0.829	0.696	0.833	0.785	**2S**					
2F	John Dashwood	0.864	0.795	0.781	0.825	0.681	**2F**				
2Q	Lucy Steele	0.916	0.873	0.918	0.839	0.799	0.671	**2Q**			
2H	Col. Brandon	0.842	0.680	0.796	0.848	0.917	0.799	0.746	**2H**		
2D	Mrs Dashwood	0.912	0.929	0.875	0.801	0.686	0.874	0.811	0.723	**2D**	
2B	EDWARD FERRARS	0.912	0.767	0.895	0.862	0.929	0.726	0.883	0.891	0.756	**2B**
2P	Anne Steele	0.817	0.684	0.726	0.883	0.694	0.708	0.761	0.756	0.690	0.765

Northanger Abbey

		ALL	1A	1B	1D	1E
1A	CATHERINE	0.852	**1A**			
1B	HENRY TILNEY	0.871	0.551	**1B**		
1D	Isab. Thorpe	0.908	0.897	0.715	**1D**	
1E	John Thorpe	0.924	0.838	0.800	0.902	**1E**
1C	Eleanor Tilney	0.935	0.843	0.818	0.901	0.897

Persuasion

		ALL	6A	6V	6P	6B
6A	ANNE	0.961	**6A**			
6V	Mrs Smith	0.918	0.856	**6V**		
6P	Mary Musgrove	0.930	0.919	0.830	**6P**	
6B	WENTWORTH	0.965	0.957	0.867	0.913	**6B**
6D	Admiral Croft	0.879	0.803	0.855	0.816	0.824

At 0.835, her husband—as he might be pleased to learn—is the furthest removed from her of the one group; and, at 0.809, Miss Bingley stands closest to her of the other. The resemblances between her and those three of her daughters who are major characters falls into a convincing hierarchy: Lydia (0.913), Jane (0.888), and Elizabeth (0.853). Mr Bennet is much closer to Elizabeth (0.938) than to his wife (0.835) or to Lydia (0.789). Lydia nowhere rises above 0.850—except with her mother (0.913). Jane's idiolect is more like her mother's (0.888) than those who regard her role as 'normative' might expect. But a not much lesser resemblance to Elizabeth (0.874) and a rather larger difference from Lydia (0.841) are reassuring.

Save for the special case of Mrs Gardiner, which was touched on a little earlier, Collins is the most isolated of the major characters of *Pride and Prejudice* with only three correlations higher than 0.770. These three comprise a slight resemblance to Elizabeth (0.818), a nodding acquaintance with Miss Bingley (0.843), and a sufficient resemblance to Darcy (0.889) to support the earlier proposal that an element of parody can be found here. (Across the whole range of the novels, Collins nowhere else exceeds 0.820, and he falls below 0.650 in fourteen correlations out of forty-seven.) At 0.838, Lady Catherine and Miss Bingley do not resemble each other very closely: but they are both closer than this to Darcy and much further from Mrs Bennet, Lydia, and Jane.

The general contrast between the two groups makes an effective test of the correlations themselves. Had they failed to register what every reader of *Pride and Prejudice* knows about the distance from Longbourn-house to Netherfield (let alone Rosings or Pemberley), they would have deserved only to be discarded. As it is, they make a framework for more far-reaching relationships.

The four highest coefficients in *Pride and Prejudice* not only make for illuminating connections between the two main groups of characters but constitute a sub-group of their own. Two of them are, as might be expected, between Elizabeth and her father (0.938) and between Elizabeth and Darcy (0.930). But that between Elizabeth and Lady Catherine (0.926) and that between Mr Bennet and Lady Catherine (0.945) are of the same order. Up to a point, these four characters are united in a firmness of manner and a control of ideas that readily distinguish them from Mrs Bennet and Lydia: and, as we have seen, such qualities affect the frequency-patterns of the very common words. But Mr Bennet and Lady Catherine are brought still closer by patterns which they share with Sir Thomas Bertram, patterns which can be associated with expressions of authority and habits of command. A very marked recourse to the second person pronouns makes one such pattern: to use them freely is to claim, at least, a right of comment and frequently a right of intrusion. (The honorific use of third person pronouns as forms of address, as in the Italian *'Lei'*, suggests that this discrimination is not peculiar to Jane Austen's use of English.) Sir Thomas's employment of 'you' as a battering-ram when Fanny, for once, resists him makes a powerful case in point: '*You* are not to be judged by the same rule. You do not owe me the duty of a child. But, Fanny, if your heart can acquit you of *ingratitude*—' (p. 319). Among the other marks of authoritative idiolects, shared by Sir Thomas, Mr Bennet, and Lady Catherine, is a pronounced avoidance of the weaker and more overt forms of emphasis: not for them to claim by emphasis what they simply claim by right. In a range of idioms of this kind, Darcy and Elizabeth do not match them: yet they approach them more closely than do the more submissive characters of the novels.

So far as I am aware, the criticism of *Pride and Prejudice*, while often touching on the exercise or the abdication of authority, does not include a direct approach to the topic. But consider how appropriately Mr Bennet, Lady Catherine, and Darcy fill the roles, respectively, of a dormant but not extinct authority-figure, an officious usurper of authority, and a worthy—though at first unrecognized and overweening—bearer of the responsibilities that should accompany a position of authority. That set of resemblances and contrasts makes a context for Lydia's mutinous resentments and Jane's submissiveness; for Collins's 'mixture of servility and self-importance', as Mr Bennet has it (p. 64); for the parodic connections between Miss Bingley and Elizabeth as well as Collins and Darcy; for the contrast between Mrs Bennet and Mrs Gardiner both as wives and as advisers to the young; for Darcy's high reputation as landlord of Pemberley and his acceptance of responsibility for Wickham's irresponsibilities; and for Georgiana Darcy's charming 'astonishment bordering on alarm' (p. 387) at young Mrs Darcy's ability to treat the master of Pemberley a little less than seriously. Consider, too, what apt questions all this raises, throughout *Pride and Prejudice*, for a swift-witted, inquiring, and not obviously submissive young woman like Elizabeth Bennet—or Jane Austen, who was twenty-one when she first worked on 'First Impressions'.[4] While the value of this line of interpretation is obviously open to debate, its particular interest is that it originates in an attempt to understand an unexpectedly close set of correlations and that these, in turn, reflect a demonstrable patterning of the very common words.

Mansfield Park offers an equally striking example of what is to be seen in the correlation-matrices set out in Table 7. In the critical discussion of that novel, much attention has been given to Fanny's place as heroine, to signs of a conflict between London values and those of the country gentry, and to the marked change of direction in the closing chapters. Without resolving any of these issues, the evidence of the very common words has light to shed on all of them.

Perhaps the most prominent feature of the correlation-matrix is the stylistic isolation of Lady Bertram. Only with Fanny does any of her coefficients exceed 0.800; and, in relation to her husband and her elder son, she falls as far as 0.650. Although Miss Maria Ward once had 'the good luck to captivate Sir Thomas Bertram . . . and to be thereby raised to the rank of a baronet's lady' (p. 3), the passage of thirty years has taught her no more than a smattering of his language. The language of Mrs Norris, more sedulous and less secure, is much closer to his and to that of the younger generation—except for Fanny.

Once Lady Bertram is set aside, the whole matrix shows an unusually high level of correlations among the rest—except for Fanny. In this way, I suggest, the claustral ambience of Mansfield is palpable even in the most commonplace of its linguistic habits. And, even here, Fanny stands as isolated as she is in matters of principle and conduct. The characterization of Fanny will be pursued in Chapter 10, when the evidence of 'character narrative' is set beside that of dialogue. But it should be noted that, while her speech idioms set her apart from her immediate fellows, they are in no way freakish: a correlation of 0.947 with Anne Elliot may lay any doubt on that point.

Despite what has been said, there are chinks in the seemingly impenetrable wall of Mansfield language. Fanny's least close correlations are with her cousin, Mr Bertram, and with the awful

---

[4] See Cassandra Austen's memorandum on the dates of composition, which is reproduced in *Minor Works*, facing p. 242.

figure of Sir Thomas. Neither of her aunts nor Edmund speaks very much like her. There is a period when her idiolect and that of Mary Crawford converge. But by far the highest of Fanny's correlations is with Henry Crawford. When it is also seen that Edmund's highest correlations—two of the three highest in the novel—are with the Crawfords, a number of interesting ideas begin to stir.

The action of *Mansfield Park* gives ample evidence of the improprieties of the Crawfords and of their unfamiliarity with the mores of the country gentry (from whom they spring). It also shows how little understanding Mansfield has of London ways, and how tenuous is the prospect of a *rapprochement*. Despite all this, criticism of the novel is often marked by an uneasiness about the treatment of the Crawfords, especially in the denouement—an uneasiness no less to be felt in over-stalwart defences of Jane Austen's purposes, like Kathleen Tillotson's, than in downright attacks upon them, like that of Kingsley Amis.[5]

The evidence of the very common words suggests a source for this unease. Such evidence cannot readily be weighed against the overt evidence of attitudes and events. But, working away beneath the surface, the unexpectedly close affinities between the glittering Crawfords and the sober Edmund and also between Fanny and the man she so frequently condemns run counter to those interpretations of the novel, not often touched by the kind of unease I have mentioned, that force it into the mould of a straightforward morality play in which the Londoners take the part of Vice to Mansfield's pastoral Virtue. The pervasive tension between surface and sub-stratum represents a newer and more imaginative enterprise than that for Jane Austen and poses more delicate questions than that for her readers. As so often, Mary Lascelles puts it more succinctly and exactly than most of her successors:

In the earlier novels, all those indefinable sympathies and antipathies which, like filaments, connect people whom kinship or fortune associates, occasionally threaten to be resolved into likes and dislikes, or even reduced to the simpler terms of approval and disapproval. These sympathies and antipathies have been adroitly complicated by misunderstandings; but such misunderstanding of the character and conduct of other people is simple compared with the Bertrams' and Crawfords' misunderstanding of the nature

---

[5] Kathleen Tillotson, 'The Tale and the Teller', in Geoffrey and Kathleen Tillotson, *Mid-Victorian Studies* (London, 1965), pp. 8–10; Kingsley Amis, *What Became of Jane Austen? and Other Questions* (London, 1970), pp. 13–17.

of their relationships, one to another and each to himself. For *Mansfield Park* is a comedy, with grave implications, of human interdependence numbly unrealized or wilfully ignored until too late.[6]

To accept this, however, is still not to be persuaded that, at the end, Jane Austen finds any better way of resolving the whole delicate system of tensions than to snap some of its chief threads. The growing indelicacies of Mary's letters to Fanny and the quiet reminders of Henry's old infirmity of purpose point towards a catastrophe which, in abstract moral terms, is certainly in keeping with the broad tenor of earlier events. But these glimpses of the Crawfords unregenerate are offset by vivid recollections of the gentle and considerate language they had gradually learnt from Fanny, Edmund, and Mrs Grant, a language that can be seen in Mary's last meeting with Fanny and, even more convincingly, during Henry's visit to Portsmouth. Especially in its management, therefore, the catastrophe rests on unsure foundations. When it comes, it includes the abrupt intrusion of the narrator: 'Let other pens dwell on guilt and misery' (p. 461). There is a convoluted account of how Henry Crawford 'lost the woman whom he had rationally, as well as passionately loved' (p. 469). There is the melodramatic shrillness of Mary's parting words. And there is the uneasily comic treatment of the recovered understanding between Edmund and Fanny:

Long, long would it be ere Miss Crawford's name passed his lips again, or she could hope for a renewal of such confidential intercourse as had been.
    It *was* long. They reached Mansfield on Thursday, and it was not till Sunday evening that Edmund began to talk to her on the subject. (p. 453)

Is there a trace of defensiveness in Jane Austen's satisfaction that her brother Henry 'admires H. Crawford: I mean properly, as a clever, pleasant man' (*Letters*, pp. 377–8)? A few days later, when he has finished the novel, she reports to Cassandra that 'his approbation has not lessened. He found the last half of the last volume *extremely interesting*' (ibid., p. 386). Not every later reader has shared his approbation: but the well-chosen phrase 'extremely interesting' may not be so unequivocal as his sister appears to have believed.

II

Each in its own way, the correlation-matrices for the other novels are as illuminating as these two. And the general validity of the figures

[6] Mary Lascelles, *Jane Austen and Her Art* (London, 1939), p. 164.

remains evident in the straightforward cases that make up a strong majority. The resemblances between Emma and Mr Knightley and between Anne and Captain Wentworth produce the two highest coefficients in those novels whereas the differences between Catherine Morland and Henry Tilney produce the second lowest of all the coefficients set out in Table 7. (Small wonder that, where the idiolects of the hero and the heroine differ so greatly that they scarcely 'speak the same language', *Northanger Abbey* is coloured by verbal games, verbal misunderstandings, and small disquisitions on semantics.) Mr Woodhouse and Miss Bates resemble each other more closely than either resembles any other character in *Emma*. Anne Steele differs much less from Mrs Jennings than from any other of her fellows. Wickham's blandness is reflected in an idiolect that neither closely resembles nor markedly differs from those of his fellows. And, even allowing for the fact that the style of each is coloured by the telling of a long and self-pitying tale, the comparative lifelessness of the dialogue of *Sense and Sensibility* is reflected in the resemblances of idiolect between characters ostensibly as different from each other as Willoughby, Brandon, and Edward Ferrars: only the coefficient for Edward and Marianne intrudes at the margin of a pattern in which each of the three resembles the other two more closely than he resembles anybody else.

And yet an occasional striking departure must be set against the weight of the predictable results. After Mr Knightley, Emma most resembles Mrs Elton. After Wentworth, Anne most resembles Mary Musgrove. (In this case, of course, the possibilities are restricted by the dearth of major characters.) The predictable resemblance between Isabella Thorpe and her brother (0.902) cannot sensibly be rated higher than the surprising resemblance between Isabella and Eleanor Tilney (0.901). Lucy Steele's closest correlation is with Marianne. And, as was noted earlier, Mrs Norris shows remarkably close resemblances not only to her nephews but also to the Crawfords. (It is regrettable that her nieces speak too little to be brought into the comparison.) Mrs Norris's correlations with Edmund (0.954) and with Mary Crawford (0.957) should be set beside that between Emma and Mrs Elton (0.945).

Both the predictable majority and the apparent departures can be more fully understood if they are set in a context where literary character, the larger workings of the language, and a little communication-theory are brought together. The questions arising will be faced in the course of the ensuing chapters.

In broad terms, a literary character—to begin on comparatively firm ground—is a construct of the words he speaks and the things he does, both of which are interpreted, for the presumable benefit of the reader, by his fellow-characters and by the 'privileged', if not always reliable, comments of the narrator. The extent to which he is 'individualized' can differ greatly not only in terms of the writer's competence in his craft but also in terms of the particular writer's larger purposes. D. H. Lawrence's celebrated attack on the individualization of character, in which he takes the allotropes of carbon—both diamond and coal—as his metaphor for a fundamental identity that transcends all differences of appearance, may be reminder enough that, among many novelists of the twentieth century, the 'classic realist' emphasis on individuality is no longer a secure criterion. By the same token, Lawrence's most memorable comment on Jane Austen is an attack upon 'that spinster' for her 'knowing in apartness'.

Questions of resemblance between literary characters and real people, whether particular persons or recognizable social types, have proved less of a distraction for the literary critic since L. C. Knights cleared the ground in 'How Many Children had Lady Macbeth?'. Mr Knightley's exceptionally marked recourse to 'her', 'herself', and 'she' offers a small but potent reminder of the force of Knights's argument, a reminder that 'whole personalities' are not the stuff of literature. No one would envisage Mr Knightley as a man whose mind was scarcely less occupied by the women of Highbury than by the men of the Donwell estate, his fellow-magistrates, and the members of his club. (In all but the fifth chapter of the novel, it should be noted, Emma is seldom the referent of these pronouns.) And yet, relative to their respective shares of dialogue, only a handful of characters in the six novels surpass his incidence for any of these pronouns. None of them surpasses his incidence for all three. His recourse to these pronouns, in short, reflects only certain aspects of what 'a man like him' would actually have to say: and these aspects, of course, are influenced by such larger forces as his role in a novel in which the heroine seizes most of the conversational initiative on most occasions.

To accept that a literary character is no mortal man but a reflection of the words he uses within the particular range of episodes that make up a novel, of certain inferences from his actions, and of the narrator's privileged comments is not to fly to the opposite extreme.

So far, at least, as Jane Austen's characters are concerned, the
evidence of the very common words is utterly at variance with the
assertion, seldom accompanied by anything so prosaic as evidence,
that 'character' itself is an abstraction, imposed by the bourgeois
reader (intent on shoring up his own precious sense of individuality)
on a more or less reluctant text. What might emerge from a
comparable analysis of those *'illisible'* texts which Barthes and his
disciples find more rewarding has yet to be seen; but the
differentiation of Jane Austen's characters is demonstrably present
in the texts themselves. (If that makes Jane Austen another misguided
bourgeois, she may conceivably be pardoned, like the virtuous pagan,
for not being converted to doctrines that had yet to be proclaimed.)

The claim that the patterns of usage in which 'character' very
largely consists are reflections of social conditioning or even
determinism rather than expressions of a genuine individuality
deserves more serious consideration. If social conditioning is
envisaged, as in some Marxist criticism, in such terms as exclude
all but gross, long-lasting influences like social rank and sexual
category, the evidence of the very common words transcends and
refines it. But if it is envisaged as admitting the influence of changing
circumstances—of the mutual adjustments and failures of adjustment
that occur when a young girl goes to Bath, an over-confident young
woman finds that she must reconsider her ruling attitudes, or two
Londoners come to live in a country parsonage and a foster-child
wins acceptance in a forbidding family; if, further, it admits the
interplay of dialogue between this one and that on such and such
a topic; and if, finally, it acknowledges the possibility, however
tenuous, that its own categories of analysis may not be all-embracing:
on such conditions as these, it converges on the same sorts of finding
as arise in traditional literary criticism at its best. (For all parties,
moreover, it is necessary to keep in mind the profound, though not
always overt, influence of earlier literary works.) Even under those
conditions, differences of emphasis will remain; but they need not
preclude debate. These matters will be discussed in Chapter 9.

There are no obvious grounds on which a similar accommodation
might be established with the more thoroughgoing of the linguistic
sceptics who follow Jacques Derrida. If—as they say—language does
not exist or lies inaccessible in a metaphysical void, there is no
more—one cannot say—to be said. On a point—(said he,
continuing)—where the lack of decisive evidence and perhaps of

evidentiality itself obliges each of us to make his own choice, I am content to take 'as if . . .' for a working basis. That preference comes the more easily when this modern scepticism is recognized as a more narrowly focused version of the scepticism of David Hume: if nothing whatever beyond the self can be shown to be (and/or to be accessible), the loss merely of language seems trifling. The preference comes more easily yet in a period of our history when even the disputes of philosophers about the demonstrability of our existence or that of our language lie under the ever-present threat of our actual extinction.

If language either exists or is regarded as if it does (and is accessible or is treated as if it is), Jane Austen has much to teach us of its intricacies. To sketch a familiar background for the less familiar argument that will follow, they include the relationship between narrative and characterization. Only in the early novels where, for instance, Mrs Dashwood correlates distinctly more closely with Elinor than with Marianne, is there often a simple discrepancy between the evidence of speech-and-action and the guidance offered by the narrator. The later novels, however, abound in subtler and more appropriate discrepancies. In *Emma*, the delicate equivocations of the narrative can leave all but the shrewdest of readers, in the course of a first reading, in an ignorance as complete if not as self-confident as Emma's own. *Persuasion*, to carry it still further, presents Jamesian narrative-complexities as the reader tries to plumb the ever-changing relationship between Anne's consciousness and the narrator's view of things.

For all its relevance to characterization, then, narrative commentary cannot be taken at face value. Even when it seems almost guileless — Frank Churchill was gone off to London 'with no more important view that appeared than having his hair cut' (p. 205) — its full meaning can be veiled. And, even where such doubts do not arise, it may do little more than mark the gap between intention and realization: against the evidence of style, we are told, of Marianne, that 'the resemblance between her and her mother was strikingly great' (p. 6). Although shibboleths are poor substitutes for perceptive reading, the notions of trusting not the teller but the tale and of having a weather eye for the 'intentional fallacy' make sensible working rules.

To the extent that the interpretation of character consists in assessing the meaning of actions and events, possibilities and problems both abound. For the present purpose, it is enough to

distinguish between cases where an uncertainty can swiftly be
resolved and those which prove more intractable. On the one side—
to choose examples where the evidence warrants a direct challenge
to some of Jane Austen's more distinguished critics—a feeling for
consistency of character is enough to dispel the idea that Elizabeth
Bennet may be serious when she makes his ownership of Pemberley
her reason for learning to love Darcy. An eye for the larger
framework of events shows why Frank Churchill really goes to
London and why Fanny Price develops so severe a migraine from
a hot morning in the rose-garden. A sense of generic decorum
suggests that, though General Tilney is an unscrupulous bully, the
parallels between him and Mrs Radcliffe's Montoni serve chiefly
comic purposes and make him a comic monster.

The more intractable cases include large parallelisms like that
between Emma's taking-up of Harriet Smith and Mrs Elton's taking-
up of Jane Fairfax; and, on an even larger scale, the possibility of
defending a full-blown 'ironic reversal' like the libertarian view of
Mansfield Park, in which Mary Crawford is taken for a defeated
heroine and Fanny for an anti-heroine, a pale convolvulus that chokes
the free play of spirit and intelligence. In the former case, a tradition-
alist would have it that the parallel exists for the sake of an emerging
contrast—that Mrs Elton epitomizes qualities which are incipient
in Emma but which she is to be seen to quell: and yet, so long as
discussion remains focused on the outward framework of events,
a Marvin Mudrick can both hold his main ground and even 'project
confirmed exploiters like Emma and Churchill into the future of their
marriages'.[7] The latter case runs counter to a body of 'intentionalist'
evidence, whether that of narrative commentary—as when we are
told of 'the really good feelings by which she [Miss Crawford] was
almost purely governed' (p. 147: my italics)—or that of such
historical facts as Jane Austen's contempt for one who was 'as raffish
in his appearance as I would wish every Disciple of Godwin to be'
(*Letters*, p. 133). But if 'intentionalist' evidence is held to be invalid
and we are left to 'trust the tale', the libertarian view of *Mansfield
Park* can be sustained plausibly enough to typify that liberty of
interpretation on which extreme forms of 'reader-response' and
'deconstructive' criticism thrive.

[7] Marvin Mudrick, *Jane Austen: Irony as Defense and Discovery* (Princeton,
1952), p. 207.

The sharper-edged evidence of dialogue must next be brought to bear: for, in most novels, characterization lies largely in the dense texture of what the dramatis personae have to say. Such interchanges as that about the place of family prayer in a great household or that about times and distances in the woods of Sotherton are too nicely balanced to prove at all conclusive. Mary's clear eye for the realities that can belie a ritual piety is well matched against Edmund's judicious and Fanny's more emotional avowals of their devotion to traditional forms of worship. In the woods, of course, Mary refuses to acknowledge what is clearly established as the fact: but her small flights of fancy can be taken either as illustrative of her essential frivolity or as a measure of Edmund's ungenial literal-mindedness.

The excursus of the last few pages will have served its purpose if it makes an adequate context for assessing the sort of evidence yielded by statistical comparisons between idiolect and idiolect. On the face of it, as the reader may recall, some of that evidence remains as 'open' as the other forms of evidence just illustrated. Mary's correlations with Edmund and with Mrs Norris are about equally close. Emma's correlation with Mrs Elton falls only a little short of her correlation with Mr Knightley and lies about as far above her correlation with Mrs Weston.

The technical question of what constitutes a 'significant' difference between idiolects can be left for Chapter 7 when a larger array of coefficients will be compared. The more immediate question bears on the basic concept of an idiolect and the legitimacy of generalizing about idiolects on no broader basis than is afforded by the thirty most common words of dialogue.

Provided the larger framework of narrative and action, the matter of the last few pages, is not neglected, it is obviously legitimate to bring the evidence of different characters' whole idiolects to bear on questions of interpretation. Over and above their evidence of verbal idiosyncrasy (or the lack of it), the words a character speaks, in such novels as Jane Austen's, make an essential part of the action in which he is engaged. At precisely this point, however, the present study turns in a different direction from such excellent analyses as Stuart Tave's:[8] whereas Tave is plainly justified in using potent thematic words like 'lively' and 'proper' to distinguish, among other things, between character and character, I have to go beyond the particular

[8] Stuart M. Tave, *Some Words of Jane Austen* (Chicago, 1973).

illustrations offered in my earlier chapters and establish an adequate general foundation for the notion of placing so much weight on the most commonplace elements in the vocabulary of character.

III

Graph 13 should be regarded as a preamble to this more general argument, an empirical demonstration that it can usefully be pursued. As a twofold 'map' of interrelationships among the major characters of *Pride and Prejudice*, based solely upon their differing recourse to the thirty most common words of dialogue, it is extracted from the earlier correlation-matrix (Table 7) by a process known as 'eigen-analysis'. The three principal 'eigen-vectors' that make the axes of the two parts of the graph—Vector B is the horizontal axis in both parts—account, all told, for almost 92 per cent of the interrelationship among these particular coefficients.[9] If the upper graph is thought of as a floor-plan or a bird's eye view, it shows a decidedly appropriate pattern of resemblances and differences among the major characters. When it is complemented by the 'side-elevation' or cross-section of the lower graph, it can be seen that Collins is more like Darcy, and Jane less like her mother and Lydia than the floor-plan alone can reveal.

How is it that mere differences in the frequency-patterns of the very common words can yield such appropriate results? If each of the very common word-types is regarded as a *separate* thread in the fabric of a character's vocabulary and if it is recalled that only thirty such threads make up 40 per cent of the whole fabric, it is tempting to envisage a skeletal pattern in which a multitude of finer but more brightly coloured threads could take their places in the interstices and contribute to the complete effect. And, given the many strong differentiations that distinguish Jane Austen's characters from each other in the use of each common word-type, it is not inconceivable that different 'mixtures' might be enough to separate the more

---

[9] Such forms of analysis are not often described in sufficiently non-mathematical language to be comprehensible to the layman. But see Joseph Woelfel and Edward L. Fink, *The Measurement of Communication Processes* (New York & London, 1980), ch. iv, for a comparatively straightforward account of eigen-analysis (in its application to sociological research). Note that, in Graph 13, the scales along the axes approximate to the relative weightings of the three vectors. Only a perspective-drawing would properly represent the angles at which the vectors meet.

'Multi-dimensional scaling' is preferable to eigen-analysis in some respects: but no satisfactory computer programme is available at the date of writing.

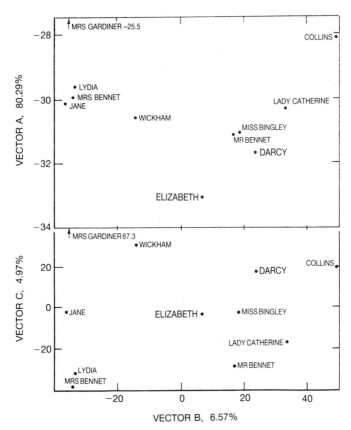

GRAPH 13. Major Idiolects of *Pride and Prejudice*
(Word-types 1–30 of Jane Austen's dialogue)

unusual idiolects. Some such line of thinking, presumably, governs those studies in which a writer's idiosyncratic use of 'with' or 'and'— or of several such words, each separately analysed—is taken as evidence that he, rather than another, was the author of an anonymous or doubtful text. Although Jane Austen's capacity to 'change style' from character to character suggests that novels may be poor material for these methods of attribution, some of the results they have yielded, especially with prose treatises, cannot lightly be dismissed.

And yet, whether it rests on an inadequate conceptual model of the language or fails of full access to a better one, this line of analysis does not justly reflect the complex relationships between word-type and word-type that yield appropriate overall differences between idiolects which are not often strongly differentiated in this particular or that. Words, after all, do not simply lie beside or run across each other like separate threads: neither warp-and-woof nor the more intricate recurrences of knitting approach their sort of relationship.

The choice, at any point, of what word to use next offers a wealth of opportunities but is subject to numerous constraints—grammatical, contextual, or habitual—of a kind touched on in Chapter 1. A more (or less) than ordinary recourse to one common word-type, moreover, inevitably affects the incidence of others. It has long been recognized, for example, that 'of' is most commonly succeeded by 'the' but that, whenever 'the' occurs, its possible successors include any of the multitude of English nouns and adjectives. Following from a comparatively secure starting-point, like 'of', an especially frequent or infrequent use of 'the' might stand as a significant idiosyncrasy; and a tendency to insert (or not to insert) an adjective before the following noun might extend the analysis a step further. The difficulty encountered by scholars who pursue this linear approach to stylistic analysis is, as George A. Miller puts it, that 'the variety of combinations of two or more words is so large that the project quickly gets out of hand'.[10] And, though subsequent advances in computing allow the exploration of a wider range of combinations than Miller could have foreseen, even the more common of the treble and fourfold word-sequences occur seldom enough to imperil statistical analysis. Despite such practical obstacles, the essential virtue of this linear approach lies in its accepting that words do not occur discretely, that each word is influenced by its predecessors and constrains its possible successors.

To illustrate a little more extensively, he who gives unusual prominence to 'I' is somewhat less likely than his fellows to find appropriate 'spaces', within a given quantum, in which to give a similar prominence to 'the' and 'a': his idiom, we might observe, is more self-oriented than most. If he flouts that probability—as the 'rules of the language' certainly allow—and also gives unusual prominence to the articles, he is less likely yet to find much room for 'you', 'he', 'him', 'she' and 'her' in the space afforded by any ordinary proportion of verbs and prepositional phrases. He is more

---

[10] George A. Miller, *Language and Communication* (New York, 1951), p. 53.

accustomed than most, we might say, to emphasize his relationships with other things and not with other people. To turn very freely, as Miss Bates does, to proper names is to impose a probable restriction on the range of pronouns employed. Any marked recourse to, or preferences among, the articles and pronouns will have a necessary bearing on choices among the inflected auxiliary verbs. A severe dearth of prepositions and conjunctions might well combine with a leaning towards 'I–you' and 'you–me' structures, as in the case of Catherine Morland. The crux is to recognize that, while the rules of English are flexible enough to allow a wide range of preferences (or tendencies, to take a less purposive word for what is perhaps not often fully purposive), any pattern of preferences whatever will exert some constraints and reflect others. The interrelationship of word-types within an idiolect, accordingly, is a probabilistic affair.

In its workings, therefore, the language is less well pictured as a fabric than as an extremely energetic force-field, like a constellation moving in space-time, a turbulent stream, or, indeed, a human organism. Even without contemplating the molecular fields of which we are composed, we can recognize that, in each of us, bones and cartilage, nerves and sinews, blood-vessels and flesh are not merely *arranged* in a unique combination: through their influence upon each other and in response to environmental influences, they *shape* that uniqueness. It is enough, for the purposes of this chapter, to envisage an — outwardly — immobile system. But, like the constellation or the human body, once again, the shape of an idiolect can respond delicately to a shift of circumstance or alter more radically with the passage of time.

Yet neither an X-ray photograph, representing the inner structures, nor an 'Identikit' composite, representing the visible features, discriminates as precisely among people of roughly the same physical type as correlation-matrices (and the 'maps' derived from them) discriminate among the idiolects of Jane Austen's characters. Comparisons with the characters of other novelists, in Chapter 8, will make it possible to assess the extent to which Jane Austen takes particular advantage of the latent resources of the language; for, unlike many plausible analogies, the notion of language as a 'force-field' can be judged by other criteria than its own evocativeness, such as that may be. It is in keeping with the method, put forward in this chapter, of extracting correlation-matrices from a large 'grid' of word-frequencies. And it is to be judged by the results which that method yields.

The curious object that follows is a skeletal representation of a celebrated passage from *Pride and Prejudice*. All but the thirty most common words have been replaced by points of suspension. Two narrative comments and a brief piece of internal quotation have been suppressed entirely. The proper names of people have been replaced by [A] and of places by [B].

... me, my ... [A], that your ..., ... you ... ..., ... to your ... . You ... have ... ... in my ... ... *not* ... ...; but ... me to ... you that I have your ... ... for ... . You ... ... the ... of my ..., ... your ... ... you to ...; my ... have ... ... to be .... as ... as I ... the ... I ... you ... as the ... of my .... But ... I ... ... with ... my ... ..., ... it will be ... for me to ... my ... for ... — and ... for ... ... [B] with the ... of ... a ..., as I ... .

My ... for ... ..., ..., that I ... it a ... ... for ... ... in ... ... (... ...) to ... the ... of ... in ... ..., that I ... ... it will ... very ... to my ...; and ... — ... ... I ... to have ... ..., that it is the ... ... and ... of the very ... ... I have the ... of ... . she ... to ... me her ...(... ...!) ... ...; and it was but the very ... ... I ... [B] — ... ... at ..., ... [A] was ... [A] ..., that she ..., '————'. ... me, ... the ..., to ..., my ... ..., that I do not ... the ... and ... of [A] as ... the ... of the ... in my ... to .... You will ... her ... ... I can ...; and your ... and ... I ... ... be ... to her, ... with the ... and ... ... her ... will ... ... for my ... ... in ... of ...; it ... to be ... ... my ... ... [B] ... of my ... ..., ... I ... you ... ... But the ... is, that ..., as I ..., to ... ... the ... of your ... ..., (..., ..., ...,) I ... not ... ... to ... a ... ..., that the ... to ... ... be as ... as ..., ... the ... ... — ..., ..., as I have ... ..., ... not be for ... . my ..., my ... ..., and I ... ... it will not ... me in your .... And ... ... for me but to ... you in the ... ... of the ... of my .... To ... I ... ..., and ... ... of ... ... your ..., ... I ... ... that it ... not be ... with; and that ... ... in the ... ... will not be ... ... your ... ..., is ... ... you ... ... be ... to. ... ..., ..., I ... be ... ...; and you ... ... that ... ... my ... ... (pp. 105–6).

The skeleton, I am afraid, is much less amusing than the complete organism: for this is Collins's proposal of marriage to Elizabeth Bennet. The point of treating it so barbarously is to show how the common words fall into little patterns and broken sequences, and how they combine to suggest the grammatical identity of many of the excised words. When even this poor frame is unjointed, the vestigial shape of the original passage still leaves traces enough for its speaker to be identified. For, when the frequency-hierarchy of the thirty most common words of dialogue, as represented in this passage of only 560 words, is correlated with the corresponding hierarchy for each of the major characters of *Pride and Prejudice*, the results, set out in Table 8, leave no reasonable doubt that Collins is the speaker.

This passage, of course, is a striking set piece. But equally convincing results can be obtained from more everyday dialogue. In the eleventh chapter of Volume III (pp. 330–8), Mrs Bennet takes a sorrowful leave of the departing Lydia; discusses Bingley's rumoured return to Netherfield with her sister, Mrs Phillips, and also with Mr Bennet; and goes on to welcome Bingley back to Longbourn and tell him the good, good news of Lydia's marriage. If her last speech in this chapter is omitted, the remainder amounts, all told, to 569 words. And, when the frequency-hierarchy of the thirty most common words in this composite passage is treated in the manner described above, it becomes evident that Mrs Bennet is much the most likely speaker.

But a total of 560 words or thereabouts makes a substantial proportion of the whole vocabulary of each of these speakers. (Collins has 4444 words all told, and Mrs Bennet 6048.) Since these words are among them, the possible influence of a part-circularity upon the results must be considered. To dispel this doubt, consider a passage of only 297 words of Emma Woodhouse's total of 21,501. The passage, again a composite of several speeches, though the last of them is much the longest, occurs when Harriet seeks to confide in Emma about her newfound affection for Mr Knightley and declares her resolution that she will never marry (pp. 341–2). Assuming that Harriet is talking of Frank Churchill, Emma refuses to have names named but advises her how to behave towards him. Once again, the results admit only one plausible candidate as speaker of these words.

In Section (*a*) of Table 8, the thirty-word frequency-hierarchy for each of these three passages is listed (and can be compared with the overall hierarchies set out in Appendix C). Section (*b*) of the Table shows how each of these passage-hierarchies correlates with the overall hierarchy for each of the major characters of the novel from which that passage is taken. Section (*c*), which is extracted from Table 7, is included here as a convenience, a reminder of the overall

TABLE 8. Comparisons between Three Passages of Dialogue and their Possible Speakers

(a) Frequency-hierarchy, for each passage, of the thirty most common words of Jane Austen's dialogue.

	A	B	C		A	B	C		A	B	C
I	21	21	12	is	3	16	7	for (pr)	9	2	1
the	21	12	5	in	8	4	3	me	7	3	0
you	11	17	13	have	6	9	3	was	2	4	1
and	13	14	4	to (pr)	6	5	3	very	3	4	3
of	14	10	11	my	18	7	0	she	2	3	0
to (inf)	13	15	7	but	5	7	3	will (vb)	6	8	4
a	3	8	3	as	9	7	0	do	1	3	4
it	8	21	8	he	0	8	2	your	9	1	10
not	7	9	7	her	4	3	0	with	4	2	0
be	10	9	8	that (cj)	12	3	3	at	1	3	3

(b) Coefficients derived by correlating the above hierarchies with the corresponding hierarchy for each major character of the appropriate novel.

	(i) Passages A and B					(ii) Passage C	
	1–30		1–20			1–30	1–20
	A	B	A	B		C	C
Elizabeth	0.738	0.793	0.671	0.703	Emma	0.745*	0.836*
Darcy	0.789	0.651	0.755	0.556	Mr Knightley	0.641	0.701
Mrs Bennet	0.585	0.861*	0.535	0.812*	Churchill	0.566	0.633
Jane	0.649	0.812	0.581	0.719	Miss Bates	0.531	0.650
Collins	0.894*	0.490	0.873*	0.312	Mrs Elton	0.632	0.686
Mr Bennet	0.679	0.823	0.574	0.765	Harriet Smith	0.542	0.643
Mrs Gardiner	0.393	0.649	0.236	0.566	Mr Woodhouse	0.604	0.686
Lady Catherine	0.673	0.694	0.567	0.624	Mrs Weston	0.594	0.683
Lydia	0.645	0.787	0.627	0.741	Mr Weston	0.644	0.783
Miss Bingley	0.711	0.648	0.640	0.505			
Wickham	0.655	0.719	0.602	0.596			

(c) Corresponding coefficients (based on words 1–30) for overall comparisons among the idiolects of the major characters of these two novels: extracted from Table 7.

	Collins	Mrs Bennet			Emma
Elizabeth	0.818	0.853	Emma		[1.000]
Darcy	0.889	0.724	Mr Knightley		0.958
Mrs Bennet	0.600	[1.000]	Churchill		0.890
Jane	0.651	0.888	Miss Bates		0.866
Collins	[1.000]	0.600	Mrs Elton		0.945
Mr Bennet	0.754	0.835	Harriet		0.809
Mrs Gardiner	0.520	0.618	Mr Woodhouse		0.868
Lady Catherine	0.776	0.730	Mrs Weston		0.923
Lydia	0.598	0.913	Mr Weston		0.901
Miss Bingley	0.834	0.809			
Wickham	0.768	0.774			

pattern of correlations between the actual speaker of each passage and his or her fellow-characters.

The first column of Section (*b*) shows a far higher coefficient for Collins (0.894) than for any of his fellows. Darcy's coefficient of 0.789 ranks second, Elizabeth's (0.738) third, Miss Bingley's (0.711) fourth, and the remainder trail off down to Mrs Gardiner's (0.393). The association of Passage A with Collins thus rests not only on his yielding much the highest single coefficient but on the broader ground that the whole succession of coefficients for Passage A so closely matches the succession listed in the first column of Section (*c*): the figures for Passage A are always lower but the *sequence* is almost identical. The speaker of Passage A, that is to say, not only resembles Collins himself in the distribution of these thirty words but also occupies Collins's unique station among his whole array of neighbours.

Despite the empirical force of this result, a statistician might justly cavil at the use of such tiny numbers as those that lie towards the foot of the word-list itself. My original object in attempting this particular experiment, I confess, was to establish the level at which the shape of an idiolect would cease to be identifiable: not for the first time, Jane Austen's language has withstood a most unreasonable trial and shown an astonishing 'tensile strength'. With that said, however, it is fair to meet the statistician's objection by excluding the last ten words from the list and repeating the correlation-calculations with words 1–20 instead of 1–30. When that is done, the level of the coefficients is reduced again: but the coefficient for Collins is still much the highest; and—as the '1–20' column for Passage A shows—the succession of the other coefficients still reinforces this indication that Passage A bears his characteristic stamp, and his alone!

After the coefficient of 0.861, which makes Mrs Bennet the most likely speaker of Passage B, Mr Bennet (0.823) stands some way above—and Jane and Elizabeth a little above—the more usual Lydia (0.787). But Mrs Bennet is on her best behaviour in the greater part of this passage, with Bingley once more in full view; and, though she is never ladylike, Mrs Bennet is capable of a more passable imitation than Lydia would deign to attempt.

The last comment implies not only that Mrs Bennet's idiolect changes somewhat as circumstances change but that our method of analysis is sensitive enough to register the effects. That large claim will be more fully investigated in Part Three. As a token of what will emerge, take the hierarchy of correlations for Emma's little passage. Even though she is talking to Harriet and still directing her behaviour, the correlation-coefficient no longer shows a close resemblance between Emma and Mrs Elton. And, to anticipate the later and more substantial evidence, when the frequency-hierarchy for the passage is correlated with those of Emma herself in successive stages of what is undoubtedly an overall line of development, the results associate the passage with Emma's *eventual* idiolect. Mrs Elton's resemblance is to the earlier Emma: but, while Emma changes, Mrs Elton has one of the most static idiolects of all. The integrity of Emma's eventual idiolect is made plain, moreover, by the fact that, towards the end, it is no longer easy to establish, from *her* manner of speech and by these methods of statistical analysis, the identity of the person she is addressing.

Even in Jane Austen's novels, it would be too much to hope that every passage of three hundred words would yield such pertinent results. (Indeed, the emergence of Mr Weston, in the correlation of words 1–20, as a not implausible claimant for Passage C, shows that three hundred words is not really a sufficient basis.) But, within safer working margins, there is good reason to test the possibility that the use of the methods proposed can give distinct indications of the identity of the speaker of a given passage, the identity of the person addressed, and — at least for the central characters — the stage of the novel at which the passage occurs. If this possibility can be sustained, there is obviously room for a closer working relationship between the literary critic, the statistician, and the student of linguistics than is common nowadays. And the fields of inquiry in which that relationship might prove effective could range far beyond the boundaries of literary criticism.

6

In Search of a Framework

To speak, in such a way, of the need for a closer working relationship is not to forget that the 'new linguistics' has profoundly influenced much recent literary theory and that, in somewhat different ways, both linguistics and literary theory reflect the ideas of de Saussure and those of the Russian Formalists and the Prague Linguistic Circle.[1] But the points of contact have usually been conceptual rather than empirical. Linguistics, regarded as a system, has furnished both models and analogues for the 'idea of literature', as variously conceived. Its actual methods of analysis, however, are still developing very rapidly and, partly for that reason, are still not widely employed in literary studies.

David Lodge, it is true, has made use of Roman Jakobson's distinction between the 'metaphoric' and the 'metonymic', itself a version of the linguistic distinction between the 'paradigmatic' and the 'syntagmatic', which was touched on in Chapter 1. (For those of us who were induced, early in life, to regard 'metonymy' as an arcane rhetorical figure whose chief—or only—function was to be distinguished from 'synecdoche', the terminology may seem as loose as it is idiosyncratic. Yet Lodge is able to apply it to matters of greater literary consequence than the Woolsack, a fleet of fifty sail, or the 'England' of a moderately successful cricket-team.)[2] Stanley Fish glances towards Chomsky, as mediated by Ronald Wardhaugh, while he charts the concealed impediments of sentences where lesser readers might tread a heedless path.[3] Faced with the truly formidable syntax of Spenser and Milton, G. L. Dillon makes fuller and more direct use of modern linguistic methods.[4] Some more orthodox essays in

<hr/>

[1] See the two editors' own contributions to Ann Jefferson and David Robey (eds.), *Modern Literary Theory: A Comparative Introduction* (London, 1982).

[2] David Lodge, *The Modes of Modern Writing: Metaphor, Metonymy, and the Typology of Modern Literature* (Ithaca, 1977).

[3] Stanley E. Fish, 'Literature in the Reader: Affective Stylistics', as reprinted in Jane P. Tompkins (ed.), *Reader-Response Criticism* (Baltimore, 1980), pp. 70–100.

[4] G. L. Dillon, *Language Processing and the Language of Literature* (Bloomington, 1978).

'stylistics' turn to linguistics for support.[5] And, overall, the number of exceptions to my generalization is steadily increasing.

Whether at the conceptual level or in more or less empirical instances like these, however, the current of trade between linguistics and literary criticism flows predominantly in one direction. And yet, especially by virtue of the works that make his stock-in-trade, the literary critic is not without—the word is Emma's before Mrs Elton debases it—'resources' of his own. To the extent that he deals in sentences less factitious than those devised by scholars to test a new linguistic hypothesis, the literary critic has special knowledge of such language as men *seem* to use. To the extent that habitual usage—whether of a striking image or a suggestive commonplace—serves to characterize an idiolect and add a dimension to its 'meaning', the literary critic is obliged to look beyond the confines of the single sentence and might help his colleague to escape them. And, to the extent that our best writers make most of the potentialities of the language, the literary critic should be especially accustomed to its subtleties.

An older generation's preference for a 'higher' style of prose than hers accounts, presumably, for R. W. Chapman's belief that, though Jane Austen is 'one of the greatest, because one of the most accurate, writers of dialogue of her own or any age', 'she is not indeed one of the great writers of English prose of the early nineteenth century' (*Sense and Sensibility*, Appendix I, p. 389). Few nowadays, I think, would accede to the second judgement. Not only from an altered climate but also on account of the long and exacting labours of literary scholars like Chapman himself, K. C. Phillipps, and Norman Page—to name but three—we are now better able to understand the ways in which Jane Austen's extraordinary powers manifest themselves in every facet of her language, and better equipped, therefore, than we sometimes recognize to repay some of our debts to a sister-discipline.[6]

Whereas traditional grammatical analysis tended to mark the differences between direct and indirect questions and to treat the

---

[5] See, for example, Roger Fowler, *The Languages of Literature* (London, 1971); Seymour Chatman and Samuel R. Levin (eds.), *Essays on the Language of Literature* (Boston, 1967); Seymour Chatman (ed.), *Literary Style: A Symposium* (London and New York, 1971).

[6] R. W. Chapman, 'Miss Austen's English', *Sense and Sensibility*, Appendix I, pp. 388–424; K. C. Phillipps, *Jane Austen's English* (London, 1970); Norman Page, *The Language of Jane Austen* (Oxford, 1972).

interrogative forms of 'who' and 'which' as a class apart from 'how, when, where, and why', modern linguistics is able to generalize about 'WH-' questions as a category. The student of Jane Austen's language can go a step further and show, with clear statistical support, that, among her characters, a pronounced recourse to questions of this kind ranges from discourtesy to downright effrontery. Mrs Jennings provides a signal instance, especially in the early episode when Colonel Brandon is unexpectedly required to go to London. As her character becomes more sympathetic, both the incidence and the tenor of her 'WH-' questions help to mark the change.

Mrs Jennings, Miss Bates, and Harriet Smith are all notable for that 'anaphoric' syntax which Coleridge, an early student of such phenomena, discerned in Shakespeare's Mistress Quickly.[7] In one characteristic form, a loose succession of items, connected by 'and . . . and', is given some sort of shape, from time to time, by an emphatic but ill-focused 'so':

By that time, it was beginning to hold up, and I was determined that nothing should stop me from getting away—and then—only think!—I found he was coming up towards me too—slowly you know, and as if he did not quite know what to do; and *so* he came and spoke, and I answered—and I stood for a minute, feeling dreadfully, you know, one can't tell how; and then I took courage, and said it did not rain, and I must go: and *so* off I set; and I had not got three yards from the door, when he came after me, only to say, if I was going to Hartfield, he thought I had much better go round by Mr. Cole's stables, for I should find the near way quite floated by this rain. Oh! dear, I thought it would have been the death of me! *So* I said, I was very much obliged to him . . . (*Emma*, p. 179: my italics)

The wide-ranging linguistic topic of 'deletion' offers another field for mutual endeavour. As an assiduous reporter of the remarks of others and an unflagging chronicler of her own hopes, Mrs Bennet might be expected to rank high in the use of the conjunction 'that'. Her actual incidence, only a little above the general average, reflects her frequent but not constant tendency to 'delete' the word: 'I began to be afraid [that] you would never come back again. People *did* say, [that] you meant to quit the place entirely at Michaelmas; but, however, I hope [that] it is not true' (p. 336). Given this strong tendency and given her comparatively sparse recourse to 'that' for

---

[7] S. T. Coleridge, 'Method in Thought', in T. M. Raysor (ed.), *Coleridge's Shakespearean Criticism* vol. ii (London, 1930), pp. 334–42.

expressions of purpose and result—whose frequent use, among Jane Austen's characters, is a mark of minds more analytical than Mrs Bennet's—the fact that she reaches even so high as the general average attests to the individuality of her syntax. The task arising here is to find means of 'recovering' a diversity of 'deleted' words either to supply a firmer basis for statistical analysis or else, more conservatively, to ensure that the statistical findings are properly understood.

If literary criticism, statistics, and the new linguistics can usefully be brought together in matters like these, the interest of the new should not be allowed to obscure the continuing value of the old. The 'diachronic' emphasis of works like *The Oxford English Dictionary* has been called into question by those who (pursuing a Saussurean doctrine more single-mindedly than he might have wished) are less interested in etymological explanation than in the different forms a language like English—if indeed, it is one language—takes in different speech-communities at a given moment.[8] Now, as the following little specimens may suggest, Jane Austen's language, so far as it represents the English of her day, supplies a wealth of occasions where the historical philologist and the literary critic can combine not merely for their own 'diachronic' purposes but also to demonstrate how powerfully usage can conflict even within the ostensibly homogeneous speech-community of the Regency gentry.

Except in legal and administrative contexts, the passage of the last hundred years has deprived the phrase 'I am determined' of its reference to the deliberative processes that end in a considered decision: in our use, the phrase is seldom more than a strong expression of intent. Yet, half a century and more before the appearance of *Felix Holt*, which supplies the *OED* with a solitary instance verging on modern usage, Isabella Thorpe consistently prefers it in a novel where the narrator, in particular, preserves the older and richer sense. In *Emma*, both old meaning and new are entangled by Harriet Smith: 'I have now quite determined, and really almost made up my mind' (p. 53). At a crucial moment in *Persuasion*, the very inappositeness of the older meaning of 'determine' gives added edge to Louisa Musgrove's display of an ungovernable impulsiveness:

---

[8] Their case is vigorously put by Roy Harris, 'The History Men', *Times Literary Supplement*, No. 4144, 3 Sept. 1982, 935–6.

'I am determined I will', she exclaims, as she leaps from the steps of the Cobb (p. 109). The older sense retains its full force in a comment on Sir Thomas Bertram: 'This was enough to determine Sir Thomas; and a decisive "then so it shall be," closed that stage of the business' (p. 368). It is from long and anxious consideration of his own prospects in life and of Miss Crawford's possible share in them that Edmund can declare, 'I do not mean to be poor. Poverty is exactly what I have determined against' (p. 214). And finally, at a point where literary considerations include but quite transcend the philological, Edmund turns twice in one page to 'determined'—and unwittingly reveals the difference between Fanny's consistency of purpose and his own betrayal of her faith in him:

'No, she is quite determined. She certainly will not act.'

'He was certainly right in respecting such [Miss Crawford's] feelings; he was glad he had determined on it.' And the morning wore away in satisfactions very sweet, if not very sound. (p. 159)

Mansfield Park gives an appropriate prominence to a conflict among the then major senses of the world 'family'. From stern traditionalism on his side and self-abnegation on hers, Sir Thomas and Fanny hold throughout to a sense—a strict version of *OED* 2—that includes the 'nuclear' family and its servants but generally excludes 'connections' like Fanny and Mrs Norris even though they dwell within the house or its environs. Lady Bertram and the younger generation almost always use the word more liberally (*OED* 3). Mrs Norris, not inexpediently, avoids it whenever she can. Among the misunderstandings, moreover, that first spark the important disagreement about family prayer lies the discrepancy, observed by Edmund, between Mary's use of 'family' in a sense, already growing archaic (*OED* 1), that includes the household but *not* its master or mistress and Fanny's yearning for a state where all can find their place:

'There is something in a chapel and chaplain so much in character with a great house, with one's ideas of what such a household should be! A whole family assembling regularly for the purpose of prayer, is fine!'

'Very fine indeed!' said Miss Crawford, laughing. 'It must do the heads of the family a great deal of good to force all the poor housemaids and footmen to leave business and pleasure, and say their prayers here twice a day, while they are inventing excuses themselves for staying away.'

'*That* is hardly Fanny's idea of a family assembling,' said Edmund. 'If the master and mistress do *not* attend themselves, there must be more harm than good in the custom.' (pp. 86–7)

Behind these conflicting senses of 'family' lies an equally potent contrast between 'difference' and 'distinction', one in which the attentive reader needs no support from the historical philologist. Sir Thomas sets it in motion, when Fanny's adoption is first resolved upon, by seeking Mrs Norris's assistance 'as to the distinction proper to be made between the girls as they grow up. . . . Their rank, fortune, rights, and expectations will always be different' (pp. 10–11). In token, that is, of certain actual differences of situation, Sir Thomas feels the need for a distinction which will take due account of them. It will be difficult, he acknowledges, to enact it without making his daughters 'think too lowly of their cousin' and 'without depressing her spirits too far' (ibid.). But Mrs Norris sees no difficulty at all. She fixes her mind, from that moment, on the preservation of an all-embracing *difference*:

There is a vast deal of difference in memories, as well as in every thing else, and therefore you must make allowance for your cousin, and pity her deficiency. . . . [For,] though you know (owing to me) your papa and mamma are so good as to bring her up with you, it is not at all necessary that she should be as accomplished as you are; — on the contrary, it is much more desirable that there should be a difference. (p. 19)

When Mrs Norris, by then widowed, makes it clear that she would wish to bequeath any 'little trifle' to his children rather than assist in Fanny's upbringing, Sir Thomas 'could not but wonder' (p. 30). Yet, loath as ever to inquire too closely, 'he soon grew reconciled to a distinction . . .' (p. 31).

Mrs Norris's idea of 'difference' continues to make itself felt in veiled attacks on Fanny and public humiliations of her. It is 'absolutely unnecessary, and even improper, that Fanny should have a regular lady's horse of her own in the style of her cousins' (p. 36). Fanny is fortunate indeed to go with the rest to Sotherton. Fanny needs to remember 'who and what she is' (p. 147). Fanny is not to behave 'as if you were one of your cousins' (p. 221). And so on to the last, when she mistakenly supposes that it is on Fanny's account that Sir Thomas denies Maria an unwanted sanctuary at Mansfield.

Although Sir Thomas's good opinion of Mrs Norris declines steadily from the time of his return from Antigua, we are not shown a moment in which he first discerns the full bitterness of her antipathy for Fanny. But, though he is not yet ready to abandon his original principle (as he will do at last), his retrospective analysis is revealing enough. And, if the original episode is echoed by his reviving the word 'distinction', it is nicely reversed by his appealing to Fanny on her aunt's behalf:

I know what her sentiments have always been. The principle was good in itself, but it may have been, and I believe *has been* carried too far in your case. — I am aware that there has been sometimes, in some points, a misplaced distinction; but . . . I am sure you will not disappoint my opinion of you, by failing at any time to treat your aunt Norris with the respect and attention that are due to her. (p. 313)

On her side, for the greater part of the novel, Fanny solaces herself with the 'wonders' of inanimate nature. (The most sententious of her reflections, on the 'wonders' of the evergreen, is directly contrasted with Miss Crawford's seeing 'no wonder in this shrubbery equal to seeing myself in it': pp. 209–10.) Fanny is scarcely less given to 'wondering' — in a censorious sense first noted by the *OED* in Samuel Richardson — *at* the behaviour of her fellows and to reminding herself that it is not her place to do so. Her emotional development, therefore, is appropriately registered when she is able to enter appreciatively into her sister's resilience in adversity: 'Her greatest wonder on the subject soon became — not that Susan should have been provoked into disrespect and impatience against her better knowledge — but that so much better knowledge, so many good notions, should have been hers at all' (p. 397). Fanny carries this capacity for a new and more generous wonder back to Mansfield, at the turning of the season, and, in a passage more evocative than those stilted 'poetic' musings, gives the human figures their due place in the landscape (pp. 446–7). The transformation from her former self is consummated in this moment of homecoming.

II

The correlation-measures of the previous chapter and of the next show that, for each of Jane Austen's major characters, the frequency-patterning of the very common words assumes a distinctive and identifiable shape. The examples of the last few pages, to which any attentive reader of Jane Austen will easily add more, may suffice as evidence of equally sharp distinctions in certain recognizable syntactical patterns and even (in territory where statistical analysis has far less to contribute) in characteristic semantic contrasts. Is there a general framework within which the statistical evidence can take its place beside the more familiar literary and semantic evidence?

The more visible, especially the more visibly controlled, examples are sometimes in keeping with the idea that the language of literature has special qualities that distinguish it from the language at large. In Jane Austen's dialogue (and even in her narrative) such special qualities are not often to be sought in traditional forms of heightening like Gibbon's splendid parallelisms, Bacon's apophthegms, Swift's towering catalogues, or Shakespeare's image-chains. There is, however, heightening of another traditional kind in such strong echoes as that of Richardson in Colonel Brandon and Willoughby; of Fanny Burney in Mrs Jennings and the Steeles; and of Samuel Johnson in the Knightley brothers, especially in John Knightley's absurdly bitter disquisition on the hardships of winter visiting. (As Marilyn Butler so clearly demonstrates, moreover, the 'buried presence' of the politically antipathetic ideas of her radical contemporaries gives an even sharper edge to some of Jane Austen's ironies.[9]) But, except in *Northanger Abbey*, Jane Austen does not customarily rely on sustained allusions to earlier works of literature or on a sustained 'self-referentiality'. (The incidence of 'I', 'we', and 'you' in passages of pure narrative makes one useful little test of 'self-referentiality'.) Her striking linguistic effects more often consist in forms of 'difference' like the 'foregrounding' and the 'defamiliarization' through which the Russian Formalists and their successors have sought to distinguish the language of literature from that of everyday.[10]

At crucial moments in Jane Austen's dialogue, that is to say, the words often call attention to themselves as words: when Edmund explicitly distinguishes between conflicting senses of 'family'; when

[9] Marilyn Butler, *Jane Austen and the War of Ideas* (Oxford, 1975).

[10] These ideas seem to have been carried furthest by A. J. Greimas. (Of Greimas, Derrida, and Jacques Lacan, it is almost ungrateful to remark that their work is simplified by those who have made an abstruse idiom more accessible.)

For helpful commentary, see Jonathan Culler, *Structuralist Poetics* (London, 1975), esp. pp. 20, 56, 75–95, 143; and Ann Jefferson, 'Russian Formalism', in Jefferson and Robey, pp. 19–23.

Edmund uses 'determined' twice in quick succession and unwittingly emphasizes the difference between Fanny's continuing steadiness and the failure of will, on his part, that is shortly to undermine her; when Emma's reaction against the insufferable conversation of Mrs Elton, 'with her Mr. E., and her *caro sposo*, and her resources' (p. 279), begins to clear her own path towards self-recognition; or when Emma and Mr Knightley debate the meaning of 'amiable' at the height of their most open disagreement about Frank Churchill (pp. 148–9). The clichés of dialogue are brilliantly 'defamiliarized' in other memorable passages: when Emma parodies the chatter of Miss Bates ('Not that it was such a very old petticoat either—for still it would last a great while—and, indeed, she must thankfully say that their petticoats were all very strong': p. 225); when half an hour or so of Mrs Elton's *bavardage* about strawberry-picking is reduced to a single elliptical paragraph (pp. 358–9); or when long passages of what people like the Musgroves (pp. 43–6) or Sir Walter and Elizabeth Elliot (p. 141) *would* inevitably say on a given occasion are compressed into a sort of choric accompaniment.

But, even though they are rendered so tellingly in Jane Austen's dialogue, it would be difficult to maintain that effects like these are peculiarly literary. We are all capable, in conversation, of 'foregrounding' a particular word or phrase, whether to emphasize a point of our own or to focus on a weak point in an opposing argument. We are all capable, in some degree, of decrying a rival's habitual catchwords and mimicking his style of speech. We are most of us tolerably adept in the management of 'straw men' and linguistic Trojan horses. Many of us have played those language-games that depend upon 'defamiliarizing' a common word by inventing a rococo definition. And all of us, alas, betray our characteristic prejudices and limitations (or even, more happily, display our saving strengths) whenever we give utterance. Whatever our various gifts in these quarters, moreover, Jane Austen's *Letters* give ample evidence of her continuing ability to play her usual verbal games when she is not on 'high-literary' duty.

An even more formidable obstacle for this line of argument emerges from the evidence, not ordinarily so visible as statistical analysis makes it, of frequency-patterning in the very common words. If patterning of the kind examined earlier is *not* to be regarded as peculiarly literary, it will be difficult, if not impossible, to draw the line between literary and non-literary effects. If Edmund's overt emphasis on 'family' is an example of literary foregrounding, what are we to make of Fanny's overt emphasis on 'I' when she rebuffs Crawford's unwary repetition of 'we' with, 'As far as *I* am concerned, sir, I would not have delayed his return for a day' (p. 225)? If examples like this are also to be included, what of the 'buried emphasis' that lies in an exceptionally pronounced recourse to 'I' itself, or 'not', or 'of'? Yet if, on the other hand, the whole range of such character-revealing tendencies as we have examined *is* regarded as peculiarly literary, the foreground will become so densely populated that little or nothing can be truly foregrounded. By then, the language of literature will have spread through the whole field of meaning and ceased, in another way, to be peculiarly literary at all.

It seems more plausible to allow the striking examples of 'defamiliarization' and 'foregrounding' to take their place among other potent forms of emphasis, available to all those who use the language, and to approach our whole range of evidence from another direction. Gregory Bateson, for whom language supplied only one class of examples in a larger field of thought, put the idea of 'difference' to an ampler, more flexible, but altogether more verifiable service than the French literary theorists were afterwards to do. A difference, he says, is one that *makes* a difference.[11] If it is to do so, it needs to stand in contrast to an array of other differences or a 'flat' background. The implication, for literary purposes, is that the background, the functional context, or (as William Empson called it[12]) the 'foil' may well range out from the immediate vicinity to embrace more distant phenomena within the same literary work, within a broader literary tradition, or in the ordinary workings of the vernacular. Approached in this way, every facet of the evidence so far considered in this study can find an effective place within a larger framework of communication-theory; and the language of Jane Austen's dialogue, perhaps that of literature more generally, can be seen as differing less in *kind* than in energy and exactness from other forms of communication.

This line of thought may well have more in common with the Russian formulations of the idea of foregrounding than with some later versions. If 'foregrounding' can consist in such pervasive forms of heightening as poetic rhythm, it is not difficult to associate it with

---

[11] Gregory Bateson, *Steps to an Ecology of Mind* (London, 1972), e.g. p. 315.
[12] William Empson, *Some Versions of Pastoral* (London, 1935), pp. 27–86.

the 'rhythms' and patterns that distinguish among the idiolects of different characters in their social intercourse or among those of the different phases of a dramatic action.[13] The crucial considerations, in my view, are that (unless compelling evidence to the contrary becomes available) literary and non-literary language should not be regarded as so different in kind that they can scarcely influence each other; and that a pattern can take effect, within a literary work and for genuinely literary purposes, without being of an elevated 'literary' tone. What goes on in the shrubbery between Tom Jones and Molly Seagrim is at least as proper to the literary purposes of *Tom Jones* as the high-flown invocation that precedes it: only when both modes are given their due can the relationship between them acquire its full effect.

When Harriet Smith says, 'I have now quite determined, and really almost made up my mind—to refuse Mr. Martin' (p. 53), her 'message' might be taken, at its simplest, to mean that she will probably do as she says or, at a second level, that she feels she should comply, albeit reluctantly, with Emma's obvious preference for a refusal. For the reader, more than for Emma, the 'message' has yet another level: that this is Harriet's way of speaking and that it is peculiar to her. Taken even as a set of discrete items, the sentence offers evidence enough to support this last proposition. 'Quite' (as noted earlier), 'now', 'really', and 'almost' are all words of which Harriet has decidedly more than her fair share and which she characteristically puts to a feebly emphatic use. With both 'and' and 'I', where statistical analysis is possible, she lies more than a standard deviation above the general mean. (The 'my', on the other hand, and the infinitive 'to' are words in which she has comparatively little property. This is one of only two occasions on which she is given access to 'mind'. And, in referring to 'Mr. Martin' as in the sense she attaches to 'refuse', she complies with social, not merely literary, conventions of that day.) 'Determined', as used here, is not only muddled in itself: in being so, it also makes a fair specimen of the many 'difficult' words that Harriet picks up at Hartfield and proceeds, half-comprehendingly, to abuse. In the balancing out of the whole sentence, it is nicely contrasted with 'made up', which lies on her more customary semantic level. These several items and also

---

[13] See Tony Bennett's account of the work of Vološinov and Bakhtin in his *Formalism and Marxism* (London, 1979), esp. pp. 75–81.

the larger contradiction between the two opening clauses are made conspicuous, in the immediate context, by their divergence from the exactness, economy, and over-definiteness with which Emma customarily marshals her ideas. In the larger context of the novel as a whole, Harriet's solecisms need also to be recognized as a concealed, perhaps unwitting, line of self-defence. Speaking of Harriet's style in general, W. A. Craik notes her 'hesitations, contradiction and tautology' and aptly comments that 'they reveal exactly the mind that never opposes an argument, but is never really swayed from its own original opinion.'[14]

Messages like 'This is Harriet speaking' open up more general issues. One of the chief objects of communication-theory is to define the conditions under which a message, verbal or otherwise, is most likely to be accurately conveyed. Everything that obscures or deflects its communication is regarded as 'noise'. The almost inevitable intrusion of 'noise' can be offset by a degree of 'redundancy' in the message itself. An elaborate form of mathematics has been developed to assess the countervailing effects of 'redundancy' and 'noise' in electronic signalling. With his customary penetration, however, Gregory Bateson translates the central idea into propositions of far-reaching relevance: redundancy (which arises at the moment when the receiver of a message can predict, with better than random success, what the remainder of the message will be) is patterning; and patterning is the very stuff of meaning. He enlarges:

The occurrence of the letter K in a given location in an English prose message is not a purely random event in the sense that there was ever an equal probability that any of the other twenty-five letters might have occurred in that location. Some letters are more common in English than others, and certain combinations of letters are more common than others. There is, thus, a species of patterning which partly determines which letters shall occur in which slots. As a result: if the receiver of the message had received the entire rest of the message but had not received the particular letter K which we are discussing, he might have been able, with better than random success, to guess that the missing letter was, in fact, K. To the extent that this was so, the letter K did not, for that receiver, exclude the other twenty-five letters because these were already partly excluded by information which the recipient received from the rest of the message. This patterning or predictability of particular events within a larger aggregate of events is technically called 'redundancy'.

[14] W. A. Craik, *Jane Austen: The Six Novels* (London, 1965), p. 144.

The concept of redundancy is usually derived, as I have derived it, by considering first the maximum of information which might be carried by the given item and then considering how this total might be reduced by knowledge of the surrounding patterns of which the given item is a component part. There is, however, a case for looking at the whole matter the other way round. We might regard patterning or predictability as the very essence and *raison d'être* of communication, and see the single letter unaccompanied by collateral clues as a peculiar or special case.[15]

Bateson's brilliant array of examples, in the course of a long book, ranges from anthropology and aesthetics to genetic coding and the language of porpoises. Let us abide, more modestly, with Harriet Smith. Most of the words of Harriet's sentence contribute, whether visibly (like 'quite' and 'really') or less visibly (like 'and' and 'I'), to the message, 'This is Harriet speaking'. While they, too, make a necessary part of her actual statement of half-intention, the statistically improbable 'my' and the unexpected 'mind' lessen the characteristic flavour of the sentence and can be regarded, in *that* aspect, as 'noise'. In its overall shape, however, as in the preponderance of its individual items, it is a thoroughly characteristic utterance in which redundancy, in its technical—to say nothing of its vernacular—sense, prevails.

The stylistic differences that *make* a difference between pattern and pattern—and, *a fortiori*, between idiolect and idiolect—can therefore, though they will not always do so, incorporate everything from idiosyncratic tropes and figures, through characteristic 'key-words' and images, syntactical forms, and local instances of 'foregrounding', to unobtrusive (but statistically demonstrable) habits of expression of the kind we have seen reflected in the most common words of all. From whatever angle an idiolect is approached, we converge on the same set of probabilistic relationships, the same

---

[15] Gregory Bateson, p. 412. Behind Bateson's version of 'cybernetics' or 'communication-theory' lies the 'information-theory' of the electronic engineers, which is usually held to have come of age in C. E. Shannon and W. W. Weaver, *The Mathematical Theory of Communication* (Chicago, 1949) and was brought within reach of students of the humanities by Colin Cherry, *On Human Communication* (Cambridge, Mass., 1957).

The daunting mathematical sophistication of the former work is offset, for our purposes, by its preoccupation with 'messages' much simpler in kind than those which usually concern the student of literature or linguistics. See Ronald Wardhaugh, *Reading: A Linguistic Perspective* (New York, 1969), pp. 53–5 for an incisive argument against too hopeful an approach, for our purposes, to 'information-theory'.

'force-field'. An exciting new development in linguistics, Noam Chomsky's recent ideas about 'core-grammar', supports that proposition.[16]

The characteristic impression of Harriet's idiolect, however, would be dissipated or extinguished if most other characters or most other people spoke in much her way. It would then be impossible to speak of particular expressions or sentence-shapes as being recognizably hers or to derive statistically significant differentiations from the incidence of the very common words. This truism bears on another important premise of communication-theory: that, in the functioning of a language as in any other system, entropy tends to prevail over ordered energy. Entropy accounts for the great mass of 'inert' cases which allow the chi-squared test to operate and which give the normal distribution curve its characteristic central peak. The enervating capacities of what might be called Flecknoe's Law, that *all* kinds of things are subject to decay, should never be ignored.

It is evident that the language affords resources enough for an energetic differentiation between pattern and pattern, idiolect and idiolect. But, since the latent probabilities *always* favour an inert sameness, the subtle and appropriate distinctions familiar to Jane Austen's readers must represent a powerful and exact marshalling of those resources, that dormant energy. Although it is not fashionable to say so, the most economical way of accounting for that remarkable release of energy would seem to lie in the labours and the intuitions of the author herself. And, instead of trying to identify specific features of a literary language, we might better consider whether the presence and the effects of a strong energy betoken a more general difference between different kinds of writing and even, perhaps, between better writing and worse.

As my use of the subjunctive indicates, the last two sentences amount to hypotheses, susceptible of testing. To what extent is it possible to distinguish between two further 'messages': 'This is Jane Austen's sort of dialogue'; and 'This is the dialogue of fiction (or of nineteenth-century fiction, or of a particular kind of nineteenth-century fiction)'? The remaining chapters of the present study will not supply adequate answers to those questions. They may show, at least, that such questions can be weighed more exactly than has been usual in the study of literary history and that they can yield verifiable answers.

---

[16] Noam Chomsky, *Lectures on Government and Binding* (Dordrecht, 1981). I owe the suggestion to N. R. Cattell.

7

Interrelationships among the Characters of Different Novels

I

In the course of Chapter 5, it was noted in passing that (for the thirty most common words of dialogue) the highest of all correlation-coefficients between any pair of Jane Austen's major characters is between Elizabeth Bennet and Emma Woodhouse (0.973) and the lowest is between Collins and Harriet Smith (0.408). The obvious appropriateness of those pairings is often matched when other exceptionally high and exceptionally low coefficients are set beside them. The highest coefficients of all are listed on the left, the lowest on the right (with the character from the earlier novel always named first):

0.973 ELIZABETH/EMMA	0.576 Willoughby/Mr Woodhouse
0.965 EDMUND/EMMA	0.558 Collins/Miss Bates
0.962 ELINOR/ELIZABETH	0.551 CATHERINE/HENRY TILNEY
0.961 Mary Crawford/EMMA	0.551 Isabella Thorpe/Mrs Gardiner
0.960 Mrs Elton/WENTWORTH	0.535 Mrs Gardiner/Lady Bertram
0.959 EDWARD FERRARS/Churchill	0.531 Collins/Mr Woodhouse
0.958 ELINOR/EMMA	0.531 HENRY TILNEY/Harriet Smith
0.958 EMMA/MR KNIGHTLEY	0.523 Anne Steele/Collins
0.957 ANNE/WENTWORTH	0.520 Collins/Mrs Gardiner
0.957 EDMUND/Mary Crawford	0.471 Collins/Lady Bertram
0.957 Mary Crawford/Mrs Norris	0.460 CATHERINE/Collins
0.956 Marianne Dashwood/ANNE	0.408 Collins/Harriet Smith

All six novels are represented at these extremities of the spectrum and four of them are represented at both extremities. (*Northanger Abbey* is missing at the upper end and *Persuasion* at the lower.) While this spreading of the results suggests that Jane Austen's capacity for differentiating among her characters continues throughout her literary career, some novels and some characters appear with particular frequency. Emma Woodhouse figures in five of the twelve closest resemblances and Collins in seven of the twelve sharpest differences. The case of Collins might seem straightforward enough in that his pompous formality stands in obvious contrast to the

TABLE 9. The Extremities of the Range of Correlations

CATHERINE
0.935   FANNY
0.917   Harriet Smith
0.909   Mary Musgrove
• • •
0.581   Mrs Gardiner
*0.551   HENRY TILNEY
0.460   Collins

HENRY TILNEY
0.925   EDMUND
0.920   Sir Thomas
0.915   Mary Crawford
• • •
0.583   Lady Bertram
*0.551   CATHERINE
0.531   Harriet Smith

Isabella Thorpe
0.930   Lucy Steele
0.928   Mrs Elton
0.917   Marianne
• • •
0.646   Collins
0.611   John Dashwood
0.551   Mrs Gardiner

John Thorpe
0.930   Mrs Elton
0.913   Henry Crawford
0.906   Mary Crawford
• • •
0.716   Willoughby
0.626   Collins
0.601   Mrs Gardiner

Eleanor Tilney
0.933   EMMA
0.929   Mr Bennet
0.927   Marianne
• • •
0.693   Anne Steele
0.692   Collins
0.691   Mrs Gardiner

ELINOR DASHWOOD
0.962   ELIZABETH
0.958   EMMA
0.950   Lady Catherine
• • •
*0.696   Willoughby
*0.684   Anne Steele
*0.680   Col. Brandon

Marianne Dashwood
0.956   ANNE
0.952   ELIZABETH
0.936   EMMA
• • •
0.771   Lady Bertram
*0.726   Anne Steele
0.661   Mrs Gardiner

Mrs Jennings
0.937   Mrs Bennet
0.929   Mrs Norris
0.914   Miss Bates
• • •
0.742   Lady Catherine
0.658   Mrs Gardiner
0.646   Collins

Willoughby
*0.929   EDWARD FERRARS
0.920   Churchill
*0.917   Col. Brandon
• • •
0.622   Mrs Gardiner
0.602   Admiral Croft
0.576   Mr Woodhouse

John Dashwood
0.902   EDMUND
0.891   Mrs Weston
0.890   Mrs Norris
• • •
0.611   Isab. Thorpe
0.610   CATHERINE
0.598   Lady Bertram

Lucy Steele
0.930   Isab. Thorpe
0.923   ANNE
0.921   Eleanor Tilney
• • •
0.673   Mrs Gardiner
*0.671   John Dashwood
0.648   Collins

Colonel Brandon
*0.917   Willoughby
0.914   Churchill
*0.891   EDWARD FERRARS
• • •
0.651   HENRY TILNEY
0.651   Lady Catherine
0.626   Mr Woodhouse

Mrs Dashwood
0.941   Sir Thomas
0.934   EMMA
*0.929   ELINOR
• • •
0.662   CATHERINE
0.626   Lady Bertram
0.624   Harriet Smith

EDWARD FERRARS
0.959   Churchill
0.947   WENTWORTH
*0.929   Willoughby
• • •
0.719   Admiral Croft
0.704   Mr Woodhouse
0.607   Mrs Gardiner

Anne Steele
*0.883   Mrs Jennings
0.851   Lydia Bennet
0.841   KNIGHTLEY
• • •
0.610   HENRY TILNEY
0.590   Lady Catherine
0.523   Collins

ELIZABETH BENNET
0.973   EMMA
0.962   ELINOR
0.952   Marianne
• • •
0.755   Col. Brandon
0.733   Anne Steele
*0.726   Mrs Gardiner

DARCY
*0.930   ELIZABETH
0.913   WENTWORTH
0.912   Marianne
• • •
0.667   Mr Woodhouse
0.665   Harriet Smith
0.651   Anne Steele

Mrs Bennet
0.937   Mrs Jennings
0.929   Miss Bates
*0.913   Lydia Bennet
• • •
0.681   HENRY TILNEY
*0.618   Mrs Gardiner
*0.600   Collins

Jane Bennet
0.915   FANNY
0.906   Marianne
0.898   Mary Musgrove
• • •
0.688   Admiral Croft
*0.651   Collins
0.618   HENRY TILNEY

Collins
*0.889   DARCY
*0.834   Miss Bingley
0.819   HENRY TILNEY
• • •
0.471   Lady Bertram
0.460   CATHERINE
0.408   Harriet Smith

Mr Bennet
0.948   ELINOR
*0.945   Lady Catherine
0.940   EMMA
• • •
0.681   Col. Brandon
0.660   Anne Steele
*0.611   Mrs Gardiner

Mrs Gardiner
0.819   Mrs Smith
*0.774   Wickham
0.768   KNIGHTLEY
• • •
0.551   Isab. Thorpe
0.535   Lady Bertram
*0.520   Collins

Lady Catherine
0.950   ELINOR
*0.945   Mr Bennet
0.933   Sir Thomas
• • •
0.613   Harriet Smith
*0.595   Mrs Gardiner
0.590   Anne Steele

Lydia Bennet
0.914   Mrs Jennings
*0.913   Mrs Bennet
0.902   Lucy Steele
• • •
0.646   John Dashwood
*0.618   Mrs Gardiner
*0.598   Collins

TABLE 9: continued

Miss Bingley		Wickham		EDMUND BERTRAM		Mary Crawford	
0.933	Crawford	0.910	Mrs Smith	0.965	EMMA	0.961	EMMA
0.916	WENTWORTH	0.904	Mary Crawford	*0.957	Crawford	*0.957	Mrs Norris
0.915	EDMUND	0.895	Mrs Weston	*0.954	Mary Crawford	*0.954	EDMUND
• • •		• • •		• • •		• • •	
0.684	Harriet Smith	*0.725	Lady Catherine	0.728	Harriet Smith	0.760	CATHERINE
0.681	Col. Brandon	0.684	CATHERINE	0.724	Anne Steele	*0.746	Lady Bertram
0.660	Anne Steele	0.680	Lady Bertram	0.688	Mrs Gardiner	0.702	Mrs Gardiner

Henry Crawford		Mrs Norris		FANNY PRICE		Sir Thomas Bertram	
*0.957	EDMUND	*0.957	Mary Crawford	0.949	Mary Musgrove	0.941	Mrs Dashwood
0.949	WENTWORTH	*0.954	EDMUND	0.947	ANNE	0.939	Mr Bennet
0.944	EMMA	0.941	EMMA	0.942	Churchill	0.935	ELINOR
• • •		• • •		• • •		• • •	
0.742	Harriet Smith	0.761	Harriet Smith	0.707	HENRY TILNEY	0.640	Mrs Gardiner
0.736	Anne Steele	0.753	CATHERINE	0.678	Collins	0.627	CATHERINE
0.644	Mrs Gardiner	0.678	Mrs Gardiner	0.678	Mrs Gardiner	0.596	Harriet Smith

Tom Bertram		Lady Bertram		EMMA WOODHOUSE		MR KNIGHTLEY	
*0.938	Mrs Norris	0.886	CATHERINE	0.973	ELIZABETH	*0.958	EMMA
*0.924	Mary Crawford	0.879	Miss Bates	0.965	EDMUND	*0.942	Mrs Weston
*0.894	EDMUND	0.878	Lydia Bennet	0.961	Mary Crawford	0.933	EDMUND
• • •		• • •		• • •		• • •	
*0.648	Lady Bertram	0.583	HENRY TILNEY	0.751	Willoughby	0.756	CATHERINE
0.646	CATHERINE	0.535	Mrs Gardiner	0.746	Collins	0.735	Willoughby
0.610	Mrs Gardiner	0.471	Collins	0.717	Mrs Gardiner	0.715	Collins

Frank Churchill		Miss Bates		Mrs Elton		Harriet Smith	
0.964	WENTWORTH	0.929	Mrs Bennet	0.960	WENTWORTH	0.923	Mary Musgrove
0.959	EDMUND	0.914	Mrs Jennings	0.952	ANNE	0.917	CATHERINE
0.942	FANNY	0.885	Mrs Norris	*0.945	EMMA	0.896	FANNY
• • •		• • •		• • •		• • •	
0.753	Anne Steele	0.688	Sir Thomas	0.766	Anne Steele	0.596	Sir Thomas
0.747	HENRY TILNEY	0.650	Mrs Gardiner	0.743	Collins	0.531	HENRY TILNEY
0.645	Mrs Gardiner	0.558	Collins	0.585	Mrs Gardiner	0.408	Collins

Mr Woodhouse		Mrs Weston		Mr Weston		ANNE ELLIOT	
*0.875	Miss Bates	*0.942	KNIGHTLEY	0.910	EDMUND	*0.957	WENTWORTH
0.873	Mrs Jennings	*0.923	EMMA	*0.901	EMMA	0.956	Marianne
0.873	Mrs Bennet	0.918	EDMUND	0.886	Crawford	0.952	Mrs Elton
• • •		• • •		• • •		• • •	
0.577	Mrs Gardiner	0.761	Lady Bertram	0.628	Mrs Gardiner	0.747	Collins
0.576	Willoughby	0.754	Mrs Gardiner	0.627	Willoughby	0.745	Anne Steele
0.531	Collins	0.707	Collins	0.605	Collins	0.685	Mrs Gardiner

Mrs Smith		Mary Musgrove		WENTWORTH		Admiral Croft	
0.936	Mary Crawford	0.949	FANNY	0.964	Churchill	0.915	Mary Crawford
0.910	Wickham	0.923	Harriet Smith	0.960	Mrs Elton	0.904	John Thorpe
0.906	ELIZABETH	*0.919	ANNE	*0.957	ANNE	0.882	EMMA
• • •		• • •		• • •		• • •	
0.744	Mr Woodhouse	0.707	Mrs Gardiner	0.774	Collins	0.631	Lady Bertram
0.701	Lady Bertram	0.693	HENRY TILNEY	0.771	Anne Steele	0.624	Collins
0.662	CATHERINE	0.604	Collins	0.688	Mrs Gardiner	0.602	Willoughby

garrulous and undisciplined speech of characters like Harriet Smith, Lady Bertram, Anne Steele, and Mr Woodhouse. But Mrs Gardiner, who is also very unlike him, stands almost as far as he does from Lady Bertram and not much closer to those others. The case of Emma Woodhouse does not even seem straightforward. To my way of thinking, the close correlations between Emma, Elizabeth Bennet, and Mary Crawford reflect definite resemblances in temperament and situation. But, though the essentially similar correlations between Emma and Edmund Bertram, Emma and Elinor Dashwood, or Emma and Mr Knightley are also appropriate enough, they do not strike me with so absolute a conviction. (Other readers, of course, may respond in other ways: my point is only that the group does not display so perfect a homogeneity as the figures would suggest.) Except for Mary Crawford—to take another tack— these characters are all heroes or heroines; and Mary could be thought of as a heroine *manquée*. Yet one might have supposed that they wore their roles with more difference than the coefficients suggest. However that may be, the mere occupancy of these leading roles does not resolve the matter: Emma also correlates very much more closely with Mr Bennet, Mrs Elton, Eleanor Tilney, and Mrs Dashwood than with Catherine Morland, Henry Tilney, or Edward Ferrars. For both Emma and Collins, then, as doubtless for some others, this little array of figures poses more questions than it resolves. There are far too many convincing resemblances, whether of personality or of role, for the figures to be dismissed; but there are oddities enough to give any of Jane Austen's readers pause.

A basic shortcoming of this line of approach is that it excludes all but the twenty-four extreme cases of a set of 1128 coefficients, the total resulting when each of the forty-eight major characters is correlated with each of the other forty-seven. To proceed in this way is like assessing the performances of cricketers without taking account of any scores except double-centuries and ducks. The weight of that objection is reduced but not removed by Table 9, which takes each of the forty-eight major characters in turn, showing his or her three closest resemblances and three sharpest contrasts. (Where a given resemblance or contrast is with another character from the same novel, the coefficient is marked with an asterisk.) Even more plainly than before, there is a large preponderance of persuasive results. To work through them seriatim would merely duplicate the table itself and insult the reader's intelligence. In many of the sets of six, however, there are one or two unexpected results.

These apparent anomalies fall broadly into three classes, of which the second and third raise the larger and more interesting questions. The first class, typified by Mr Knightley's location as third closest to Anne Steele, is that of the isolated anomaly. (There is nothing anomalous, obviously, in the fact that Anne's closest neighbours are Mrs Jennings and Lydia Bennet or in the fact that, after Mr Knightley, she next resembles Harriet Smith.) The second class, typified by John Thorpe's resembling Mrs Elton and the Crawfords more closely than he resembles anybody else, is that where a given character resembles a whole set of others more closely than might have been expected. (Apart from a predictable resemblance to his sister and another, truly surprising, to Eleanor Tilney, Thorpe's next closest resemblances are to characters from the late novels including Admiral Croft, Captain Wentworth, and Emma Woodhouse.) The third class, less obvious but more pervasive, is that in which whole groups of characters figure more or less frequently than might have been expected in these exceptionally close resemblances and exceptionally sharp contrasts. In the upper register of Table 9, where the three closest resemblances for each of forty-eight characters are listed, the twelve heroes and heroines might be expected to appear in a quarter of the 144 cases. They actually appear almost twice as often as that; and only six of the forty-eight characters do not have a hero or heroine among the three with whom they correlate most closely. In the lower register, meanwhile, the heroes and heroines figure in far less than a quarter of the 144 sharpest contrasts; and none of them save Catherine Morland and Henry Tilney ever appears there. We are brought back, in a larger framework, to the problems raised, a little earlier, by Emma Woodhouse. It is somehow 'easier' for any character to stand comparatively close to most of the heroes and heroines than to stand in sharp contrast to them. It seems 'easier', likewise, for any character to stand comparatively close to the characters of the later novels than to those of the earlier. Without forgetting the salient truth that most of the resemblances and contrasts carry a strong air of conviction, we should turn our attention to the seeming anomalies.

II

The isolated anomalies represented by Mr Knightley's comparatively close proximity to Anne Steele become less anomalous as the full

TABLE 10. The Thirty-Word Correlation Matrix

Relative frequencies of the thirty most common words in Jane Austen's dialogue for all the ma[...]
characters.

```
        ALL
1A  CATHERINE        85 1A
1B  HENRY TILNEY     87 55 1B
1D  Isab. Thorpe     91 90 72 1D
1E  John Thorpe      92 84 80 90 1E
1C  Eleanor Tilney   94 84 82 90 90 1C

2A  ELINOR           93 76 88 86 82 92  2A
2C  Marianne         96 84 79 92 88 93 91 2C
2K  Mrs Jennings     93 82 74 84 90 87 80 87 2K
2S  Willoughby       83 68 65 74 72 75 70 83 79 2S
2F  John Dashwood    86 61 84 61 76 79 80 78 83 68 2F
2Q  Lucy Steele      92 88 72 93 85 92 87 92 84 80 67 2Q
2H  Col. Brandon     84 69 65 69 74 75 68 80 85 92 80 75 2H
2D  Mrs Dashwood     91 66 91 78 82 90 93 88 80 69 87 81 72 2D
2B  EDWARD FERRARS   91 81 73 86 84 83 77 90 86 93 73 88 89 76 2B
2P  Anne Steele      82 69 61 69 75 69 68 73 88 69 71 76 76 69 77 2P

3A  ELIZABETH        97 81 90 90 87 92 96 95 84 79 81 90 76 93 86 73 3A
3B  DARCY            91 71 84 83 80 87 87 91 77 88 76 85 82 86 89 65 93 3B
3D  Mrs Bennet       91 87 68 89 86 85 82 87 94 71 72 83 75 78 81 82 85 72 3D
3E  Jane Bennet      88 87 62 84 78 84 80 91 84 76 70 85 76 79 84 79 87 79 89 3E
3K  Collins          78 46 82 65 63 69 75 79 65 80 72 65 74 80 77 52 82 89 60 65 3K
3C  Mr Bennet        92 74 89 87 86 93 95 89 83 69 78 87 68 92 77 66 94 85 84 76 75 3C
3O  Mrs Gardiner     73 58 61 55 60 69 70 66 66 62 71 67 70 71 61 75 73 70 62 72 52 61 3O
3L  Lady Catherine   89 70 90 88 80 89 95 86 74 70 75 86 65 90 75 59 93 89 73 69 78 95 60 3L
3H  Lydia Bennet     90 85 67 90 86 83 80 86 91 78 65 90 74 74 88 85 84 76 91 84 60 79 62 73 3H
3J  Miss Bingley     92 69 89 79 83 82 84 83 85 81 82 77 85 86 86 74 90 87 81 75 83 85 64 84 77 3J
3V  Wickham          90 68 75 74 76 78 81 88 84 84 84 78 85 82 84 82 86 86 77 84 77 74 77 73 80 8

4B  EDMUND           97 76 93 83 89 90 93 91 87 79 90 85 82 93 85 72 95 90 84 78 81 93 69 91 80 9
4C  Mary Crawford    97 76 92 86 91 90 91 93 91 78 87 86 80 92 87 81 95 89 85 82 79 90 70 87 87 9
4D  Crawford         96 80 88 85 91 88 86 90 88 80 86 85 83 88 90 74 93 88 84 80 78 89 64 87 82 9
4J  Mrs Norris       96 75 88 81 87 87 86 88 93 81 89 85 84 88 87 83 91 84 86 78 78 88 68 85 86 9
4A  FANNY            94 94 71 90 88 90 84 93 87 83 76 91 81 79 92 75 91 86 87 92 68 83 68 79 86 8
4E  Sir Thomas       89 63 92 78 76 86 94 87 76 66 79 83 65 94 75 68 93 86 74 74 82 94 64 93 74 8
4G  Tom Bertram      88 65 86 70 83 79 78 80 86 72 87 74 75 85 81 77 83 76 76 69 74 80 61 74 80 8
4F  Lady Bertram     83 89 58 85 75 77 75 77 83 68 60 86 68 63 78 72 77 67 88 76 47 76 54 71 88 7

5A  EMMA             98 84 89 89 90 93 96 94 90 75 87 90 77 93 85 78 97 88 89 86 75 94 72 92 85 8
5B  MR KNIGHTLEY     95 76 86 81 86 86 92 87 89 74 87 83 80 90 80 84 92 82 88 82 72 90 77 85 81 9
5E  Churchill        94 84 75 87 86 85 82 92 88 92 78 88 91 78 96 75 89 89 86 74 78 82 65 80 86 8
5D  Miss Bates       89 82 70 81 83 80 79 79 91 73 76 79 77 73 80 83 81 72 93 79 56 76 65 72 88 8
5I  Mrs Elton        96 84 83 93 93 89 87 93 90 82 79 90 81 84 92 77 92 88 88 83 74 88 59 87 83 8
5M  Harriet Smith    84 92 53 81 80 79 73 80 86 69 64 84 70 62 79 84 77 67 86 86 41 68 71 61 88 6
5P  Mr Woodhouse     86 79 73 79 84 78 77 79 87 58 77 75 63 73 70 81 79 67 87 75 53 79 58 73 81 7
5O  Mrs Weston       94 79 79 78 86 83 86 86 87 79 89 79 86 85 84 78 88 83 83 83 71 81 75 79 78 8
5N  Mr Weston        89 75 81 77 88 85 84 83 87 63 89 73 72 86 73 70 85 74 86 78 61 84 63 78 74 8

6A  ANNE             96 87 80 92 88 89 91 96 85 81 78 92 79 87 91 75 95 91 85 89 75 87 69 87 87 8
6V  Mrs Smith        92 66 86 78 82 84 87 86 85 78 80 84 76 87 81 84 91 87 78 78 75 84 82 82 84 8
6P  Mary Musgrove    93 91 69 88 80 84 81 89 89 75 74 88 77 77 87 83 87 78 91 90 60 79 71 74 90 8
6B  WENTWORTH        97 83 83 90 91 88 87 92 88 87 79 90 88 84 94 95 77 93 91 85 84 77 86 69 86 88 9
6D  Admiral Croft    88 67 87 76 90 81 81 79 83 60 83 73 67 85 72 75 84 75 76 69 62 82 67 77 76 8
```

continued

```
4B  EDMUND           4B
4C  Mary Crawford    95 4C
4D  Crawford         96 94 4D
4J  Mrs Norris       95 96 94 4J
4A  FANNY            87 87 91 85 4A
4E  Sir Thomas       90 91 84 87 75 4E
4G  Tom Bertram      89 92 89 94 78 81 4G
4F  Lady Bertram     76 75 77 78 85 65 65 4F

5A  EMMA             97 96 94 94 91 92 86 81 5A
5B  MR KNIGHTLEY     93 92 90 92 85 87 83 79 96 5B
5E  Churchill        90 88 93 90 94 76 80 85 89 87 5E
5D  Miss Bates       86 85 82 89 83 69 78 88 87 86 85 5D
5I  Mrs Elton        92 93 94 92 92 84 82 83 95 89 94 86 5I
5M  Harriet Smith    73 78 74 76 90 60 68 87 81 80 81 86 80 5M
5P  Mr Woodhouse     81 83 80 85 79 72 77 80 87 83 76 88 85 80 5P
5O  Mrs Weston       92 89 91 90 90 77 82 76 92 94 91 85 88 81 81 5O
5N  Mr Weston        91 88 89 86 82 76 82 70 90 87 79 86 85 73 84 87 5N

6A  ANNE             91 92 93 87 95 86 79 82 95 89 92 80 95 82 78 89 82 6A
6V  Mrs Smith        89 94 85 89 81 87 85 70 89 90 82 80 84 77 74 84 78 86 6V
6P  Mary Musgrove    84 87 89 86 95 73 78 87 90 88 91 87 91 92 86 89 80 92 83 6P
6B  WENTWORTH        93 92 95 97 94 82 82 82 93 91 96 85 96 80 79 92 82 96 87 91 6B
6D  Admiral Croft    86 92 85 87 76 80 85 63 88 87 76 77 85 70 85 86 85 80 86 82 82 6D
```

Note. In order to present so large an array of figures, the coefficients have been rounded to two decimal plac[...] and the decimal points excluded: 0.817 is represented as 82 and so on.

picture begins to take shape. None of the other characters, in fact, is very much like Anne. Even her correlation of 0.883 with Mrs Jennings is among the lowest 'top readings' of all: only Mrs Gardiner and Mr Woodhouse lie further from their nearest neighbours; even Collins is a trifle closer to his. Anne's correlation of 0.841 with Mr Knightley is fractionally the highest of a cluster of more or less average coefficients in which she participates and which thins out, beneath the average, into some very low coefficients indeed. And, while he stands third highest in her list, she stands only thirty-first in his.

To study the complete picture is a formidable but necessary task. Table 10 shows, in an abbreviated form, the entire set of 1128 coefficients derived from the forty-eight frequency-hierarchies of the thirty most common words of dialogue. This makes it possible, in the manner of an inter-city mileage grid, to examine the degrees of resemblance between each of the forty-eight major characters and the other forty-seven. The first column of the matrix, headed 'ALL', shows, in addition, how each of the forty-eight characters correlates with the overall frequency-hierarchy of these thirty words in Jane Austen's dialogue *taken as a whole*.

So large a matrix does not readily yield up the wealth of information it contains. To form a first impression, it is best perhaps to follow the fortunes of one or two idiosyncratic characters like Harriet Smith and Sir Thomas Bertram. It quickly emerges that the pattern of resemblances and differences between any such character and those of his or her own novel is reinforced by corresponding patterns throughout the six novels. Harriet, for example, is comparatively remote not merely from Emma and Mr Knightley but from all the other heroes and heroines save Catherine and Fanny. Her mild resemblance to Miss Bates, in her own novel, is matched or surpassed by her resemblances to Mrs Jennings, Mrs Bennet, Jane, Lydia, Lady Bertram, and Mary Musgrove. The impression of an emerging group is confirmed when it is seen that, with some exceptions in Jane Bennet's case, those named tend also to resemble each other. Sir Thomas Bertram develops an almost antithetical pattern, with close resemblances to all of the heroes and heroines except Catherine, Fanny, and the self-abnegating Edward Ferrars; with especially close resemblances to those in positions of domestic or semi-public authority; and with sharp contrasts to Harriet and all those who much resemble her. While Harriet's group comprises

only female characters, Sir Thomas's includes both men and women.
On a point of some delicacy, it seems fairer to say that Jane Austen's
vulgarians are mostly women and her authoritarians mostly men than
that she discerns a generic vulgarity in her own sex and a generic
authoritarianism in the other. Her most likeable characters, certainly,
include both men and women.

By gradually broadening and deepening such impressions as these
(and thus developing a recognition that, in general, the patterns
emerging from the matrix are self-consistent and consistent with each
other), a growing acquaintance with the figures shows that they
deserve to be approached more systematically. It is useful, as a first
step in that direction, to establish a distribution-curve like those
discussed in Chapter 3. The mean-point on that curve is 0.814 and
its standard deviation is 0.093: in the abbreviated format of Table
10, these would amount to 81 and 10 respectively. (If the two most
aberrant hierarchies, those of Collins and Mrs Gardiner, are
excluded, the mean rises to 0.827 and the unit of standard deviation
falls to 0.080.) The shape of the distribution-curve is heavily skewed
towards the upper end, where the very highest coefficients lie around
1.5 units of standard deviation above the mean and within half a
unit of a perfect correlation of 1.00. At the lower end of the scale,
eight extreme cases lie more than three units of standard deviation
below the mean while the lowest of all lies beyond four units.
Although it includes 1128 scores instead of forty-eight, the curve
is no less abnormal than those examined in Chapter 3.

With this information in hand, the unimportance of the 'isolated
anomalies' is plain. Especially in the middle of the range, between,
say, 0.76 and 0.86, it is not merely reasonable but requisite to
disregard isolated anomalies of less than half a standard deviation
or so. Anne Steele is not *significantly* less like Mrs Norris (0.83) or
Mary Crawford (0.81) than she is like Mr Knightley (0.84) or Lydia
Bennet (0.85). The difference between her resemblance to Mrs
Jennings (0.88) and that to Jane Bennet (0.79) is more worthy of
remark. And, in terms of the general consonance of the results, her
resemblance to Harriet Smith (0.84) and to Miss Bates (0.83) can
safely be given more weight than her resemblance to Mr Knightley.

To argue that it is necessary to distinguish between significant and
negligible differences is not to descend to the simplicities of a binary
system in which everything is to be categorized as black or white,
paradigmatic or syntagmatic, metaphoric or metonymic, diachronic

or synchronic, cooked or raw. Computer switches, no doubt, can register nothing but 'off' or 'on': but thermometers, barometers, and many timepieces register no less real differences through a succession of imperceptible changes. A well-informed account of the differences between digital and analogical methods of reckoning, a convincing demonstration that each has a necessary but distinguishable part to play in our affairs, and a searching assessment of the harm done to our ways of thinking by a recent overemphasis upon digital models run through Anthony Wilden's *System and Structure*.[1]

A hierarchical succession of only forty-eight scores or even a matrix of 1128 leaves gaps of different sizes but remains analogical in principle: any number of additional scores might be inserted at any point; and, whether the actual intervals are large or small, the progression from one extremity to the other allows cumulative effects to register subtler truths than any single bald contrast. Although it is easy to devise exceptions, few of us would ordinarily prefer a clock that distinguished only between 'day' and 'night' or a thermometer that distinguished only between 'hot' and 'cold'. When a subtler analysis is practicable and its findings pertinent, bald categorization is comparatively uninformative: by suppressing part of the evidence, it can become profoundly 'disinformative'.

Statistical analysis includes processes by which it is possible to assess precise degrees of 'significance' in the resemblances and differences between correlation-coefficients. The simpler of these processes are not germane to our evidence because they are designed to assess relationships among *independent* variables. Now, as I hope I have sufficiently established and as the generally high level of our correlation-coefficients attests, the complex probabilistic relationships bound up in the varying incidences of the very common words make a classic specimen of a set of mutually dependent variables.

A genuine statistician would be able to introduce what are known as 'transform-formulae' into the analysis of such data and hence to

---

[1] Anthony Wilden, *System and Structure: Essays in Communication and Exchange* (London, 1972). There are important areas of his argument, however, where Wilden recks not his own rede. They are well illustrated by his turning to Eldridge Cleaver for an epigraph: 'You either have to be part of the solution, or you're part of the problem. There ain't no middle ground.' A notable democrat's 'two cheers for democracy'—a single cheer, or even half a cheer—might have caught a more appropriately analogical note.

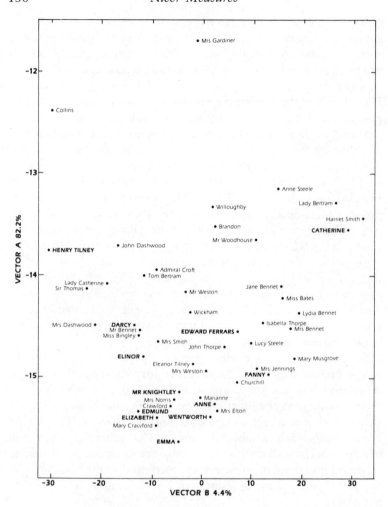

GRAPH 14. Jane Austen's Major Characters
(Word-types 1–30 of her dialogue)

establish the appropriate 'orders of freedom' for assessing the precise degrees of mutual dependence among such variables. Yet he would be severely handicapped by the dearth of comparable data for other writers than Jane Austen and for English conversation in the real world. His best efforts, that is to say, would yield only the beginnings of an understanding of a complex set of probabilities. Lacking both his skills and the range of data necessary for such an analysis, I am content to propose that such figures as those of Table 10 should be treated conservatively; that, especially around the mean, differences of less than half a standard deviation should be regarded as negligible; and that an 'eigen-map' will show the differences that matter.

Graph 14 is such a map, derived from Table 10 and illustrative of the kinds of pattern discussed in the present chapter. In Graph 13, in Chapter 5, the pattern of interrelationships among the characters of *Pride and Prejudice* needed a second projection of the map before an adequate picture could be obtained. But, by virtue of the more complex influences of forty-eight cases upon each other, a single projection suffices here. As it stands, it casts a new and revealing light upon the resemblances and differences among Jane Austen's major characters; and, while doing so, it does not conceal the kinds of anomaly we have yet to consider.

Where the variables analysed are mutually dependent, the several 'eigen-vectors' tend to function only as statistical abstractions, ordering the data intelligibly but not easily definable in other terms. In the present case, however, it is possible to find 'real' meaning in Vectors A and B. The hierarchical order of Vector A, ranging up the map from Emma and Mary Crawford to Collins and Mrs Gardiner, is almost identical to the hierarchical order of the 'ALL' column in Table 10, ranging from Emma's entry of 0.98 to Mrs Gardiner's entry of 0.73. The position occupied by each character along the north–south axis of the map corresponds, that is to say, with the degree to which each of them conforms to the general norms of Jane Austen's dialogue (as represented in the incidence of the thirty most common words); and, at least in this technical sense, Emma is the most 'normal' character of all. (The reasons why she should be so are of both literary and statistical interest. As we shall see, it is not enough to say that, having much the largest speaking-part, she does most to establish the norms themselves: her 7 per cent share in the whole dialogue of Jane Austen's novels is enough of itself to make a potent factor but hardly enough to make a controlling influence.) Since Vector A accounts for 82 per cent of the whole pattern of the correlation-matrix, the hierarchical ordering it affords is of great force: that point, too, is borne out by its close correspondence with the 'ALL' column of Table 10 which rests upon an analysis in which all Jane Austen's dialogue and not merely that of the major characters is brought into account. Vector B, which accounts for a further 4.4 per cent of the whole pattern of the matrix, also affords an appropriate ordering of the characters. In moving across the map from Harriet Smith to Collins, we see a gradual transformation from garrulousness and intellectual indiscipline, through a middle area of civil and articulate speech-habits, to formality and dignity, and onward to pomposity. That transformation coincides with a transformation from brief or straggling sentences, highly personalized in cast, to the composed and impersonal disquisitions that make one point of resemblance between characters who, as Vector A shows, are otherwise as unlike each other as Collins, Henry Tilney, and Sir Thomas Bertram.

By virtue of the combined effect of so many interrelationships, the more isolated anomalies evident here and there in Table 10 have been extinguished. Anne Steele, to recur to that example, is as remote from Mr Knightley as she should be. But the more 'systematic' anomalies of the second and third classes, those where a character or even a set of characters seems oddly placed, are clearly visible in the eigen-map and should now be considered.

III

A careful study of Graph 14 reveals an overall contrast between the characters of the earlier novels and those of the later. Towards the lower extremity of the map, the location of those who conform most closely to the general norm, Marianne Dashwood and Elizabeth Bennet are alone among a dozen characters from the last three novels. At the upper extremity, Lady Bertram, Harriet Smith, and Mr Woodhouse are almost as heavily outnumbered by characters from the first three novels. There is also a preponderance of characters from the earlier novels towards both the left and the right-hand extremities of the map.

Because they seem to have been revised in different ways at different times before they were eventually published, there is room for disagreement about the sequence of composition of Jane Austen's first three novels and even about the meaning of 'sequence of composition' in such a case. These considerations scarcely bear on the broad division between two groups — the three novels that she first undertook in the late 1790s (though none of them was published until after 1810) and the three 'Chawton' novels of her resumed career. Of the latter group, *Mansfield Park* is first heard of on 24 January 1813 (*Letters*, pp. 291–6); and it was published in May

1814. *Emma* quickly followed it and, unless Jane Austen's brother or her publisher made any minor changes after her death, *Persuasion* was brought to the state in which we have it by early 1817. Brian Southam has argued that *Northanger Abbey* was very thoroughly revised in the last months of Jane Austen's life.[2] Even if his case were accepted as conclusive—though all the evidence of the very common words runs counter to it—the two groups of three novels would still stand apart. As Cassandra Austen's memorandum (*Minor Works*, p. 242) attests, three novels were undertaken and carried to what might be called a 'first completion' when Jane Austen was in her early twenties. The other three were undertaken and completed in her late thirties and early forties. It is difficult to conceive of substantial revisions that would not affect the patterning of the very common words. And yet, though the eigen-map shows that Jane Austen's management of these words remained comparatively consistent throughout her literary career, it also shows evidence of change. To move vertically down the map or to move, from either side, towards the centre is to move away from the majority of characters from the first three novels and towards those of the last three. As a further map will show, in the next chapter, the scale of the changes is much less than that which separates Jane Austen's characters from those of *The Waves*. It is greater, however, than that which separates many of her characters from the central characters of *The Awkward Age*, *Howards End*, and *Frederica*.

Once it is perceived, this kind of patterning introduces a 'double standard' into the argument. John Dashwood lies somewhat further from the general norm than Admiral Croft, Jane Bennet further than Miss Bates: but, relative to the characters of their respective sets of three novels, Admiral Croft and Miss Bates stand further from the 'sub-norm' than do the other pair from their 'sub-norm'. This more discriminating way of looking at the map accords with what is obviously the case: that the idiolects of Miss Bates and Admiral Croft are decidedly more idiosyncratic than those of Jane Bennet and John Dashwood and that they stand out more conspicuously among the idiolects of their immediate fellows in the novels themselves.

To refine the contrast between two sets of three novels into a series of contrasts in which each of the six novels is distinguished from

[2] Brian Southam, '*Sanditon*: the Seventh Novel', in Juliet McMaster (ed.), *Jane Austen's Achievement* (London, 1976), pp. 1–26.

the rest will call for other methods of analysis. But the present map is capable of showing that *Northanger Abbey* is the most distinctive novel of the six and that, in some respects, *Sense and Sensibility* is not much less so. I shall pursue the former case and touch only lightly on the latter.

Of the five major characters from *Northanger Abbey*, only Eleanor Tilney and Isabella Thorpe seem entirely at home among their neighbours in the map. Eleanor's highly appropriate location in the lower centre, beside Mrs Weston, is closer to the overall norm than that of any other character from the first three novels except Elizabeth and Marianne. What more need be said of Isabella than that her next neighbours are Mrs Bennet, Lydia, and Lucy Steele? But John Thorpe stands nearer to the general norm, Catherine and Henry much further from it, than might have been expected. Relative also to each other and, yet again, to Eleanor and Isabella, all three seem oddly placed.

The criticism of *Northanger Abbey* shows a division, not always strongly marked, between those who attach more weight to Catherine's essential 'candour', in the old sense of the word, than to her ingenuous speech-habits and those who reverse this balance. With Henry, the two groups tend to exchange places. For the former party, his good sense is offset by a condescending and sometimes almost priggish treatment of Catherine and his sister. For the latter, attracted by his wit and, in particular, by his mockery of Gothic clichés and Gothic hyperbole, his criticism of the young women is justified by its good sense and also by its consonance with the spirit of Jane Austen's most light-hearted narrative commentary. But neither party carries its argument so far as to imply that Catherine is a prototype of Harriet Smith or an incipient Lady Bertram or that Henry is more coldly dignified than Sir Thomas Bertram, more pompous than John Dashwood, or more overbearing than Lady Catherine de Bourgh. And no one, I think, would propose that John Thorpe speaks more courteously than Henry or less colloquially than Catherine; that he resembles the later heroes and heroines more closely than either Catherine or Henry does; or that he has anything important in common with Edward Ferrars, Mrs Smith, and Eleanor Tilney, his neighbours of the map.

The map itself offers a first indication of what has gone amiss. If a small number of secondary characters, ranging up an imaginary centre-line from Wickham and Mr Weston to Mrs Gardiner, are momentarily shut out of mind, the pattern of the entries is that of an outspread pair of wings. With Emma as their hinge, the wings spread out towards Henry and Collins on the one side, towards Catherine, Harriet, and Lady Bertram on the other. The more composedly spoken of the heroes and heroines run inward from Henry, Darcy, and Elinor and on past Mr Knightley, Edmund, and Elizabeth to Emma. Those who speak less formally, more personally, and often more effusively lie along a corresponding inward path from Catherine and Edward Ferrars towards Fanny, Wentworth, and Anne and on again towards the biaxial Miss Woodhouse. Except for Edward, so much less composed than Elinor in attitude and style, each of the heroes stands on the same 'side' of his heroine. The crucial consideration, however, is that the 'wing-span' diminishes greatly as Jane Austen's literary career proceeds.

All this makes for the argument, highly attractive on empirical grounds, that Jane Austen's increasing command—or discovery— of her own kind of fiction bears her ever further from the stiff stylistic oppositions between heroes and heroines that characterize the novels of many of her predecessors, including Fanny Burney, Maria Edgeworth, Mrs Radcliffe, and Richardson.[3] Jane Austen is unusual in an even-handedness that denies her heroines the better of every case. She is more unusual yet in her capacity to register increasingly close compatibilities between distinguishable styles of speech without sacrificing their distinctiveness entirely.

Just such aspirations are evident in *Northanger Abbey*. The narrative makes it clear, from the first, that Catherine is to be regarded as less—or is it really more?—than a conventional heroine; and Henry's amused intelligence is closely akin to that of the narrator (who exercises it, at times, on him). But, in an apprentice-piece, these aspirations are sadly betrayed by overstatement. Catherine's idiolect takes a shape that will afterwards be matched only by Harriet Smith and the young woman whose captivation of Sir Thomas Bertram made all Huntingdon exclaim; and, of all Jane Austen's major

---

[3] Those who were fortunate enough to study under Wesley Milgate may recall the argument that similar, though less exaggerated, contrasts between heroes and heroines are to be found as early as Shakespeare's comedies. With Dorothy Osborne and Sir William Temple as leading examples, Milgate attributed the literary contrasts to differences in 'real language' stemming, in turn, from the differences between the formal schooling to which boys of the educated minority were subjected and the freer self-tutelage that lay within the reach of generations of enterprising and intelligent young women from the Pastons to the Brontës.

characters, only Collins surpasses Henry in 'talking like a book'. The idiolects of Collins and Henry, that is to say, correlate more closely with that of Jane Austen's *pure narrative* than do those of any of their fellow-characters. Collins, a brainless ancestor of Casaubon, undoubtedly deserves and might even welcome such a fate. In Henry's case, however, it seems fair to infer that Jane Austen had yet to learn the art of 'distancing' the idiolect of a character whose attitudes and habits of expression are often reminiscent of her own early letters to Cassandra: 'There seems no likelihood of his coming into Hampshire this Christmas, and it is therefore most probable that our indifference will soon be mutual, unless his regard, which appeared to spring from knowing nothing of me at first, is best supported by never seeing me' (*Letters*, p. 28).

Overstatement, however, is not the only explanation for what has gone amiss. When it is set in the context of evidence that will shortly be presented in more detail, the eigen-map reveals a second, not much less powerful reason why the idiolects of Catherine and Henry stand in so much more extreme a contrast than do those of their successors in the leading roles. Of the seventeen of Jane Austen's major characters who speak more than six thousand words apiece — a tolerable but not ample working minimum for calculations of this kind — Catherine and Mrs Elton show least change in their idiolects as the novels unfold. And, though Henry is carried some way up the list by differences arising from his stylistic games and, in particular, from his long passage of Gothic pastiche, he changes less than most. In the later novels, the idiolects of the heroes and heroines change in a manner that can only be interpreted as a consistent and appropriate development; and it is secondary characters like Mrs Elton — 'flat' characters, as E. M. Forster would have it — who show least change. If it is accepted that Catherine and Henry should show signs of development, that *Northanger Abbey* is notionally akin to Jane Austen's later form of *Bildungsroman*, it follows that their unchanging idiolects betray a comparative failure in her art. (The generic question, however, must not be overlooked: none of the characters of our 'other' novels, from *The Awkward Age* to *Frederica*, changes much more than Catherine; and we shall need to consider whether it is proper to expect that they should do so.)

Whereas a 'fixed' character finds and holds his or her appropriate location in the eigen-map, a character whose idiolect changes at all markedly tends to average out into a sometimes misleading conformity to the general norm. The very energy with which such idiolects change erodes itself into a seeming entropy. That is why it is 'easier' for other characters to correlate unexpectedly closely with the characters of the later novels and especially with the later heroes and heroines. That is why the handful of exceptionally close correlations with which this chapter was introduced includes some resemblances that seem a little less convincing than the rest. That is why *Northanger Abbey* does not figure at the upper extremity of the spectrum or *Persuasion* at the lower.

And, in a nice variant of the same argument, that is why Marianne Dashwood, Mrs Jennings, and (so far as his three thousand words can bear this form of analysis) John Thorpe conform more closely to the general norm than might have been expected. Theirs, too, are changing idiolects: but the evidence is of unsubtle change. With Marianne, whose idiolect changes most of all, there are fluctuations as striking as her shifts of attitude and role. With Mrs Jennings, there are the concomitants of a change in dramatic function. And, with John Thorpe, there is evidence of a failure in authorial imagination or control.

An overall eigen-map cannot show more, on such questions, than that a number of unexpected characters find their way towards the lower centre, where some of them keep better company than they deserve. To support the explanations that have been offered, further evidence is required. That evidence is to be found by turning from the concise generalities of a correlation-matrix (and the 'map' derived from it) to the patterns upon which it rests — by turning back, with an increased understanding, to the differing incidences, for different characters, of the common words themselves.

Graph 15 is an array of miniature bar-graphs, derived in precisely the same manner as those described in Chapter 3 but dealing with only a single pair of characters at a time. To move down the first column is to see the degree of difference (or, even, of resemblance) between Catherine and Henry in each of the thirty most common words. On the very first line, for example, they differ so greatly in the incidence of 'I' that Catherine lies almost two units of standard deviation above the centre-line, the general mean for Jane Austen's dialogue, while Henry lies the better part of two units below it. Thus the difference between their respective 'z-scores' for this word approaches four, an exceedingly strong contrast in any ordinary field of individual difference. With 'the', in the second line, the difference

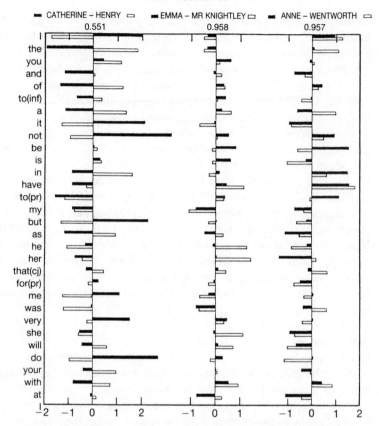

GRAPH 15. Comparative z-Scores for Three Central Couples
(Scores based on distribution among forty-eight major characters)

is of the same order but it is Henry who runs high. With 'not', the difference is even greater; and with 'it', 'but', and 'do', it is not much less. There are examples like 'at' where the two characters stand, once more, on opposite sides of the mean but where the distance between them is negligible. There are examples like 'be' and 'is' where they stand on the same side of the mean but at a negligible distance from it. In the whole set of thirty, however, the prepositional 'to' affords the only instance where Catherine and Henry stand near each other but at a distinct remove from the mean.

Neither the greater nor the lesser differences are especially associated with the more lexically or the more grammatically oriented of the thirty words. The chief point of consistency is of quite another kind: where two characters so frequently diverge in opposite directions from the mean, even the less 'significant' of their particular differences help to form a cumulative contrast. (If it were possible to render it clearly, the column would be better represented as an inverted triangle: the much greater frequency of the words near the head of the list gives them a comparatively powerful influence upon the cumulative effect.) Only in a few instances, of which the prepositional 'to' is easily the most pronounced, is the overall contrast offset by a divergence in the same direction from the mean.

With Emma and Mr Knightley, in the second column of the graph, and with Anne and Wentworth, in the third, an entirely different case obtains. Not only are most of the z-scores much smaller: in these columns, unlike the first, even $+ / - 1.5$ is an uncommonly large score. Beyond that, there is scarcely an example of marked divergence in opposite directions. 'At' is the least negligible example for Emma and Mr Knightley and, even there, they lie only one unit or so apart. 'Be', 'her', and 'a' carry Anne and Wentworth a little further apart than that: but only 'be' affords a difference of two units. And, while Anne and Wentworth both diverge somewhat more often and more considerably from the mean than do Emma and Mr Knightley, the former pair so often travel side by side that the divergences rarely amount to significant differences between them. For the rest, Mr Knightley's comparatively strong recourse to 'he', 'she', and 'her' — the subject of an earlier comment — affords some of the few divergences worthy of remark.

Small wonder, then, that the three correlation-coefficients should be as they are: only 0.551 for Catherine and Henry as compared with 0.958 and 0.957 for the other pairs. There is no doubt that, in this respect, as in many others, *Northanger Abbey* is different. There is no doubt that the contrast between Catherine and Henry is both strongly stated and many faceted. Whether that contrast amounts, as I argued a little earlier, to an overstatement, a ground for comparing *Northanger Abbey* with the novels of Jane Austen's immediate predecessors and for preferring her own later novels, is a question of critical judgement.

Up to a point, the examples chosen for Graph 15 show signs of the further difference between 'fixed' and 'changing' idiolects. Although they are not directly represented in this graph, the variations within the idiolects of Emma and Mr Knightley combine

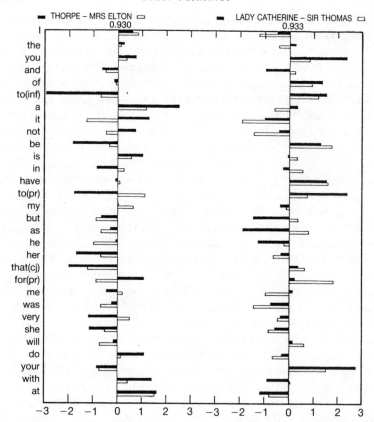

GRAPH 16. Comparative z-Scores for Two Secondary Couples
(Scores based on distribution among forty-eight major characters)

with the effects of comparative understatement to produce those
many z-scores where there is only a negligible divergence from the
mean. But, if even the most negligible examples are admitted, both
the second and the third columns include numerous small divergences
in opposite directions. These idiolects are not unvaryingly similar:
the differences between them in some phases of *Emma* and *Persuasion*
respectively are eroded, overall, by the averaging effects of change.

No serious argument could be based on these small divergences
alone. But Graph 16 makes the same point more firmly. It is time
to recognize that unusually high correlation-coefficients can arise in
more ways than one. In cases like those of Emma and Mr Knightley

and of Anne and Captain Wentworth, the close overall resemblance rests on a *dearth of sustained differences*. In cases like that of Lady Catherine and Sir Thomas, in the second column of Graph 16, close overall resemblances—and the high coefficients that derive from them—rest on the more or less *continuous presence of striking similarities*. Considered as a set, the z-scores for Lady Catherine and Sir Thomas are scarcely less strong than those for Catherine and Henry. But, whereas the former pair usually diverge from the mean in opposite directions, these two tend to diverge in the same direction. With 'you', 'your', and the prepositional 'to'—to take only the most outstanding instances—Lady Catherine's z-scores are so high as to separate her sharply from almost all of the other forty-seven characters: but, without quite matching her, Sir Thomas travels sufficiently far in the same direction to keep the difference between them within bounds. With 'it' and 'not', in her turn, she travels some way after him. With 'be', 'have', and the infinitive 'to'—all markers of the compound verb-forms and hence, when they are freely used, of a comparatively ornate conversational style—these two characters score almost equally strongly. (Like 'that', the infinitive 'to' is commonly deleted by Jane Austen's less formal speakers.) Their scores are also similar for several other words among those listed.

The whole set of scores includes differences enough to dispel the thought that these two idiolects might be mistaken for each other. (The differences between the scores for the connectives 'but', 'as', and 'and' are especially suggestive of actual differences in syntax.) By virtue of such differences, the correlation between Lady Catherine and Sir Thomas does not rise above 0.933. Yet there is a sense in which the resemblance between them is more 'real' than those between Emma and Mr Knightley and between Anne and Wentworth. It is 'easier', at least, for other idiolects to correlate comparatively closely with those where most z-scores lie near the mean than with those where there are numerous strong divergences.

Since the idiolects of Lady Catherine and Sir Thomas never vary greatly in the course of their novels, the association between strong z-scores and fixed idiolects and that between weak z-scores and changing idiolects grow firmer. But, as the column treating of John Thorpe and Mrs Elton indicates, the other side of our argument—that treating of strongly and less strongly *stated* idiolects—should still be kept in mind. Thorpe and Mrs Elton travel often enough in the same direction to achieve an unexpectedly high correlation-coefficient: the highest, it will be recalled, in which he participates. Tempting as it is to leave them to each other's mercy, we should rejoice in an opportunity to *use* them.

Mrs Elton shows an obvious dearth of high z-scores. By the standards of the later novels, she remains strident enough to stand out among her companions. And yet, if she is even temporarily to resemble Emma, her worst qualities cannot be represented as nakedly as those of Mrs Bennet or Lady Catherine. Given that her idiolect varies as little as any, it is for such larger reasons and not from an averaging effect that her z-scores are mostly weak and, accordingly, that hers is one of those idiolects which are accessible to high correlations. (Apart from a correlation of 0.585 with Mrs Gardiner, she never runs lower than 0.74.) The fact that Emma's resemblance to her is transient suggests that she is not to be seen, as Marvin Mudrick would have it, as Emma's double but only as a credible and revealing parody of Emma: the evidence on which this last distinction rests will be offered in Part Three.

John Thorpe's case is different again. There is a handful of exceptionally strong z-scores, including those for several major connectives in each of which he lies far below the mean. (Only a Harriet Smith would cavil at a short letter: there is more reason to harbour doubts about a man who can manage only short sentences.) The highest of all Thorpe's z-scores is for 'a', which is associated with his anecdotes about a bottle of wine I drank, a distinguished old fellow I outplayed in a game of billiards, or a devilish good horse I bought at a price you would scarce believe.[4] Except for these few words, however, John Thorpe shows a weak array of scores. Merely to hear him speak is to recognize that his is no understated idiolect. With him, as was suggested earlier, the weak z-scores arise from an averaging-out of inconsistencies between the 'sub-idiolects' of the braggart, the bully, the Brummel-manqué, and the elephantine suitor of his last appearance. The handful of strong z-scores reflect those chiefly superficial tricks of expression through which the young Jane Austen seeks to cobble up a highly-coloured patchwork. Too stern a response to so comical a monster? Perhaps so: but largely because

---

[4] See my article '"Nothing out of the Ordinary Way": Differentiation of Character in the Twelve Most Common Words of *Northanger Abbey*, *Mansfield Park*, and *Emma*', *British Journal for Eighteenth-Century Studies*, vi (1983), 35–6, for a somewhat more detailed contrast between this particularizing use of 'a', Mr Knightley's generalizing use, and Henry Tilney's typifying use.

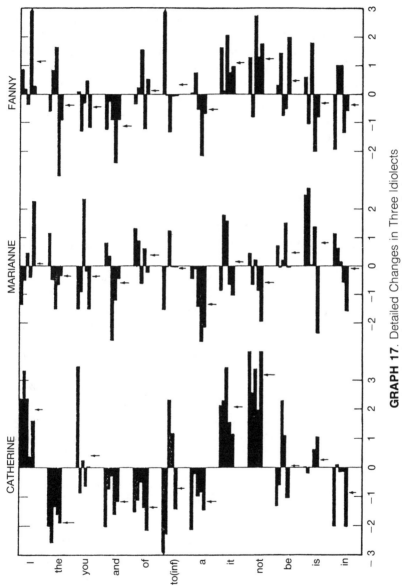

GRAPH 17. Detailed Changes in Three Idiolects
(z-scores for the use of each word at each stage)

a Mrs Elton, a Mrs Norris, or a Mary Musgrove spoils the appetite for a Thorpe, a Captain Mirvan, or a Branghton.

The means by which it is possible to distinguish more directly between mere inconsistency, sustained development, and a delicate attunement to an altered situation are the main subject of Part Three. But, in order to draw the threads of the last few pages together, we should anticipate something of the later argument by considering Graph 17.

Here, again, is an array of miniature bar-graphs. On this occasion, however, the whole speaking-part of each chosen character has been divided into five equal segments. For each word treated, the comparison now shows how its incidence changes through five successive phases of a given idiolect. (The three characters chosen have speaking-parts of about the same size as each other.) Only the twelve most common words have been recorded because, except in the very largest speaking-parts, only they occur often enough to support this degree of segmentation: but even these dozen words amount to a quarter of each character's speaking-part. Against the pattern for each word in each column, a marker-point indicates the overall z-score of the kind treated in Graphs 15 and 16.[5]

The striking feature of Catherine Morland's column is the frequency with which, in all five segments of her speaking-part, the scores diverge strongly in the same direction. That pattern is very marked in seven of the twelve cases and is almost maintained, albeit in a weaker fashion, in another two. Only with 'you', 'to' (inf.), and 'be' does her incidence diverge markedly in opposite directions at different stages of the novel. This means, for example, that while she turns most often to 'I' in the second of her five segments and least often in the fourth, she *always* uses it more often than the average for the other major characters of Jane Austen's novels. The same point holds for 'it' and 'not'. With 'the', 'and', 'of', and 'a' she lies always below the average. Here, then, is direct evidence of extreme consistency in an overstated idiolect.

[5] The scores registered for each segment are not true z-scores in that they, too, are derived from the *overall* mean and the *overall* unit of standard deviation for the use of the word in question by Jane Austen's forty-eight major characters. While this approach overstates the absolute size of the scores, it avoids the worse distortion that would follow from dividing the smaller speaking-parts into five segments. And it does allow an exact parity of comparison between segment and segment and also between character and character.

In Marianne's column and, at first sight, in Fanny's, the signs are all of inconsistency. 'A' is the only word where Marianne runs consistently to one side of the mean. For Fanny, 'and' and 'it' are the only words to do so. But, though Fanny's column includes a few exceptionally strong divergences, a tally of the more sizeable scores indicates that, overall, both Catherine and Marianne diverge substantially from the mean more frequently than she does.

Upon more careful inspection, Fanny's column shows an underlying consistency of pattern. Especially in the upper part of the column, the fourth segment often yields the most unusual score. Fanny's fourth segment has 'I' running to much the highest level of all the scores shown in Graph 17. 'The' runs to an extremely low level. 'You' does not run significantly high: but the score for the fourth segment remains the odd one out. To turn from the graph to the text of Fanny's speaking-part is to discover that this fourth segment, which begins (p. 279) near the end of the Mansfield ball, portrays her reception of Crawford's proposal and her stalwart defence against a succession of attempts to bully or cajole her. It treats, in other words, of a Fanny who speaks more plainly and firmly than she has ever dared.

But she does not speak 'out of character'. Unusual as it is, the fourth segment does not yield the most divergent of the five correlation-coefficients derived by relating each segment, in turn, to Fanny's overall hierarchy for the twelve most common words. (The most divergent, in fact, is for the third segment, which treats of the period preceding the ball, when Fanny's connection with Mansfield Parsonage is strongest.) Further study of the graph shows why this should be so. Although the scores for the fourth segment are exceptional, especially in sheer magnitude, they often tend to run in the same direction as (and not often in the opposite direction from) the scores for the first and last segments. The correlation-coefficients are as follows:

1	0.940	pp. 15–102	childhood; Sotherton
2	0.843	pp. 102–99	theatricals; return of Sir Thomas; the family alone
3	0.740	pp. 199–279	association with Mary; Crawford's interest; ball
4	0.948	pp. 279–349	Crawford's proposal; defence against his advocates
5	0.950	pp. 349–456	last interview with Mary; Portsmouth; return to Mansfield

Fanny speaks least like herself, then, in the unhappy period of the theatricals and in the period of her uneasy intimacy with Miss Crawford. Even there, as the level of the coefficients suggests, her idiolect shows a capacity to adjust and not a fundamental change. And its integrity survives pressures as severe as those she experiences in the powerful series of chapters that begins when Sir Thomas informs her of Crawford's wish to marry her.

To show the comparative fixity of Catherine's idiolect, it is enough to record the corresponding set of five correlation-coefficients: 0.927, 0.958, 0.974, 0.966, 0.980. But Marianne calls for the more thorough treatment accorded to Fanny:

1	0.597	pp. 14–47	apostrophe to Norland; comments on Elinor and Edward
2	0.860	pp. 47–99	Willoughby at Combe; Edward's visit
3	0.751	pp. 99–188	(Palmers and Steeles); London; crisis with Willoughby
4	0.938	pp. 188–311	end of London phase; Cleveland and onset of illness
5	0.951	pp. 311–72	delirium; convalescence; resolutions for future

The disparities among these correlation-coefficients make it easier to understand why Marianne Dashwood has made for controversy among Jane Austen's critics. To fix on the Marianne of any one phase and argue, in effect, that this is 'the real Marianne' is to be at odds with those who would locate 'the real Marianne' elsewhere. To set any of these Mariannes beside the (comparatively) unchanging Elinor is to make the novel revolve on only one of several possible axes. Are we to take Marianne as the enthusiastic dogmatist we first encounter? The pitiable but morbid introvert of the London episodes? The eventual mistress of high-flown resolutions? From the evidence of Graph 18, it is more appropriate to avoid such choices; to note that, if the third segment is regarded (reasonably enough) as *sui generis*, the remainder lie in a rough line of development; and to argue, accordingly, that Jane Austen approaches the eventual Marianne from afar. Yet that argument is more convincing in the abstract than when it is seen to entail the acceptance of some unconvincing pieties and of the implausible idea that the various Mariannes can be united as Colonel Brandon's wife. I think it fair to conclude that, while a rough line of development can be observed,

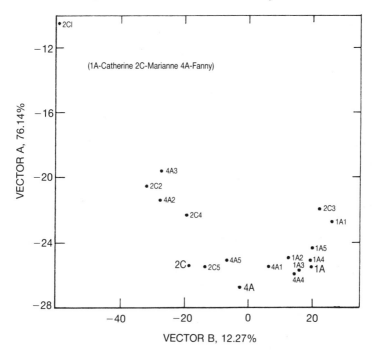

GRAPH 18. Overall Changes in Three Idiolects
(Word-types 1-12 of dialogue)

Marianne is not so much a character as a succession of loosely-fitting roles—the enthusiast, the victim, the regenerate; that, for all the stiffness of her portrayal, Elinor makes a better point of departure for an understanding of this novel; and that, while *Sense and Sensibility* is far more ambitious than *Northanger Abbey*, it fails to realize some of its chief aims.

Graph 18 makes a concise summary of the evidence touched on in recent pages. Derived by the same processes as the earlier 'eigenmaps', it locates Catherine (1A), Marianne (2C), and Fanny (4A) relative to each other and shows relative locations for the five segments of each speaking-part. The remote location of '2C1'—that is, of Marianne as the reader first encounters her—has a marked effect upon the remainder. Merely by requiring a smaller-scale map than might otherwise be drawn, it suggests that the remainder are closer to each other than they would otherwise appear. Beyond that, however, this method of mapping allows a remote value to exercise a disproportionate pressure on the remainder and actually to drive them together. Despite that disadvantage, the map makes its main points well.

The choice of the three characters is designed to illustrate three different patterns in speaking-parts of roughly the same size. The choice of five segments, rather than three or ten, is a mere practicality, a matter of acceptable working minima. (Ten segments will be employed, in Part Three, to give a suitably detailed picture of the different kinds of change.) The choice of equal segments instead of a more 'natural' division into 'real' dramatic phases is born not of statistical necessity but of a considered policy of non-intrusion. To base a similar line of analysis on 'real' divisions in the action of a novel would not only sharpen the statistical findings but also enrich and reinforce the larger argument. And yet, in an exploratory study, it would be a pity to risk the suspicion that my prejudices as reader lay concealed behind the statistics themselves. Those prejudices are evident enough, no doubt, in the more literary facets of the discussion: and, so far as possible, that is the proper place for them. The reader who discerns a fundamental ideological bias in the decision to study characters and idiolects must take his case to the novels—to texts which incorporate inverted commas at one point rather than another and which associate particular proper names with the passages so enclosed.

IV

To bring the present phase of the discussion to a close, Graph 19 is an eigen-map composed in precisely the same fashion as Graph 14 save that it treats of the sixty (rather than the thirty) most common words of Jane Austen's dialogue. (Table 11, from which it is derived, corresponds to Table 10 save that it includes the extra thirty words.) Table 11 and Graph 19 thus embrace more than half of all the words of each major character. The first two eigen-vectors now account for almost 90 per cent of the whole shape of the correlation-matrix. The close overall correspondence between these two large 'maps' adds weight to the proposition that idiolects are highly cohesive 'force-fields' in which the pervasive effects of the probabilistic relationships among word-frequencies outweigh any small anomalies and, at least in a language as energetic as Jane Austen's, register differences worth studying.

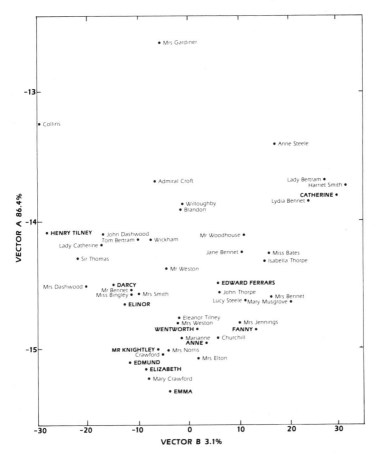

GRAPH 19. Jane Austen's Major Characters
(Word-types 1–60 of her dialogue)

The composition of the main groups of characters remains essentially unchanged as does the general pattern of interrelationships between group and group. The group of vulgar women grows rather more compact and Jane Bennet stands further from it. John Thorpe, Lydia Bennet, and Admiral Croft are perhaps the only ones to shift location far enough to indicate that their 'second thirty words' are not consonant with their first. Mrs Norris moves a little away from Edmund and the Crawfords. Anne and Wentworth move a little further from the bottom centre of the map.

TABLE 11. The Sixty-Word Correlation Matrix
Relative frequencies of the sixty most common words in Jane Austen's dialogue for all the major characters.

```
                         ALL
1A  CATHERINE            89 1A
1B  HENRY TILNEY         91 68 1B
1D  Isab. Thorpe         92 92 78 1D
1E  John Thorpe          94 87 85 92 1E
1C  Eleanor Tilney       95 88 88 91 91 1C

2A  ELINOR               95 81 91 87 86 93   2A
2C  Marianne             96 87 86 92 90 94   92 2C
2K  Mrs Jennings         95 86 82 87 92 90   86 90 2K
2S  Willoughby           89 77 78 80 79 83   80 88 85 2S
2F  John Dashwood        91 72 88 72 83 85   87 84 88 79 2F
2Q  Lucy Steele          94 90 80 94 88 93   89 93 88 85 78 2Q
2H  Col. Brandon         89 77 77 76 80 83   79 85 88 94 85 81 2H
2D  Mrs Dashwood         94 75 92 82 85 92   94 90 86 79 92 86 81 2D
2B  EDWARD FERRARS       93 85 81 88 87 87   83 91 89 94 81 90 91 82 2B
2P  Anne Steele          86 77 71 76 80 76   75 78 90 77 77 82 81 76 81 2P

3A  ELIZABETH            98 85 92 91 90 94   97 96 89 85 88 92 83 95 89 80   3A
3B  DARCY                93 78 89 85 85 90   91 93 83 92 83 88 88 89 91 74   95 3B
3D  Mrs Bennet           94 90 79 91 89 90   86 89 95 81 82 89 82 85 86 86   90 80 3D
3E  Jane Bennet          91 88 74 86 83 87   87 92 88 82 80 88 83 86 86 82   91 85 91 3E
3K  Collins              85 62 88 74 74 80   83 85 76 86 81 75 82 85 84 64   87 92 74 76 3K
3C  Mr Bennet            94 81 92 89 89 94   95 92 87 78 84 90 77 92 83 74   95 89 88 83 83 3C
3O  Mrs Gardiner         81 67 71 66 70 76   80 75 75 74 79 75 80 81 71 79   80 80 73 81 66 72 3O
3L  Lady Catherine       92 78 92 87 85 91   94 89 82 78 82 88 75 91 82 68   94 91 82 78 84 95 70 3L
3H  Lydia Bennet         89 86 72 90 87 83   79 86 90 79 71 90 75 76 86 87   84 77 90 83 67 81 65 76 3H
3J  Miss Bingley         94 78 91 84 87 87   88 87 89 87 87 84 87 89 89 79   93 90 87 83 88 89 73 88 80 3J
3V  Wickham              91 74 81 77 80 82   88 90 86 86 87 82 87 88 85 81   89 89 82 89 81 80 85 78 77 85 3V

4B  EDMUND               98 82 95 86 91 93   94 93 91 86 92 88 87 93 89 79   96 92 89 85 87 94 77 93 81 93 87
4C  Mary Crawford        98 83 94 89 93 93   93 94 94 85 92 90 86 94 90 85   97 92 90 87 86 93 79 90 87 94 9
4D  Crawford             97 86 92 88 93 91   90 92 92 87 90 89 88 91 92 80   95 91 89 85 85 91 74 90 84 95 8
4J  Mrs Norris           97 82 91 86 91 90   89 90 94 87 92 89 89 91 90 86   93 88 90 83 84 90 76 88 87 92 8
4A  FANNY                95 95 79 92 90 91   87 93 90 87 83 94 86 85 93 81   93 89 91 93 78 87 77 84 87 87 8
4E  Sir Thomas           92 73 94 82 82 90   95 90 83 78 85 87 78 94 82 74   95 90 82 83 88 95 75 93 76 88 8
4G  Tom Bertram          91 74 90 77 87 85   82 85 90 80 89 81 81 88 85 81   87 81 83 78 81 84 70 80 84 87 8
4F  Lady Bertram         88 91 70 88 83 83   80 82 87 77 72 89 76 73 83 78   83 75 90 82 64 81 64 78 89 79 7

5A  EMMA                 99 88 92 91 92 95   96 95 93 84 92 93 85 95 89 83   98 91 93 90 83 95 80 94 86 93 89
5B  MR KNIGHTLEY         97 82 90 85 89 90   95 90 92 83 92 88 87 94 86 86   95 88 92 88 82 92 84 89 81 92 90
5E  Churchill            96 88 83 89 89 90   86 93 92 94 85 91 93 84 96 81   92 92 90 87 86 93 79 90 87 91 87
5D  Miss Bates           92 86 78 85 87 85   83 83 92 81 83 85 82 81 84 85   86 79 94 84 70 82 74 79 88 86 8
5I  Mrs Elton            97 89 88 94 94 92   89 94 92 87 85 92 85 87 94 82   94 90 92 87 82 91 69 90 89 92 8
5M  Harriet Smith        88 93 66 85 84 83   80 84 89 78 74 89 78 73 83 87   83 76 89 88 58 77 78 71 88 75 8
5P  Mr Woodhouse         91 85 81 85 88 85   83 84 91 73 84 83 75 82 80 83   86 78 92 83 70 75 71 81 83 81 8
5O  Mrs Weston           95 84 85 83 88 87   90 89 90 85 92 86 90 90 88 82   92 88 88 89 81 87 84 84 79 90 9
5N  Mr Weston            93 81 86 83 91 89   88 88 90 76 92 81 80 91 80 77   90 82 90 84 75 88 74 84 78 87 8

6A  ANNE                 96 90 85 93 90 91   92 96 88 86 84 94 84 88 92 80   96 92 89 92 90 76 89 87 89 87
6V  Mrs Smith            94 75 89 82 85 88   91 89 89 85 87 88 85 91 85 86   93 91 85 85 82 88 88 85 82 88 9
6P  Mary Musgrove        94 93 77 91 90 87   85 90 91 81 81 91 82 82 90 89   90 83 93 91 72 84 77 80 91 85 8
6B  WENTWORTH            96 86 86 89 91 89   88 92 89 90 84 90 81 86 95 82   93 93 87 85 82 87 76 87 85 91 8
6D  Admiral Croft        88 73 86 79 91 83   82 83 85 69 84 78 73 85 75 79   86 78 81 75 71 83 72 79 81 82 8
```

continued

```
4B  EDMUND               4B
4C  Mary Crawford        97 4C
4D  Crawford             97 96 4D
4J  Mrs Norris           96 96 95 4J
4A  FANNY                90 91 93 89 4A
4E  Sir Thomas           93 93 89 90 82 4E
4G  Tom Bertram          92 94 91 94 83 86 4G
4F  Lady Bertram         83 82 84 84 89 75 75 4F

5A  EMMA                 97 98 96 96 94 94 90 86   5A
5B  MR KNIGHTLEY         95 95 93 94 90 91 87 84   97 5B
5E  Churchill            94 92 95 93 95 83 86 89   93 91 5E
5D  Miss Bates           89 89 87 91 87 77 84 90   90 89 89 5D
5I  Mrs Elton            94 95 96 94 94 88 87 88   96 92 96 89 5I
5M  Harriet Smith        80 84 81 83 92 71 75 90   85 85 86 89 85 5M
5P  Mr Woodhouse         88 89 86 91 86 81 84 86   91 89 84 91 89 86 5P
5O  Mrs Weston           93 92 92 92 92 85 86 82   94 96 92 88 91 86 87 5O
5N  Mr Weston            93 92 91 90 86 84 87 79   93 91 85 89 89 80 89 91 5N

6A  ANNE                 92 94 94 90 95 89 84 87   96 91 94 85 96 86 84 91 87   6A
6V  Mrs Smith            91 95 89 91 86 90 87 77   92 93 87 84 87 83 82 90 85   88 6V
6P  Mary Musgrove        88 90 91 89 96 80 83 90   92 90 92 89 93 94 90 91 85   93 86 6P
6B  WENTWORTH            94 92 94 92 92 86 85 85   93 91 96 86 95 84 84 92 85   95 88 91 6B
6D  Admiral Croft        87 91 86 87 80 82 89 72   88 86 80 80 86 74 86 86 88   83 85 84 82 88 6D
```

Note. In order to present so large an array of figures, the coefficients have been rounded to two decimal places and the decimal points excluded: 0.817 is represented as 82 and so on.

Among the more energetic members of this second set of thirty are the modal auxiliary verbs, 'would', 'must', 'can', 'should', and 'could'; the main verbs 'know' and 'think'; the pronouns 'him', 'his', 'we', and 'they'; the demonstrative 'that', the adjectival form of 'no', and 'so' as an adverb of degree. But 'am', 'are', 'had', 'has', and 'been', as well as 'if' and 'or', are also worthy of remark.

The more obvious connections between a number of these words and the small changes between map and map can be dealt with in a brief space. Those verb forms that are associated with the past tenses and the subjunctive mood are of particular relevance to Anne and Wentworth and tend to distinguish them (and Edward Ferrars) from the other heroes and heroines. On the whole, however, these verb forms stand with 'that', 'no', and 'so' (in the senses mentioned above) and also with 'if' as tending, when they are freely used, to distinguish the vulgar and the discontented. Save in an unusual situation like Anne Elliot's, Jane Austen's more admirable characters are not much accustomed to dwelling on the past or speculating about the future:[6] they therefore have comparatively little need for several of these verb forms. (Marianne's nostalgic hankerings and Mrs Bennet's inordinate hopes may point sufficient contrast.) And, as we have seen, the more admirable characters are not much given to the feeble gestures of emphasis associated with a pronounced recourse to the demonstratives and the intensifiers.

When they figure strongly in the idiolect of a particular character, 'know' and 'think' tend to reflect an uneasy self-assertiveness that is even plainer in Mrs Norris's habitual 'I am sure'. It is almost always a good thing to think and sometimes a better thing to know. But, when they are freely used in dialogue, these forms of the verbs tend to appear in the first person, present tense of redundant parentheses in which the speaker—not content to know or to think—must remind others that he does so. (The usual second person versions, like 'you know' and 'don't you think so?' serve similar purposes a little less overtly.) Poor Mr Rushworth makes an exception to prove the rule. When he first appears in person, he produces three versions of 'I do not know' within a single page (p. 53). When he last appears, the narrator comments that 'Mr. Rushworth hardly knew what to

[6] As I have argued elsewhere, even Anne learns something, in this respect, from Mrs Smith. See my '*Persuasion* and its "Sets of People"', *Sydney Studies in English*, ii (1976-7), 3-23.

do with so much meaning' (p. 186). And, in between, the phrase 'I do not know' serves as a little Rushworth-motif, especially in contexts where he ponderously but ineffectually appeals to Miss Bertram's better knowledge.

As the discussion of 'we' in Chapter 1 implies, these words of the 'second thirty' repay as close attention as those that lie above them in the hierarchy of frequencies. But it is enough, for the present purpose, to recognize that their overall effect is to differentiate Jane Austen's characters in a manner that strengthens, not alters, the lines evident in the first thirty. Taken as a whole, therefore, the half of each idiolect made up by the sixty most common words of Jane Austen's dialogue shows a decided homogeneity, a remarkable integrity of shape. Given the argument advanced about John Thorpe, it is no surprise to find him among the few noteworthy exceptions.

8

Larger Patterns and Interrelationships

I

COMPARISONS BETWEEN JANE AUSTEN'S DIALOGUE AND THAT OF OTHER NOVELISTS

The methods of eigen-mapping, which have yielded so many apt comparisons across a range of idiolects, can equally be brought to bear upon comparisons between novel and novel, both in and beyond the field of dialogue. By treating the whole dialogue of each novel as a single entity and establishing the frequency-hierarchy of its common words, we can try to judge whether the differences (concealed but not deprived of influence) among its several idiolects outweigh, or are outweighed by, more general differences in the 'style of dialogue'—as among the novels of Jane Austen or between that of Jane Austen and those of other novelists.

Graph 20 makes a first step in that direction. With the thirty most common words of dialogue as a base, each of the six sets of dialogue is compared with the others and also with the full set, the overall frequency-hierarchy of those words in Jane Austen's dialogue as a whole. Taken together, the three eigen-vectors account for over 99 per cent of the pattern of the correlation-matrix from which they are derived. In both projections of the map, the entry for the full set, marked 'DIALOGUE', shows the effect, by now familiar, of an averaging-out of all the idiolects of all six novels.

As in Graphs 14 and 19, the ordering of the entries of Vector A, the north–south axis of the upper section of the map, corresponds almost exactly with the hierarchy of coefficients set out in the 'ALL'

TABLE 12. Jane Austen's Six Sets of Dialogue

	ALL					
1 *Northanger Abbey*	0.969	*NA*				
2 *Sense and Sensibility*	0.989	0.948	*SS*			
3 *Pride and Prejudice*	0.985	0.943	0.979	*PP*		
4 *Mansfield Park*	0.990	0.951	0.972	0.969	*MP*	
5 *Emma*	0.992	0.965	0.977	0.964	0.977	*E*
6 *Persuasion*	0.983	0.930	0.971	0.969	0.974	0.973

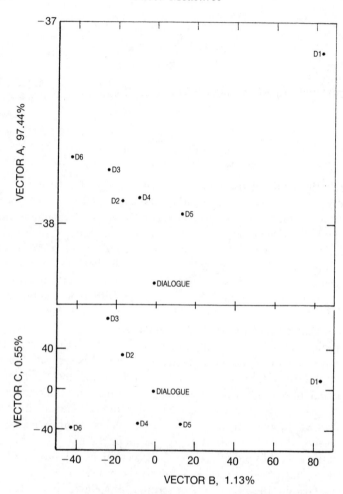

GRAPH 20. The Dialogue of Jane Austen's Six Novels
(Word-types 1-30 of her dialogue)

column of the correlation-matrix. (On this occasion, however, that result does not carry its former corroborative weight: useful as it is in locating the general norm, the inclusion of the entry marked 'DIALOGUE' cannot be achieved except by taking the 'ALL' column into the reckoning and thus allowing it a direct influence upon the configuration of the map.)

Once again Vector B, the east–west axis of both projections of the map, affords a graduated contrast between more and less disquisitive forms of dialogue. The pattern is not one of continuous development in Jane Austen's style. It better represents the different mixtures of idiolects that mark each novel. In *Northanger Abbey*, at one extremity, Henry Tilney is the only truly formal speaker among the major characters: his contribution (to which his father adds a little) is far outweighed by the combined contributions of Catherine, Isabella, and—among the minor characters—Mrs Allen, Mrs Morland, Mrs Thorpe, and a brace of incipient Isabellas. In *Persuasion*, at the other extremity, Mary Musgrove is the only major character who tends in Catherine's direction (so to call it): and, though the other Musgroves appear to resemble Catherine more closely, the entire contribution of Uppercross is far outweighed by those of Mrs Smith, Lady Russell, the Elliot circle, and the naval officers. Among the 'normal' characters, Anne and Wentworth make for a larger steadying influence upon the one set of figures than that of Eleanor Tilney (and John Thorpe) upon the other. It would be easy to refine this rough tallying of effects and counter-effects: but, rather than labour the obvious, it may suffice to note that a similar tallying accounts for the contrast, like in kind but lesser in degree, between *Emma* and the other three novels. The combined influence of the idiolects of Miss Bates, Mr Woodhouse, Harriet Smith, and Isabella Knightley represents a stronger injection of rambling anecdotage than can be found in any of those novels; and, except for John Knightley's small part, *Emma* alone does not include a single idiolect of the more disquisitive sort. Vector B suggests, in short, that the local combination of idiolects in one novel or another is a force that cannot be ignored in an analysis of possible developments in Jane Austen's 'style of dialogue'.

Yet Vector C supports the belief, widespread among her readers and critics, that Jane Austen's style of dialogue does change and that, even in this respect, the Chawton novels stand some way apart from those undertaken in her youth. For, on the north–south axis of the second projection of the map, the Chawton novels lie together, well below the general norm, while the three earlier novels range above it. Graph 20 does not afford evidence enough for a definite interpretation of this contrast. But, from a comparison with Graph 14 (and a prior knowledge of Graph 21), I suggest that it has to do with an overall relaxation in Jane Austen's style, with the emergence of a more conversational fluency in her dialogue, and with a more complete assimilation — though never an abandonment — of the disciplines of Augustan prose. Were *Tom Jones* and *Amelia* to be added to such a map as Graph 21, I venture to predict that they would lie at least as far beyond Jane Austen in one direction as *The Awkward Age*, *The Waves*, and *Howards End* lie in the other.[1]

In order to compare Jane Austen's dialogue with that of more recent novelists, it is necessary to modify the word-list that has carried the argument so far. Since Jane Austen remains the subject of this study, there is no occasion to form a new (but not much different) set of word-types. But the dialogue of James, Forster, and Georgette Heyer includes so many contracted forms like 'I'll' and 'don't' that it would be misleading to exclude them. The totals (for every novelist) for 'I', 'you', 'it', 'not', 'is', 'have', 'he', 'was', 'she', and 'will' have therefore been adjusted. Since the totals for 'not' will now include 'can't', I have also included 'cannot'. And — as might have been done from the first — 'a' will now include 'an'.[2]

The effect of these modifications upon the word-list for Jane Austen is very slight, amounting to an addition of only 1647 word-tokens to the 123,137 that make up the thirty most common word-types of her dialogue. (If 'an' and 'cannot' are set aside, the true contracted forms of the words mentioned above amount to fewer than 200 in the six novels. A third of these are to be found in *Sense and Sensibility*, where they belong to the obvious claimants. ''Tis' accounts for half of the twenty that occur in *Northanger Abbey*.) Jane Austen's total of 1647 is easily surpassed in *each* of those three 'modern' novels where they are used at all. Thus, in the dialogue of *The Awkward Age*, there are 619 instances of 'do', but another 544 of 'don't'; 588 of 'is' but 1204 of its contracted forms; 122 of 'can't' — and none at all of 'cannot'.

[1] The location of *Northanger Abbey* least far above the general norm is not seriously at odds with this interpretation. Given the 'ownership' of most of its dialogue, as noted in the preceding paragraph, only a 'degraded Augustanism' could suffice to carry it so far towards the other early novels. While Jane Austen's more Augustan dialogue can best be seen in Henry Tilney, Elinor Dashwood, Brandon, and Darcy, some of its characteristics can be seen in Catherine Morland and even in the cheap stylishness of Isabella Thorpe. They emerge, for example, from a close comparison of Catherine's idiolect with those of Lady Bertram and Harriet Smith, her neighbours of Graph 14.

[2] My original decision to exclude 'an' rested upon the fact, long recognized in the study of literary statistics, that the incidence of 'an' rarely corresponds (at its lower level) with that of 'a': 'an' tends to be associated with adjectives and nouns that bear Latinate prefixes and, accordingly, to run high in more formal kinds of prose.

TABLE 13. The Whole Dialogue of Twelve Novels

		ALL											
1	*Northanger Abbey*	97	*NA*										
2	*Sense and Sensibility*	99	95	*SS*									
3	*Pride and Prejudice*	99	95	98	*PP*								
4	*Mansfield Park*	99	95	97	97	*MP*							
5	*Emma*	99	97	98	97	98	*E*						
6	*Persuasion*	98	93	97	97	97	97	*P*					
7	'Sanditon'	89	82	87	88	92	87	92	*S1*				
8	*Sanditon 2*	96	92	95	95	96	94	96	93	*S2*			
9	*Frederica*	91	95	88	90	88	92	87	70	86	*F*		
10	*The Waves*	73	63	71	73	77	69	78	92	79	51	*TW*	
11	*The Awkward Age*	86	91	83	84	84	86	79	66	81	94	48	*AA*
12	*Howards End*	92	95	89	89	92	92	88	79	89	93	67	93

The modified frequency-hierarchy yields Table 13, the correlation-matrix (presented in the abbreviated form) for the 'whole dialogue' of the twelve novels; and this, in turn, yields the eigen-map of Graph 21.

Just as Graph 20 isolated *Northanger Abbey* from Jane Austen's other novels, especially in the first projection, so Graph 21 sets *The Waves* apart from all the rest. Its extreme remoteness is brought out by considering how slight a distance now separates *Northanger Abbey* from *Emma*. We have moved from a map on which Gravesend stands far from Wimbledon and Richmond to one that also includes Coventry or Chester.

The Waves, of course, is marked off by the fact that, while its self-absorbed meditations are couched in a kind of direct speech, they are scarcely touched by the ordinary give-and-take of dialogue. The pronouns 'you' and 'your' slide far down the frequency-hierarchy and make a simple illustration of a pervasive set of differences. Taken on their own, the characters of *The Waves* are aptly differentiated from each other. Taken in comparison with those of other novels, they huddle uneasily together. Collins, alas, is much the least distant from them of Jane Austen's major characters: but theirs is 'formality' of another kind.

There is no more than a shallow paradox in the fact that 'Sanditon' stands so much further from the main group of Jane Austen's novels than does *Sanditon 2*, the Other Lady's imitation. In terms of the size of their idiolects, the manuscript fragment lacks a hero and scarcely has a heroine: Charlotte has only 562 words and Sidney Parker only 38. The characters whose idiolects make up almost the entirety of its dialogue and give it so idiosyncratic a shape range from egoists to monomaniacs; and most of them pay only enough attention

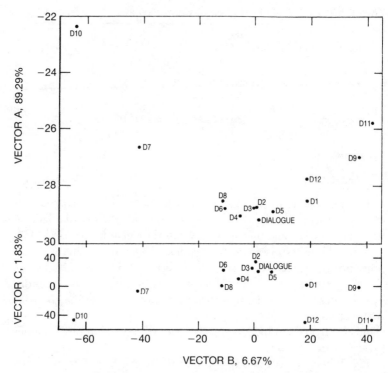

GRAPH 21. The Dialogue of Twelve Novels
(Word-types 1–30 of Jane Austen's dialogue including their contracted forms)

to what others say to ensure a prompt recapture of the
'conversational' initiative. The inevitable effect is to carry 'Sanditon'
some distance towards *The Waves*, where uninterrupted discourse
serves other purposes than those of Jane Austen's unfinished satire,
splendid in its absurdity, on the 'new men' and 'old women' — not
always different people — of a score of little Brightons.

As was noted much earlier, the Other Lady effects a creditable
imitation but errs always on the side of caution and 'normality'. One
necessary kind of normalizing lies, of course, in her introducing a
hero and giving the heroine a more adequate part. But each of them,
along with the rest, broadly resembles a Jane Austen 'type' while
lacking the individuality of any of the originals. (Her Mr Parker is
nearest to the mark, her Lady Denham furthest from it. Her Charlotte
is too like a Lucy/Isabella. And Sidney Parker's idiolect is that of

a *more* ponderous Edmund Bertram.) The overall effect is to locate the dialogue of *Sanditon 2* at the fringe of the group of Jane Austen's novels, about as far from the 'DIALOGUE' entry in one direction as *Northanger Abbey* is in the other. The most noteworthy variation in any of the idiolects arises when Charlotte is abducted by Sir Edward Denham and, unabashed, proceeds to tell him what she thinks of him and to gull him into driving in the direction of her home. In this episode, undeniably, she departs somewhat from her usual style of speech. A detailed analysis of characteristic specimens, in the manner described at the end of Chapter 5, readily distinguishes the Other Lady's dialogue from Jane Austen's. With these things said, the case requires no more. The Other Lady comments that her completion of the manuscript was intended not for 'literary critics' but 'for the lay readers of Jane Austen' (*Sanditon 2*, p. 326). Her close knowledge of and obvious devotion to Jane Austen's novels enable her to serve those readers well.

Howards End, *Frederica*, and *The Awkward Age* all lie in the opposite direction from the novels already mentioned. Little study is required to see that, in Forster generally and at this stage of James's career, dialogue usually consists in interchange and that few characters are given much opportunity to hold the floor. Without having known quite what to expect, I regard the location of *Frederica* as appropriate. While Georgette Heyer's dialogue may be closer to Jane Austen's in broad generic and overt thematic terms, Forster's is more akin to Jane Austen's in spirit and in the concealed exactitudes of language. And, though *Washington Square* and *The Europeans* might well yield results even more like Jane Austen's, the James of the late 1890s had begun to play a different game.

To turn to the second projection of Graph 21 is to see one of the most remarkable patterns of all. The north–south axis, Vector C, aligns the three more directly modern novels (including *The Waves*!) at the foot; the two modern pieces of Regency pastiche some distance above them; and the majority of Jane Austen's novels above them again, with *Sense and Sensibility* at the head. Without being aligned precisely as they were on the corresponding axis of Graph 20, Jane Austen's Chawton novels (and 'Sanditon' also) still lie a trifle below *Sense and Sensibility* and *Pride and Prejudice*. Only *Northanger Abbey* fails, presumably for reasons already offered, to meet the earlier suggestion that Vector C registers a *progressive* relaxation, an increase of conversational fluency, in the style of dialogue. If it

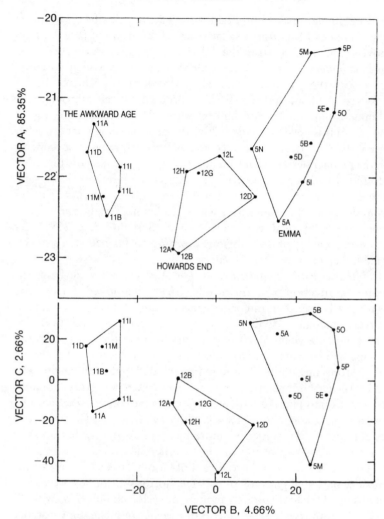

GRAPH 22. The Major Characters of Three Novels
(Word-types 1-30 of Jane Austen's dialogue including their contracted forms)

were to prove that, in spite of their generic differences — and in spite of an occasional *Northanger Abbey* — a larger assortment of novels fell into a similar historical succession, the general pattern would justify a closer analysis of historical changes in and *as reflected in* the common stuff of dialogue. That is a daring proposal, based on too few cases: but on every occasion on which it has been practicable to test a striking pattern in the figures, the pattern has held its shape and a meaningful result has emerged.

The last few pages have shown that local combinations of idiolects, differences between novelist and novelist (whether in their imaginative capacities or in their generic preferences), and a possible historical tendency in prose style can all be discerned and, to some extent, distinguished from each other when the whole dialogue of a dozen novels is compared. Graph 22 is designed to test these distinctions more rigorously by offering comparisons among the twenty-one major characters of three novels that stand comparatively close to each other in Graph 21: *Emma*, *Howards End*, and *The Awkward Age*.[3] The 'ALL' column has been left out of the reckoning to allow the twenty-one idiolects to find their own locations, free of the constraint of an overriding norm.

The most striking feature of Graph 22 is that, in both of its projections, the characters of each novel make a distinct 'family group', attesting to underlying differences between novelist and novelist in the style of dialogue. In the first projection, it is true, Helen Schlegel is not far removed from Emma. Mr Weston— influenced, as ever, by a promiscuous 'open-heartedness' (*Emma*, p. 320)?—strays towards Leonard Bast and Mrs Munt. But, as the second projection indicates, these are not pervasive resemblances. In both projections, to take another general point, the characters of *Emma* cover a larger area than those of the other novelists. That remains true even if Harriet and Mr Woodhouse, the most sharply differentiated of all, are shut out of mind. Any of Jane Austen's first three novels would cover a larger area again.

The statistical dynamics of eigen-mapping bear Margaret Schlegel and Mr Wilcox towards the lower centre of the first projection. (If the

[3] This sample is offered, also, as a manageable and not unrepresentative illustration of interrelationships among the eighty-one major characters of the whole twelve novels. To correlate each of 81 with each of the other 80 yields 3240 coefficients and a revealing but intolerably over-burdened eigen-map. The vast distances it spans require small-scale mapping: yet many of the idiolects are so closely grouped as to call for an ampler scale.

As Graph 21 would suggest, the characters of 'Sanditon' and *The Waves* lie far removed from the rest. Those of the other four novels mostly lie around the fringes of Jane Austen's main group, congregating, especially, just outside a line running from Fanny Price to Miss Bates in Graph 14. Of the few who approach the lower centre of Graph 14, 'Sidney Parker' can be taken as a successful imitation. No other character enters the inner circle of Jane Austen's heroes and heroines.

'ALL' entry were allowed its influence, both *Howards End* and *The Awkward Age* would be driven towards the western side of the map and the gap between them and *Emma* would be increased.) A sustained development, unusual in the 'other novels', causes Margaret's idiolect to 'average down' to the lower centre. It is fluctuation, rather than development or an unexpected affinity of style, that sets Mr Wilcox beside Margaret. (The point will be taken up again in Chapter 10.) Beyond that, their proximity to each other reflects the influence of countervailing pressures from *The Awkward Age* and *Emma*—and especially from characters who do not much resemble either of them.

The relativism of these methods of comparison is even more evident elsewhere in Graph 22. Notwithstanding an intellectual inferiority in which they are well matched, Harriet and Mr Woodhouse do not much resemble each other. (Their correlation-coefficient is 0.798 for the thirty most common words and 0.796 when the contracted forms are included.) But, because each of them is even less like most of the characters of James and Forster, they stand close together at the upper margin in the first projection of Graph 22. The correlation between Emma and Mr Knightley rises negligibly from 0.958 to 0.959 when the contracted forms are included. But, because she bears a closer resemblance than he to the characters of James and Forster, their own correlation is made somewhat 'anomalous' and they stand further apart than usual.

The immediate discomfort of anomalies like these can easily be assuaged: Vector C, in the second projection, brings Emma and Mr Knightley back together and restores the distance between Harriet and Mr Woodhouse. It is better, however, to press upon the thorn and learn from the discomfort. In one of the more enduring though less original of their doctrines, the structuralist critics of the sixties and early seventies did well to insist that relativisim need not be untruth. (Whether relativism is the only not-untruth is quite another question.[4]) Presumably a set of characters from Beckett or Fielding

---

[4] To recognize that 'near' and 'far', or 'tall' and 'short', are relative terms is only to maintain that altered 'bench-marks' do affect comparisons and that it is important to know what 'bench-marks' are being used. It is not, of itself, to argue that a brick ceases entirely to be a brick when it is used as a door-stop. It is certainly not to argue that all customs and opinions are of equal or indistinguishable merit or that 'merit' has no useful meaning. Consider the occasion when Miss Bates goes on from 'our good Mrs. Elton' to describe her as 'the most indefatigable, true friend. She would not take a denial. She would not let Jane say "No"' (p. 380). Is there a reader of

would have even more 'anomalous' effects upon the shape of a map like Graph 22: as a representation of *systematic* resemblances and differences throughout a correlation-matrix, the map would not be the worse. It might seem so, of course, to those who enshrine statistical analysis—like Conrad's women-characters—among those deities they do not care to think about. But, like other instruments of complex interpretation, statistical analysis cannot help us to see until we bring our minds to bear.

The 'historical' ordering of the idiolects in Vector C gains in subtlety and force when its relativism is acknowledged. The most 'correct' speakers of each novel lie at the upper extremity of their respective sets. But, through the passage of three-quarters of a century, the 'correctness' of Mr Knightley, the Westons, and Emma—relaxed as it is by Jane Austen's earlier standards—leaves them almost isolated at the head of Vector C. Their stylistic register is no longer approached by the Schlegels or even Mr Longdon but rather by the Duchess and Mrs Brookenham, grotesquerie in the one and affectation in the other. At the lower extremity, where Leonard Bast and Harriet Smith lie far beyond the rest, Harriet's idiolect is aptly registered as even less consonant with the general tone of her novel than Leonard's is with his. The dialogue of novelists like Iris Murdoch and Anthony Powell— *Hearing Secret Harmonies*, perhaps, comes nearest to the usage of our time—would shed light on more recent changes. And yet, relative to the linguistic standards of the 1980s, even *their* more relaxed speakers might emerge as old-fashioned and 'correct'.

II
COMPARISONS BETWEEN DIALOGUE AND NARRATIVE

At the moment, early in life, when anyone first senses a difference between 'Once upon a time . . .' and 'Grandmamma, what great teeth you have got!', he begins to discover that, besides the interplay of dialogue, the language of fiction is usually characterized by the interplay of dialogue and narrative.

Emma who thinks the better, for this, of Mrs Elton? Whether to think the worse of Miss Bates is a more difficult question, embracing such considerations as her ignorance of Jane's real situation, her experience of the poverty from which Jane may now be saved, her ever-generous construction of other people's behaviour—and her complete incapacity to imagine that anyone might be as Mrs Elton is.

I have written a little more extensively on such matters in '"A Measure of Excellence": Modes of Comparison in *Pride and Prejudice*', *Sydney Studies in English*, v (1979–80), 38–59.

Narrative (at least in the familiar mode that comes down from ballads and fairy-tales to Jane Austen and some more recent fiction) is most visibly distinguished from dialogue by tense-changes in the verbs and changes of person in the pronouns. But that visible distinction is so strongly marked as to conceal other, more interesting differences in—and as reflected in—the incidence of the very common words. If the frequency-hierarchy of the common words in the whole of each novel of Jane Austen's is compared with the corresponding hierarchy in each of the other five, the results show unexpected resemblances between *Sense and Sensibility* and *Emma*, on the one hand, and between *Northanger Abbey* and *Mansfield Park* on the other. These implausible results derive from nothing more interesting than that the proportion of narrative to dialogue runs decidedly lower in the former pair.

To attempt more rational comparisons between dialogue and narrative, it is necessary, as a first step, to establish a fresh word-list. In replacing 'the thirty most common words of Jane Austen's dialogue' by 'the thirty most common words of Jane Austen's literary vocabulary', I have also taken the opportunity to assess what happens when the homographic forms are *not* separated and each 'word-type' is taken at face-value: 'to' (inf.) and 'to' (prep.) are now united as 'to'; the distinct forms of 'that' are all made one; and so on. For the purpose of close linguistic analysis that amounts to a (temporary) suppression of information. But, so great is the 'tensile strength' of the linguistic 'force-field' that the broader statistical comparisons between idiolect and idiolect are not greatly affected by the change. The new list of thirty word-types is as follows, its incidences calculated in relation to the 709,917 words that make up the six novels:

37.06	the	15.08	in	10.32	he*	6.68	at
33.61	to	14.41	it	9.92	as	6.68	is*
31.60	and	14.37	she*	9.21	for	5.48	all
29.81	of	12.07	not	8.43	his*	5.31	very
18.72	a	11.50	be	8.33	with	5.13	him*
18.52	her*	11.45	that	8.27	but	5.08	could*
16.98	I*	10.88	you*	7.42	have*	4.93	by
15.79	was*	10.32	had*				

A correlation-matrix, based on this list, in which the six frequency-hierarchies for the 'whole dialogue' and the six for the 'whole narrative' of Jane Austen's novels are compared, yields the obvious result. The coefficients of dialogue with dialogue range from 0.944 to 0.985. Those of narrative with narrative range from 0.966 to 0.993. *But* those in which narrative and dialogue come together range from 0.133 to 0.453. An eigen-map derived from this matrix is like a geographical map in which London and Paris are both to be shown—but on a scale that allows the suburbs of each city to be distinguished.

The asterisked words in the list are the most common of the 'deictics', words that directly express such relationships as those of time and person; words that are most directly affected by the universally acknowledged, highly visible, and all-consuming point of contrast between dialogue and the most familiar mode of narrative; words whose frequency-patterns are changed utterly by the simple shift from 'I am ready, if the others are' to 'She said that she was ready, if the others were'. If the twelve asterisked words are excluded, a correlation-matrix based on the remaining eighteen will reflect any subtler differences between dialogue and narrative and (on my 'force-field' hypothesis) will not fail to reflect the residual effects of the words that are excluded. Although the results are less pronounced, they are far more revealing. The coefficients of dialogue with dialogue are scarcely altered, ranging from 0.938 to 0.991. Those of narrative with narrative, likewise, still range from 0.974 to 0.997. But those in which narrative and dialogue are brought together *now* range from 0.778 to 0.947. An eigen-map, which I have not reproduced, now assumes a manageable scale and shows the six sets of dialogue ranged out along one wing, the six sets of narrative more closely grouped along the other. By virtue of the two highest correlations between narrative and dialogue, it shows—near the point where the two wings meet—that the dialogue of *Persuasion* and that of *Mansfield Park* have a good deal in common with the narrative of *Emma*. (At those points, of course, the correlations between dialogue and narrative—0.947 and 0.933, respectively—have reached the level of the lowest correlations between dialogue and dialogue.) On closer inspection of the matrix, it emerges that the eventual overlapping is the culmination of a steady, though not perfectly regular, development over the course of Jane Austen's literary career.

This increasing affinity between narrative and dialogue arises chiefly from the fact that, in the hands of some novelists—the later Jane Austen notable among them—the 'familiar mode of narrative' to which I have referred has more than one constituent. Without venturing far into the realms of 'narratology' (where *common* words are rare), we must now take account of the distinction, touched on in the Introduction of this study, between 'pure narrative' and 'character narrative'. In such novels as Jane Austen's, the narrator not only performs the conventional functions of supplying necessary information, shaping and pacing the action, and commenting on the characters' ideas, but also renders the thoughts of the characters, especially the heroines. At its simplest, as in Georgette Heyer's *Frederica*, character narrative can scarcely be distinguished from dialogue except in its observance of the forms of indirect speech. At its subtlest, as in *Mansfield Park*, *Emma*, and *Persuasion*, it affords the heroines something like 'second idiolects', more—or less—akin to their speech-idiolects but adapted to the expression of ideas too private or, as frequently in Emma's case, too outrageous for open utterance. These complexities will be considered in due course.

For the moment, it need only be recognized that character narrative has a far greater share in the narrative of Jane Austen's Chawton novels than in *Sense and Sensibility* or *Pride and Prejudice*. On my reckoning, character narrative amounts to about a fifth of all Jane Austen's narrative: but the proportion rises from less than 5 per cent in *Sense and Sensibility* and 10 per cent in *Pride and Prejudice* to almost a third in *Mansfield Park* and *Emma*.[5] In *Mansfield Park*, characters other than the heroine have unusually large shares of character narrative. In both *Mansfield Park* and *Persuasion*, the character narratives of the heroines are considerably larger than their spoken parts. Fanny speaks 6117 words and, on my reckoning, 'thinks' 15,418. For Anne, it is 4336 as against 5667. But, for Emma, it is 21,501 as against 19,730. Another reader might well include a greater part of *Persuasion* in Anne's character narrative: while the general distinction between pure narrative and character narrative holds good, there are passages—as on the walk to Winthrop—where it is more than usually difficult to sustain and where the moments of transition from one mode to the other are very lightly marked.

---

[5] The figures for 'character narrative' rest, of course, on no more objective foundation than my capacity to recognize the 'cues' that Jane Austen offers when she turns from one mode of narrative to the other. While this is not a matter in which any two readers would arrive at identical results, the *general* efficacy of the distinction (made possible by Jane Austen's exactitude) is put beyond question by the separateness of the three sets of entries in Graph 23.

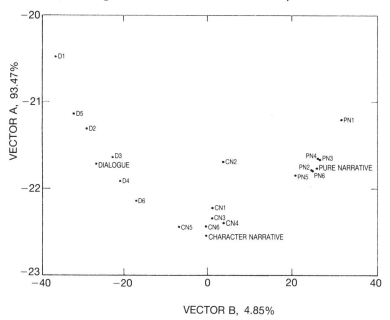

GRAPH 23. Major Components of Jane Austen's Novels
(Non-deictic word-types 1-18 of her literary vocabulary)

Once again *Northanger Abbey* is *sui generis*. Though it is managed in a comparatively simple way and though Catherine's thoughts do not *seem* to differ much from what she is prepared to say, character narrative does play a larger part (15 per cent) than in the other early novels. In *Sense and Sensibility* and in *Pride and Prejudice*, I suggest, the comparative dearth of character narrative arises from the fact that the ideas of Elinor and Elizabeth do not need to be distanced so firmly as those of Catherine. If that point is granted, it is not difficult to accept that, in those novels, there is seldom an inescapable requirement for anything more than a running commentary on what the heroine is thinking. With Fanny and Emma, in their different ways, the requirement is inescapable; and Jane Austen's art attunes itself to a new demand. With Anne, in turn, subtler requirements call for yet subtler attunements.

The analysis of these matters should begin with a plain demonstration that, when pure narrative and character narrative are distinguished from each other, the three main component parts of Jane Austen's kind of novel enter into thoroughly appropriate statistical relationships and occupy convincing locations in an eigen-map. Graph 23, I believe, is adequate to that task. The discriminations among the three constituents are so uniform and so exact that Vector A accounts for 93.47 per cent and Vector B for a further 4.85 per cent of the interrelationships in the correlation-matrix from which they are derived. (It would be idle, in those circumstances, to give any space to Vector C: 0.65 per cent.) The twenty-one entries in the map fall into distinct clusters, with no suggestion of an overlap at any point.

Despite the considerable changes in the word-list, from the thirty most common words of dialogue to the eighteen most common non-deictic words in Jane Austen's literary vocabulary, the entries for dialogue preserve much the same relationship among themselves as was discussed in the preceding section of this chapter. The entries for character narrative form a closely-knit group save that the brief and simply rendered character narrative of *Sense and Sensibility* is forced some way into the no man's land reserved for that which (like the speech-idiolect of Wickham) is neither one thing nor another. The entries for pure narrative are even more closely grouped save that *Northanger Abbey* shows itself as more formal than the rest. The extreme distance between PN1 and D1, the pure narrative and the dialogue of that novel, shows, yet again, that it deals in stronger contrasts than do Jane Austen's later novels. While it is even more pronounced, this contrast between pure narrative and dialogue is along just such lines as the contrast between Henry and Catherine.

When the corresponding frequency-hierarchies for the three component-parts of our 'other novels' are to be compared with those for Jane Austen, *The Waves* must be excluded. As any reader of that novel is aware, the choric voice of its 'narrative' sections bears little resemblance to ordinary narrative and there is no equivalent of character narrative.[6] If the hierarchy of its narrative-frequencies for the eighteen commonest non-deictic words is correlated with the

---

[6] What of the possibility that, as a rendering of the characters' thought-processes, the 'dialogue' of *The Waves* has something in common with Jane Austen's character narrative? If the deictic words are set aside, that line of comparison proves to have a place. As compared with the eighteen-word hierarchy for Jane Austen's dialogue, the 'dialogue' of *The Waves* yields a coefficient of 0.717. But, as compared with the corresponding hierarchy for her character narrative, it yields a coefficient of 0.837. Such possibilities might usefully be pursued by a critic whose chief interest was in the novels of Virginia Woolf.

corresponding hierarchies for the narrative, whole or 'pure', of the other novels, the average coefficient is about 0.83. Much as Forster's and James's narrative styles differ from Jane Austen's and from each other, 0.90 is an unusually low coefficient in such correlations as these; and, among Jane Austen's own narratives, as was mentioned earlier, 0.97 is as low as any of the coefficients run. The only relevance of *The Waves*, therefore, in this phase of the inquiry, lies in its unequivocal demonstration that, even though they are applied to only eighteen 'inert' word-types, the present methods of analysis suffice to locate it, appropriately, in a territory of its own.

The character narrative entries for 'Sanditon' and *The Awkward Age* might also have been excluded and, suggestive as they are, should not be given undue weight. On my reckoning, the former includes only 1211 words of character narrative, of which a thousand are divided almost equally between Charlotte and Mr Parker. The latter includes only 1303, spread widely among the leading characters. Over the long course of his literary career, James takes an increasing interest in the possibilities of character narrative. In the Preface to the New York edition of *The Portrait of a Lady*, for example, looking back across a quarter of a century, he singles out Chapter 42, the rendering of Isabel's melancholy vigil, as 'obviously the best thing in the book' (p. xxi). And Strether, Milly Theale, and Maggie Verver are reminders enough of the weight laid on an exceedingly complex form of character narrative in the novels of his last phase. In *The Awkward Age*, however, an unusually marked recourse to dialogue seems to drive character narrative from the centre of the action; and, dialogue aside, the rhythm of the pure narrative is not often broken except by some passages (which I have not separated out into a further category) treating of what 'an observer . . . might have fancied' (p. 130) or what 'another person present might have felt' (p. 269).

Graph 24, then, adds four novels and a fragment to Jane Austen's six. To make the picture clearer, the entries for Jane Austen are not labelled individually: within each of her three groups and between group and group, the interrelationships are very close to those of Graph 23. And the overall entries, marked 'DIALOGUE', 'CHARACTER NARRATIVE', and 'PURE NARRATIVE', each surrounded by the appropriate set of six individual reference-points, attest to the *comparative* uniformity of her artistic practices over the course of her literary career.

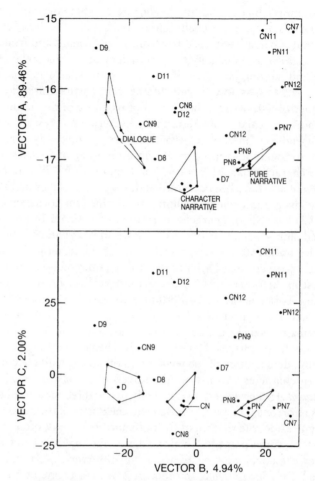

GRAPH 24. Major Components of Eleven Novels
(Non-deictic word-types 1-18 of Jane Austen's literary vocabulary)

As the first projection of the map indicates, the other novels most resemble hers in the broad distinction between dialogue and pure narrative. None of the entries for pure narrative strays towards those for dialogue: in three cases of the five, indeed, the pure narrative is in some sense 'purer' than Jane Austen's, a point to which I shall return. The entries for dialogue adhere less closely to the alignment of the dialogue 'wing'. But, while the dialogue of *Howards End* lies in no man's land, only the dialogue of 'Sanditon' penetrates into the territory of narrative. Its proximity to character narrative is further evidence that those characters do not converse but merely express their *idées fixes* aloud.

Its location also sheds light on the widely scattered entries for character narrative in the 'other' novels. In both *Frederica* and *Sanditon 2*, dialogue and character narrative are less sharply distinguished from each other than in all the rest. The relative locations of D9 and CN9, and of D8 and CN8, indicate—as is in fact the case—that Georgette Heyer and the Other Lady, especially the former, offer only a rudimentary form of character narrative, lacking in real inwardness and assuming the shape of that which, though not spoken, might very well be spoken. Among all the rest, *Sense and Sensibility* has the only character narrative that lies in the general vicinity of CN8 and CN9.

At the opposite extremity, so far as the numbers bear analysis, stand 'Sanditon' and *The Awkward Age*. The location of their character narratives at the tip of the north-eastern wing can best be understood when the other inhabitants of that neighbourhood are also called to witness. The presence there of the pure narrative of *Howards End* discountenances the simple interpretation that, in 'Sanditon' and *The Awkward Age*, it merely *happens* that pure narrative and character narrative are not very clearly differentiated. A sounder interpretation, I believe, lies in a characteristic that takes these five entries beyond the usual boundaries of the formal, the impersonal, the disquisitive, and makes them the polar opposites of the dialogue of *Frederica* and *Northanger Abbey*. In their different ways—as the map shows, they are not identical to each other— they are all marked by an uncommon generality of subject, an uncommon meditativeness of expression, ranging from the satirical generalities of the pure narrative of 'Sanditon' to the attempts, by James's characters, to grasp what 'it all means'. In Forster's pure narrative, in his character narrative, and even—less strongly—in his dialogue, the generalizing strain spreads out from comments on St Pancras or on what will become of Wickham Place or of a countryside into which 'London's creeping' to troubled thoughts about the poor and oppressed and troubled meditations on England's future.

If that is a valid interpretation, it accounts for the fact that character narrative of this more generalizing kind lies even further from dialogue than does pure narrative. Save in cases as unusual as *The Waves*, the generalizing strain in pure narrative is offset by the requirements of that other language in which the action is carried forward. (Even in *The Waves*, 'Bernard said', 'said Louis', and the like take up 476 of the five thousand words of narrative.) If it is a valid interpretation, it can well make its presence felt in the statistics by a disturbance in the ordinary frequency-relationships between the definite and indefinite articles on the one hand and the pronouns, excluded but not deprived of all influence, on the other; in the residual effects of the excluded auxiliary verbs; and, perhaps above all, in a higher than usual recourse to prepositions and the more 'formalizing' of the connectives. A different kind of sentence-shape has widespread effects: and a number of memorable passages in *Northanger Abbey*, not often matched in Jane Austen's later novels, show those effects, those sentence-shapes, at work. The raillery of the opening pages; the stalwart defence of the novel as a respectable literary form; the reminder that novelist, reader, and principal characters 'are all hastening together to perfect felicity' (p. 250); the final question 'to be settled by whomsoever it may concern, whether the tendency of this work be altogether to recommend parental tyranny, or reward filial disobedience' (p. 252): these passages and others like them contribute to the fact that, notwithstanding its light-heartedness, the pure narrative of *Northanger Abbey* lies nearer to the generalizing style than any other main component of Jane Austen's six novels. And, finally, if this interpretation has any validity about it, it might well encourage a student of narrative method to refine on my simple distinction between pure narrative and character narrative. Once he had completed the arduous task of differentiating, case by case and as consistently as possible, between narrative passages of several distinguishable kinds, he would be well placed to examine large questions of 'narratology' with an unusual precision.

In Graph 24, then, Vector A maintains its usual role of showing the succession from the most to the least 'normal' members of the set. Vector B confirms, but increases the force of, earlier distinctions between formal and informal extremities. But Vector C, in the second projection of the map, takes on a new and revealing function. For, on the north–south axis of the second projection, the several components of each novel find something like common ground. The three topmost entries are those for *The Awkward Age*, the next three for *Howards End*, and the next for *Frederica*. The pattern holds good for Jane Austen but is broken a little by the entries for 'Sanditon' and *Sanditon 2*. Whatever the internal differences of 'tone' or 'stance', 'style' or 'subject' between components, the map displays the presence of a Jamesian, a Forsterian, an Austenian quiddity in their respective novels. The same truth even holds good for the narrative components of 'Sanditon' and—almost—for its dialogue. Meanwhile the historical dimension, discernible in earlier maps, has been driven down among the lesser vectors by the more energetic presence, in the correlation-matrix, of these 'authorial' resemblances between component and component.

Considered in retrospect, therefore, the evidence of this chapter suggests that, for historical analyses of prose style, it may prove best to compare dialogue with dialogue, narrative with narrative. But, for studies in attribution or authentication, a valuable corroborative effect may be obtainable when several distinct components of a work are taken side by side. Such possibilities need more extensive testing, over a wider range of writing. For the central purposes of the present study, however, it is time to resume the analysis of Jane Austen's novels. While that analysis is consolidated by a range of larger comparisons, the exactness of her effects is obscured by comparisons in which, by virtue of their common difference from the work of other novelists, her novels are made to look one like another. The differences among her six pure narratives afford an excellent case in point. Relieved of the cross-pressures from the pure narrative of other novelists and from her own dialogue and character narrative, the six pure narratives move away from each other and form a small but illuminating map. When it is derived from the thirty most common words of all—the whole of our new set—that map places Jane Austen's six pure narratives in what is usually regarded as their order of composition. *Northanger Abbey* and *Sense and Sensibility* lie, not far out, along the north-eastern wing. *Pride and Prejudice* and *Mansfield Park* lie either side of the lower centre. And *Emma* and *Persuasion*, on the north-western wing, perfect the symmetry of Graph 25.

When the major thought-idiolects are separated from the main body of character narrative and examined in their own right, the results are even more persuasive. With the exception of Elinor Dashwood, whose 'thinking' runs to 1976 words, the characters included in Graph 26 are all those who have more than two thousand words of character narrative apiece. The whole set consists of the

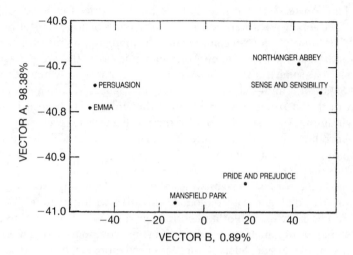

GRAPH 25. Jane Austen's Six 'Pure Narratives'
(Word-types 1–30 of her literary vocabulary)

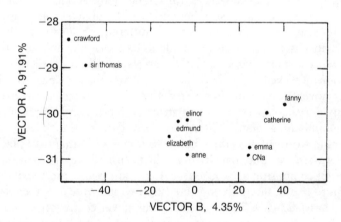

GRAPH 26. Jane Austen's Chief 'Thought-Idiolects'
(Word-types 1–30 of her literary vocabulary)

six heroines, Henry Crawford, Edmund Bertram, and Sir Thomas. The other entry on the map, CNa, is for the six heroines treated as a group.

As the last in a series of maps characterized by appropriate distinctions between character and character, narrative and narrative, novel and novel, Graph 26 may not display its full potency at first sight. What else might be expected (by now) than that Crawford and Sir Thomas should be the polar opposites of Catherine and Fanny? That Anne should stand at the 'true centre' (as distinct from CNa, whose location is much influenced by the very large thought-idiolects of Emma and Fanny)? That Anne should be the innermost of a little group from which Elinor is technically—and Emma imaginatively?—displaced? That, in the second projection of the map, which I have not reproduced, the characters of *Mansfield Park* should be nicely aligned on Vector C, with Emma and Anne located nearby as their fellows in a 'Chawton style' of character narrative while the three earlier heroines stand some way apart? Taking all that for granted, one might attend rather to such unexpected details as Crawford's lying even further out than Sir Thomas. The reason is that Sir Thomas's thoughts are most extensively rendered in the closing pages of the novel when he tries to understand why three of his children have gone so much amiss and, humbly and frankly, accepts his own share of the blame. Crawford's thoughts, on the other hand, bear chiefly on his attempt to 'excite the first ardours of her [Fanny's] young, unsophisticated mind' (pp. 235–6) and on the consequences of that attempt. It is Crawford, rather than Sir Thomas, who thinks *de haut en bas*.

But these things are not what Graph 26 most notably displays. Its real force is as an illustration of the capacities of genius. In differentiating among thought-idiolects, Jane Austen's characterization extends into regions where she has few, if any, predecessors in English fiction. The distinctions drawn there lack even a speech-idiolect's foundation in the cut-and-thrust of dialogue. They are measured only in their effects upon the distribution of the most common words. And the very accuracy of the distribution is contingent upon a reader's ability to recognize the tiny cues that mark the transitions from commentary on to rendering of the thoughts of the characters. These impediments notwithstanding, Jane Austen's sense of language is so delicate and so exact that the set of thought-idiolects assumes a pattern as compelling as any we have seen.

Part Three

LIVELY MEASURES

O chestnut-tree, great-rooted blossomer,
Are you the leaf, the blossom, or the bole?
O body swayed to music, O brightening glance,
How can we know the dancer from the dance?

W. B. Yeats, 'Among School Children'

9

Changes of Mode and
Differences of Aspect

I

Although Part Three can only be a coda to the present study, I hope that it may serve as the overture of future work, not merely of my own, in which the broad integrity of literary idiolects and the fact that they are often sharply differentiated from each other can be taken as a point of departure and in which there is less need to establish that the very common words make a useful (but, *ex hypothesi*, not the only useful) way of approaching them. The very uncommon words, for example, may lead by different paths to similar conclusions. Of all those word-types that occur only once apiece in *Northanger Abbey*, an overwhelming majority belong to the narrator. Of the remainder, however, a not dissimilar proportion belong to Henry Tilney.

To choose Yeats's noble lines as an epigraph is, first, to indicate that, with Jane Austen's major characters suitably disposed about the dance-floor, it is almost time to allow the music to begin. It is to imply a deliberate analogy between the dynamics of the language, 'the stream of words', and the rhythms of a musical performance. And, in the light of evidence already offered and shortly to be offered, it is to suggest that, suitably developed, statistical analysis may provide a way through a central and long-recognized impasse in literary criticism to firmer ground beyond.

The dancer, most of us acknowledge, can tell us little of her art save in the very act of dancing: yet the dance itself remains an abstraction until the dancer gives it life, form, substance. When we regard the author as dancer (rather than choreographer?) and consult *her*, we turn from literary criticism towards literary biography and background studies—and do not always return. Our efforts to describe the dance usually result in heavy-footed paraphrase. When we single out particular motifs or pluck rare figures of rhetoric from their proper habitat, we tend to elevate the part above the whole. When, working in a larger frame of reference, we compare one dance with another (and thus, perhaps, set up a 'great tradition', trace out a 'line of wit', or seek 'new bearings'), we are hard put to prevent broad resemblances from obscuring subtle differences. Among our best critics, as with Coleridge's ideal poet, a 'judgement ever awake and steady self-possession',[1] manifesting itself in a continuing awareness of what criticism entails, has done much to alleviate such difficulties. Better to emulate those critics, so far as we are able, than to preserve a supposed purity of response in unchallengeable silence. And better that than — weary of walking on the razor's edge? — to join in the brisk new game of 'deconstruction' in which the (admitted) rights of the reader are so enlarged as to supplant the hard-earned privileges of the author; in which the fact that the music of the past cannot be recovered in its entirety becomes an argument for resetting it, entirely, to the tempos of our day; and in which the belief that Jane Austen's novels are *better* than those of Barbara Cartland, Judith Krantz, or Thomas Keneally is dismissed as a 'high-literary' affectation or an exercise in cultural politics.

Suppose it were possible, however, to register the changing postures of the dancers themselves and the very rhythms of the dance; to follow the dance through its successive phases or compare one phase with another; to redefine the chosen phases, mark new moments of transition, and begin again; to see what differences ensue when the music alters; to trace a particular gesture without losing sight of the larger pattern; or even to stop the action and inspect a single 'frozen frame'. Suppose it were possible, too, to show that some music is merely derivative and that some takes advantage only of the most obvious potentialities of the medium.

The central doctrine of organic unity, that form and content are inseparable constituents of the whole, might then be assessed on its merits as a doctrine without remaining an impasse. In terms of the comparative frequency-distributions of different types of cell and of their interrelationships, a botanist *can* determine whether 'the leaf, the blossom, or the bole' is under the microscope at any given moment and can establish, at a high level of probability, whether his specimens have the distinctive characteristics of chestnut, eucalypt, or elm. Even at the points of transition, he can show that a particular section is more or less leaf-like than another.

---

[1] S. T. Coleridge, *Biographia Literaria*, ed. J. Shawcross, vol. ii (London, 1907), p. 12.

Accordingly, it is seldom if ever necessary for him to attempt impossibilities, seeking 'pure' specimens or constructing mutually exclusive categories. For the purposes of literary criticism, likewise, we can accept that, while 'form' and 'content' may not be absolutely separable, they are not entirely indistinguishable. We need not even give up the use of terms like 'form' and 'content'; 'grammatical' and 'lexical'; 'action' and 'character' and 'theme'. We need only acknowledge that our pleasant vice of categorizing is of our own making and is not *sent* as an instrument to plague us.

On the evidence already offered in this study, the differing configurations of the very common words—whether the more lexically oriented, the more grammatically oriented, or both taken indifferently—make remarkably accurate epitomes of the differences between one 'style' and another. If that conclusion held good across a wider range of literary texts, then statistical analysis, suitably refined, might well become an instrument that would make it possible to realize the suppositions I have described. The measures illustrated in earlier chapters show how the more static of them might be approached. Whenever a sufficient body of words is available, the more dynamic of them are made feasible by a form of correlation known as 'time-series analysis'. We would never be relieved, by these forms of analysis, of the need for a 'judgement ever awake and steady self-possession'. Neither is the botanist.

Long before computation was sufficiently advanced to permit the analysis of a proper body of evidence, an eminent student of linguistics touched on the essential point: 'I shall say nothing here concerning the troublesome matter of style save to hint, in passing, at a definition: the STYLE of a discourse is the message carried by the frequency-distributions and the transitional probabilities of its linguistic features, especially as they differ from those of the same features in the language as a whole.'[2] The gathering of evidence from 'the language as a whole' has yet to be undertaken on a sufficient scale: but Bernard Bloch's passing hint is upheld by evidence that, not only between one discourse and another but within a single discourse, there can be sustained differences of the kind he envisaged.

---

[2] Bernard Bloch, 'Linguistic Structure and Linguistic Analysis', in the *Report of the Fourth Annual Round Table Meeting on Linguistics and Language Study*, ed. Archibald A. Hill, Monograph Series on Language and Linguistics, vol. iv (Washington, 1953), p. 42. The series is now better known as the papers of the *Georgetown University Round Table* and is usually catalogued under that title.

Such differences even make themselves felt as a single idiolect changes and as different idiolects converge or diverge in the movement of the dance.

II

The most obvious of all the larger changes within any of Jane Austen's idiolects arise from the unconversational propensities of the epistolary mode and those, not unlike them, of that 'historian's mode' which runs down the line of English fiction from Fielding's Man of the Hill and Johnson's Imlac to Georgette Heyer and beyond. The long letters of Darcy and Frank Churchill make a sizeable enough proportion of their idiolects to alter their essential shape. With Mrs Gardiner, a letter makes up 1781 of her 2865 words and is largely, though not entirely, responsible for her remote location in the eigen-maps. But a few characters, like Collins and Lucy Steele, write so much as they speak that no strong epistolary influence can be discerned.

Among the more extensive 'histories', those of Willoughby and Brandon depart furthest from the style—even their rather stilted style—of conversation. Like Miranda, in the long expository scene near the beginning of *The Tempest*, and like the hapless interlocutors of Socrates, Elinor is allowed a few words here and there: but they are not enough to transform chronicle into conversation. Notwithstanding the widespread belief that Mrs Smith's part in *Persuasion* had not been fully assimilated by the time Jane Austen was obliged to put the manuscript aside, the effects of a mature artistry can be seen in the comparatively conversational flavour of Mrs Smith's long tale. (Like Mrs Gardiner, she has little else to say: but the great distance between their respective locations in Graphs 14 and 19 outweighs the fact that everyone else is even less like Mrs Gardiner.) It may be fairer, indeed, to say that Mrs Smith's idiolect was itself made good and that the sense of something unassimilated has to do with the content of her history, the unduly tortuous machinations of William Walter Elliot.

When Willoughby's history and the letters of Darcy and Frank Churchill, to take those three examples, are separated from the remainder of their idiolects, the 'intrusions' move far towards the extremities of an eigen-map in which the entry for 'DIALOGUE' supplies a general norm. (The base for these calculations is the original set of the thirty most common words of Jane Austen's dialogue.) It is satisfying to find that, despite some differences between the epistolary and historical modes, these special entries for Willoughby and Churchill stand close to each other, in token of their obsequiousness and self-absorption, and that they are far removed from the entry for Darcy's letter. (All three, be it noted, are broadly similar in substance: the speaker or writer offers his version of an earlier episode and attempts to justify his own behaviour.) The 'conversational' idiolects that now remain for each of them are located much closer to the general norm: but only Darcy finds a place among the majority of other heroes and heroines. When the locations of Darcy, Willoughby, and Churchill in Graph 14 are contrasted with these new locations for their separate sub-idiolects, it can be seen that, where a complete change of literary mode is involved, the processes of averaging-down towards the lower centre do not operate in the usual way. As conversationalists, all three move inward: as letter-writers or historians, they move towards Mrs Gardiner and beyond. This point is of particular importance as a reminder that it is desirable to compare like with like and, if that is not practicable, to make the necessary allowances.

III

Subtler and more revealing differences within an idiolect can be discerned in those cases where the different 'aspects' a character displays in various personal relationships become a central issue. Of all the anomalous locations noted in earlier maps, only that of the abominable Mrs Norris has not yet been considered. In what possible sense, it must be asked, does she resemble the younger generation at Mansfield Park (or those heroes and heroines who are their neighbours in the maps)? They do not fawn upon Sir Thomas or treat the elder Mrs Rushworth so unctuously as she. They cannot emulate the affectation of sisterliness with which she tries, usually in vain, to manage Lady Bertram. They do not bully Fanny from first to last. Almost any passage serves to show that she speaks in a manner—in several manners—very much her own.

With one proviso, there is no great difficulty in breaking an idiolect into a set of sub-idiolects, each defined by the identity of the person addressed. The proviso bears on the desirability, which I have treated strictly, of setting aside all those passages where there is any doubt about who is being addressed. This gives the analysis a proper purity but at the price of excluding many highly characteristic utterances.

With characters like Miss Bates, whose omnivorous style knows little respect of persons, the price is easily paid. But, in a further study, it would be useful to find a subtler answer than exclusion in such cases as Mary Crawford's. Save in undramatized episodes, like the later part of the escapade at Sotherton, she rarely speaks to Edmund except in public: it is a question of the social conventions of the day. And yet there is no doubt that her 'public' remarks, in the early chapters, are often directed to Tom Bertram in particular and that, in later chapters, the younger brother takes his place. The exclusion of their 'public' utterances carries some of the secondary characters beneath a sufficient quantum of words; and some of them, of course, have speaking-parts too small to be broken into workable sub-idiolects. Within these rather self-consistent fields, I have taken a thousand words as a substantial enough body to be treated as a sub-idiolect.

The need to recognize 'bench-marks' was touched on when three different novels were being compared. For comparisons like those that occupy the remainder of this chapter, it is especially valuable to identify them precisely. In each of the next three eigen-maps, therefore, four of the more strongly contrasted of Jane Austen's characters supply a framework within which the degrees of contrast among a given character's sub-idiolects can be assessed. The four characters used as bench-marks are Henry, Catherine, and the elder Bennets. The dynamics of eigen-analysis do not allow the bench-marks to remain in absolutely fixed positions: but any sub-idiolect that lies beyond *that* framework is different indeed.

The framework makes no barrier for Mrs Norris. In Graph 27, her overall location (4J) stands as close to the general norm as Graphs 14 and 19 indicated. Her 'miscellaneous' sub-idiolect (4JX), in which her public utterances are joined with those of her sub-idiolects that do not amount to a thousand words apiece, lies some little way out in no man's land. Sir Thomas's Mrs Norris (4JE), fawning and servile, lies in the centre of the map with no closer neighbour than Mrs Bennet. Her affected ingenuousness towards her sister (4JF) carries her into a region far out on Catherine's wing of the map. And, for any reader who finds Henry Tilney a trifle overbearing, the location of poor Fanny's Mrs Norris (4JA) shows a truly authoritarian style at its most naked.

From a statistical point of view, therefore, Mrs Norris's overall location (4J) is not so much anomalous as ill-measured, clear evidence

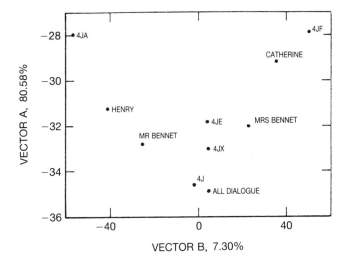

GRAPH 27. Mrs Norris's Sub-idiolects
(Word-types 1–30 of Jane Austen's dialogue)

of an averaging-out so marked that the original analysis is inadequate. I have taken this example because no other is so pronounced. Instead of presenting forty-seven other maps, I suggest that the general pattern of relationships in Graphs 14 and 19 shows plainly that (while many other characters, especially the central characters of the later novels, do change in 'aspect' from one conversational relationship to another) they move within a relatively narrow range. If that were not true, the entries in those graphs would lie in a muddle and it would be impossible to discern those little groups of the like-minded which they display.

From a critical point of view, however, there is a question of judgement to consider. At what point does a set of sub-idiolects become so disparate that it is no longer reasonable to speak of an idiolect, a character, at all? Like old Mr Graysford and young Mr Sorley, in *A Passage to India*, we shall doubtless draw the line at different points, finding a place within the divine hospitality for monkeys but not perhaps for jackals . . . or wasps . . . or the bacteria inside Mr Sorley. . . . For my part, as was indicated earlier, I cannot accommodate John Thorpe. The disparateness of his idiolect is not made good by meaningful shifts of aspect except in his particularly

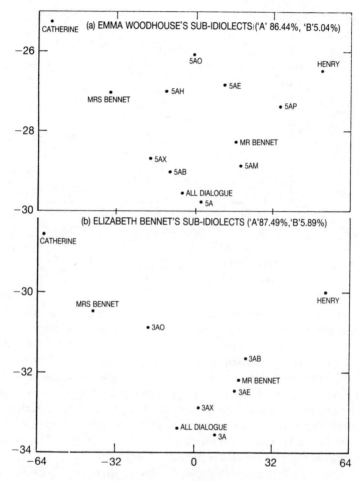

GRAPH 28. The Sub-idiolects of Two Heroines
(Word-types 1-30 of Jane Austen's dialogue)

objectionable treatment of his mother and sisters, which occupies only a handful of words. But with Mrs Norris, I find no difficulty at all. Extreme as they are, her shifts of aspect spring from consistent and identifiable motives; and each of her three main sub-idiolects has its milder simulacrum. Her manner towards Maria and Julia is not unlike her manner towards Lady Bertram. She fawns on

Tom Bertram, especially after she persuades herself that his father is unlikely to return. And, so far as her courage allows it, she tries to bully Edmund, younger son, advocate of the deplorable Fanny, and chief impediment to her darlings' improprieties. Her whole portrayal amounts to a classic display of what the modern sociologist, David Riesman, was to describe as 'other-directedness' in contradistinction to 'inner-directedness' (like that of Fanny and even Lady Bertram who is too somnolent to change in any way).[3]

Graph 28 shows how Emma Woodhouse and Elizabeth Bennet change in aspect from relationship to relationship. Except in her frank and submissive conversations with her aunt (3AO), Elizabeth remains very much herself. And, even in that extreme case, she lies well within the framework of the bench-marks. Emma's sub-idiolects are more sharply differentiated. Her condescension, affectionate as it is, towards her father (5AP), is suitably registered and easily understood. Her extraordinary capacity for hauteur is well registered by the fact that her manner of speaking to Mr Knightley (5AB) is not *more* unlike her manner of speaking to Harriet Smith (5AM). The other three entries are driven up the centre of the map by their dissimilarity to the rest. In what sense is her manner towards Mrs Weston (5AO) akin to those more natural neighbours, 5AH and 5AE, the manner she adopts towards Elton and Frank Churchill respectively? All three sub-idiolects are delicately controlled unions of the authoritarian and the submissive, the iron hand and the velvet glove. The courteous deference towards Mrs Weston is genuine: but, as Mr Knightley does not hesitate to tell the latter, 'ever since she was twelve, Emma has been mistress of the house and of you all. In her mother she lost the only person able to cope with her' (p. 37). With Churchill she shows her hand a trifle more openly and, all unknowing, tells him what he ought to think about Jane Fairfax and the rest. But, with Elton, a mock-modest affectation of submissiveness remains the keynote until the splendid episode where she recognizes and dismisses his presumptuousness.

If I interpret the figures justly, the matter of dominance and submissiveness comes so much to the fore in the analysis of these sub-idiolects partly because of the examples I have chosen and partly because the associated contrasts between the formal and the colloquial, the disquisitive and the rambling, are not usually

---

[3] David Riesman, *The Lonely Crowd* (New Haven, 1950), *passim.*

important variables *within* a single idiolect.[4] It is not because Sir Thomas's manner is unfailingly 'correct' that Mary Crawford exclaims, 'if he wrote to his father, no wonder he was concise. Who could write chat to Sir Thomas?' (p. 288).

In the course of Chapter 5, I suggested that, despite differences of emphasis, Marxists and traditionalists share certain common ground. That suggestion is well illustrated by Tony Bennett's account of the work of V. Vološinov and M. Bakhtin. Vološinov, it seems, proposed 'that the word should be understood not only along the axes of its relationship to other words but in the context of its functioning within the dialogic relationships between speaker and listener'. He went on to argue that '"speech-genres" might themselves be explained with reference to the objective "conditions of socio-verbal interaction" on which they are predicated'. By virtue of this interaction, meaning consists partly in '*whose* word it is and *for whom* it is meant'. Up to this point, clearly, Vološinov's argument has much in common with Coleridge's analyses of Shakespeare's language and with some versions of the 'close reading' that has played so large a part in academic criticism throughout the last half-century. Vološinov went on, however, to interpret socio-verbal interaction as '"an arena of class-struggle", as words are mobilized and fought for by different class-based philosophies'.[5]

The evidence of the present study is often in keeping with the proposition that the social standing of Jane Austen's characters manifests itself in '*whose* word it is and *for whom* it is meant' and, accordingly, has an influence upon the whole shape of their idiolects. The patterns of dominance and submissiveness, to pursue that example, support the proposition more subtly and powerfully than overt contrasts between the 'correct' usage of one social class and the solecisms—comical or deplorable—of another. The contrasts between Mrs Norris's sub-idiolects support the further proposition that the effects of different 'dialogic relationships' upon the shape of an idiolect must be weighed against those of an essential individuality. All this makes it necessary to entertain the possibility that social relationships are the crux of the whole affair and that 'essential individuality' is indeed a bourgeois fiction.

To give that possibility a fair hearing, it is necessary, in the first place, to take the liberty of insisting that the class-divisions

[4] Among the exceptions that come to mind is the full-frontal contrast between the everyday discourse and the 'bed-language' of Connie Chatterley's gamekeeper.

[5] Tony Bennett, *Formalism and Marxism* (London, 1979), pp. 77–81.

of dialectical materialism are too crude to meet the case. So far as modern ideas of class-distinction are relevant, almost all of Jane Austen's characters are members of a single social class: the struggle of the proletariat is only rarely glimpsed. Within the 'class' of the gentry, however, there are sub-classes or gradations enough to admit the kinds of social conflict that Jane Austen does portray. It is necessary, in the second place, to insist that, in Jane Austen's novels as in the real world, considerations of rank are not the only arena of conflict and that the usefulness of the word 'class' is greatly reduced when it is appropriated by those who would distinguish only between the proletariat and the bourgeoisie. (The nobility, in which even Sir Thomas Bertram and Sir Walter Elliot have no place, is almost as unimportant in Jane Austen's novels as it is in modern society.) We are all of us members of many 'classes' and, as Jane Austen so richly demonstrates, we can enrol under any or several of their banners. The conflicts she portrays are not merely between a Sir Walter Elliot and his social inferiors (all the other gentlemen of England among them?) but between the sexes, between the generations, between men of estate and men of the new professions, between rivals in love, between ill-matched siblings, and so on. When the complex interconnections between these and similar 'determinants' are given their due, the different characters assume particular roles and 'social class' becomes one factor among many. The social insecurity of being a mere connection of the family weighs heavily upon Mrs Norris and goes far towards uniting her different sub-idiolects. But, with Emma Woodhouse, whose 'class-status' is not at risk, the struggle that most matters is for self-definition and the chief need is to reconcile her own aspirations with the expectations of those closest to her. Although the eventual union between Hartfield and Donwell enshrines Emma's class-status, a union between Hartfield and Enscombe (which she never seriously entertains) would have done as much or more. It is not merely on 'class' grounds, therefore, but in token of her individuality and his that 'it darted through her, with the speed of an arrow, that Mr. Knightley must marry no one but herself' (p. 408). And only the hardiest veteran of the class struggle, I suggest, would find Emma's preference of Mr Knightley to Frank Churchill a matter of little importance for her future.

When 'class' determinants of *every* kind are set beside those of social status, there still remains the '*je ne sais quoi*' which attracts Mary

Crawford, for once, to a younger son; which draws Darcy, against his conscious system of beliefs, towards a social inferior; and which sustains Fanny's fidelity to the less eligible and, seemingly, less available of two young men. Even before she knows his history, a '*je ne sais quoi*' turns Anne Elliot away from any thought of marrying her father's heir, Lady Russell's preferred candidate, the most eligible man she knows, the only man who can ever offer her the title (cherished for her mother's sake) of Lady Elliot of Kellynch. Such actions are not really enigmatic. Like much behaviour in real life, they are made to seem so when only 'class' interpretations are admitted. In these and many other cases, the characters' speech-idiolects show the effects of the various 'dialogic relationships' through which the action of the novels is (in part) carried forward: but those relationships are not entirely shaped by the determinants of 'class'. With the thought-idiolects of the later heroines, the effects of dialogic relationships become a vestigial influence and the particular emotional and intellectual attributes of Fanny, Emma, and Anne do more to explain the differentiations noted at the end of Chapter 8.

Despite the congeniality of Vološinov's analysis, I turn back, therefore, to Coleridge's less categorical approach to language as social intercourse; to the emphasis on *domestic* politics in Mr Knightley's comment that Emma is 'mistress of the house and of you all'; and, finally, to the profound insight of one of Jane Austen's earliest critics. Writing anonymously in 1870, Richard Simpson commented on her 'thorough consciousness that man is a social being, and that apart from society there is not even the individual'. Hence, he argued, 'the individual mind can only be represented by her as a battle-field, where contending hosts are marshalled, and where victory inclines now to one side, now to another'. But he does not reduce the complexities of the battle to a straightforward affair of social class or define individuality as a bare emblem of one category or several. Simpson's later argument anticipates the subject of my remaining discussion:

A character therefore unfolded itself to her, not in statuesque repose, not as a model without motion, but as a dramatic sketch, a living history, a composite force, which could only exhibit what it was by exhibiting what it did. Her favourite poet Cowper had taught her,

'By ceaseless action all that is subsists.'[6]

---

[6] [Richard Simpson], 'Jane Austen', *North British Review*, ns xii (1870), 137.

10

The Changes that Time Brings

I

The basic concept of 'time-series analysis' and the method of calculation upon which it depends are scarcely so much as an extension of the forms of correlation employed in recent chapters. If a character's whole speaking-part is cut into an appropriate number of successive segments, the frequency-hierarchy for any segment can readily be correlated with any or all of the others; with the frequency-hierarchy for the original whole; or with those of other idiolects (whether in *their* entirety or in their successive segments). This method of analysis was employed, in fact, in the earlier discussion of changes in the idiolects of Catherine, Marianne, and Fanny.

Despite its essential simplicity, the method requires more delicate handling than most and the results it yields can be distorted by bad management. If the original body of data is too small or if it is cut into too many segments, the dearth of numbers may yield aberrant results. If it is too large or if too few segments are allowed, the effects of 'averaging out' can produce undifferentiated results. With our particular data, moreover, the steep decline in relative frequencies from the most common word-types to the twentieth, the thirtieth, and onward at gathering speed can soon deplete the numbers beyond safe working limits.

An abundance of trials and a multitude of errors suggest that the twelve most common words of Jane Austen's dialogue, about a quarter of the vocabulary of her characters, yield tenable results for those seventeen characters who speak more than six thousand words apiece. If Virginia Woolf's Susan (with 5960 words) is included, eighteen characters from the 'other' six novels can be added. Since some comparisons with them are to be undertaken, the contracted and ancillary forms of the twelve word-types have been incorporated.

My trials have also shown that, though some ten segments are required to give a clear enough picture of the sustained development which characterizes many of Jane Austen's major idiolects and which distinguishes them from those of the other novelists, that number

allows marked fluctuations in some of the idiolects of only six or
seven thousand words. To employ different numbers of segments
for idiolects of various sizes would complicate discussion and almost
preclude comparison. The recognized solution is to translate the
original segments into 'rolling phases'. This elegant procedure not
only shows up underlying trends and brings the numbers to a safer
working level but also prevents the arbitrariness of the original
boundaries between segment and segment from distorting the whole
picture. On occasion, however, the rolling phases can conceal
meaningful aberrations. It is desirable to consider both sets of results.

'Rolling phases' are most familiar in the analysis of seasonal patterns
like those of rainfall. Comparisons of the amount of rain that falls in
successive months are greatly affected when there are several days of
exceptionally heavy rain in, say, the last week of a month. Had it
begun three or four days later, the figures for the two months might well
have been reversed. Had it begun only a day or two later, the figures
for both months might have been higher than usual. Yet, from the
farmer's point of view, what really matters is that the rain came in the
right—no, no, the wrong—season of the year. Instead of treating the
month-endings as real boundaries, that is to say, we might analyse the
rainfall-patterns for January/February/March, for February/March/
April, for March/April/May, and so on. Those are rolling phases
and we encounter them whenever we are told, early in each new
month, of what happened 'in the three months ended 31st . . .'.

The rising and falling patterns of change through ten successive
segments, for three major characters of *Emma*, are illustrated in the
upper part of Graph 29. Each character is treated separately in the
sense that the frequency-pattern for each segment is correlated *only*
with the corresponding pattern for his or her whole idiolect: the
higher the coefficient for a given segment, the nearer the entry lies
to 100 (or + 1.000). The graph does *not* show that Emma and Mr
Knightley's idiolects resemble each other in their third segments, the
time of their bitterest disagreements: it shows that, at that time, they
are both extremely unlike themselves. It also shows that they both
'come to themselves' as the novel continues and end, Emma
especially, rather more 'like themselves' than they were at the
beginning. With Mrs Elton, the fluctuations are less marked but the
graph distinguishes accurately between the many episodes where she
is 'quite' her usual self and those others where she tries to ingratiate
herself with Emma (1) and Mr Knightley (8). In the last phase, the

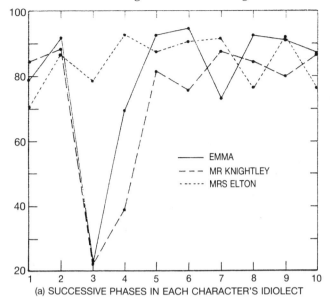

(a) SUCCESSIVE PHASES IN EACH CHARACTER'S IDIOLECT

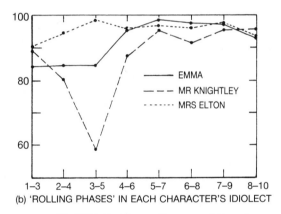

(b) 'ROLLING PHASES' IN EACH CHARACTER'S IDIOLECT

GRAPH 29. Linear Patterns of Development
(Word-types 1-12 of Jane Austen's dialogue including their contracted forms)

coefficient falls still lower for a different reason. The patterns there
are coloured by her attempt to conceal her failure to organize Jane
Fairfax's future and by the irritable little contretemps about her
husband's appointment to meet Mr Knightley. As we take leave of
her, Mrs Elton is not quite so composed or elegant as usual.

Mr Knightley's sixth segment (pp. 228–330) and Emma's seventh (pp. 261–79) both fall in a part of the novel where they have less to say to each other, and she to Harriet, than usual. For Emma, this segment is chiefly characterized by things that she 'said to herself', passages that would be classified as character narrative if the stage-direction 'said' and the direct speech-form were disregarded. What she 'says' in these passages bears on her realization that her attitude to Frank Churchill does not amount to love; on the—fortunately fleeting—self-delusion that Harriet is much her own superior because 'there is no charm equal to tenderness of heart' (p. 269); and on her immediate dislike for Mrs Elton. Her actual dialogue in this segment consists almost entirely in the artificial pleasantries of her first meetings with that newcomer. Thus, while the irregularity in the rising curve of the graph reflects differences in Emma's speech-patterns, it can justifiably be regarded as an aberration.

The irregularity in the sixth segment of Mr Knightley's curve is slighter but more illuminating. The very fact that his sixth segment covers a hundred pages of the novel shows how little part he is taking in the dialogue at this time. His jealousy of Frank Churchill increases during the young man's first visit to Highbury and is refreshed when he reappears. It is in this period that Mr Knightley remains uncertainly outside Miss Bates's window, unable to decide whether to join the company or ride on to Kingston: as Samuel Beckett has it, '"Let's go." (They do not move.)'. And, in his longest conversation with Emma at this time, he is obliged, for once, to talk about himself. When she tests Mrs Weston's suspicion that he may be attracted to Jane Fairfax, he finds no difficulty in repudiating the suggestion, thus settling her half-comprehended fear of losing him. His real difficulty, the source of an unusually personal and hesitant manner of speaking, stems from the idea that, if she is willing—as it seems—to make him over to Jane Fairfax, her own affections must certainly be engaged by Churchill. The segment ends more happily for him in the *rapprochement* at the ball. The rising curve of his coefficients is restored (only to fall again when he is confronted by Frank Churchill's letter). And the irregularity in his sixth segment can be seen as the reflection of an emotional crisis.

So far as the relationship between Emma and Mr Knightley is concerned, the analysis can be refined by excising what they say to each other from the rest and treating the excised parts as sub-idiolects: with consistency of 'aspect' thus secured, it is possible to concentrate on the changes that time brings. We shall soon return to that procedure. For the moment, however, my purpose is to contrast the upper and lower parts of Graph 29. When ten distinct segments are converted into eight rolling phases, the larger tendencies of each idiolect are emphasized and all but the most marked irregularities are smoothed out. It becomes even clearer that, once established in Highbury, Mrs Elton changes very little until her plans are thwarted at the end. It becomes clearer that the changes in Emma and Mr Knightley amount to sustained developments of the kind that Coleridge, treating of Shakespeare's characters, was the first critic to discern. And, especially with Emma, it is as if the mature Jane Austen no longer needs to 'establish' an idiolect firmly before exposing it to the effects of changing circumstance. In a passage whose location I have lost, Henry James has words to the effect that, 'My characters, once in motion, tell me what they have to say'. While this doctrine says much of the shaping of literary idiolects in general, the changing portrayal of Emma suggests that Jane Austen had something more than a Jamesian 'germ' of an idea of what the 'heroine whom no one but myself will much like'[1] would *eventually* become. And yet, even in *Bildungsromane,* where psychological development is especially important, it is necessary to turn a little away from Coleridge and emphasize that literary idiolects are artefacts. The novel itself assures us of 'the perfect happiness of the union' (p. 484) between Emma and Mr Knightley; and — *pace* Marvin Mudrick — enough is shown of their development to justify that assurance. The novel is silent on the question of Mrs Elton's future with her *caro sposo*: but enough has been shown to suggest that she will be as happy as she deserves. To ask for more is to ask for the diffuse continuance that distinguishes life from art or, less misguidedly but no less vainly, to ask for another story.

In the topmost section of Graph 30, the frequency-pattern for each of Emma's eight rolling phases is correlated, in turn, with those for the whole idiolects of Elizabeth Bennet, Mary Crawford, and Mrs Elton. The parodic resemblance between Emma and Mrs Elton can now be seen in all its power — and in all its transience. As the majority of Jane Austen's readers and critics have always recognized, the two characters are not fundamentally, or finally, alike. Having already seen that Mrs Elton's own development is limited, we can treat her

---

[1] J. E. Austen-Leigh, *A Memoir of Jane Austen* (London, 1870), p. 203.

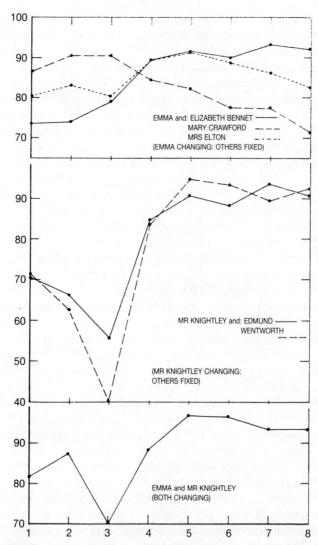

GRAPH 30. Changing Resemblances as Evidence of Development
(Word-types 1–12 of Jane Austen's dialogue including their contracted forms)

as a bench-mark for the curves in which Emma comes increasingly to resemble Elizabeth Bennet and differs increasingly from Mary Crawford. The three stand in close proximity to each other in Graph 14: and so they should. But, beneath the broad resemblances, there are recognizable differences that make themselves felt when even one of the three is allowed to 'dance'.

When all three of them are allowed to do so, the resemblance between Emma and Elizabeth is not much reduced but Mary moves away from them. In Elizabeth's case, the curve of eight rolling phases shows the firm establishment of an initial idiolect; a gradual divergence from it in the first half of the novel; a very marked irregularity at the time of Lydia's elopement and the hasty return from Pemberley; and a culminating upward movement, marking a recovery of her initial idiolect and a development beyond it into something nearer than ever to her 'full self'. When Emma's idiolect and Mary's are taken as wholes, the correlation between them, registered in Table 10 and illustrated in Graph 14, is 0.961. Yet, even at her most sympathetic, in the fifth of her eight rolling phases, Mary comes no closer to the final Emma than 0.868. At her most remote, the coefficient is 0.395; and, in the finale, it is only 0.598. All this casts doubt on the notion that Mary is the 'secret' or 'ironic' heroine of *Mansfield Park*. To establish that she *never* much resembles what Emma and Elizabeth become—and that she is unlike Anne Elliot, first to last—does not settle the whole matter: but, at the very least, it poses a sharp question for Mary's advocates.

The middle section of Graph 30 compares Mr Knightley's development with the overall frequency-patterns for Edmund Bertram and Captain Wentworth. His eventual resemblance to them is to be expected. But the extent of his change should surprise those of Jane Austen's critics who regard him as the novelist's 'privileged' spokesman. The most striking of his changes, registered in Graph 29 as a departure from 'himself', now reappears as a divergence from the heroes of the other Chawton novels. Throughout the whole range of Jane Austen's major characters, I have been unable to find a close match for the frequency-pattern of Mr Knightley at this stage of his career. Only one resembles this Mr Knightley more closely than he resembles the Mr Knightley of most other phases. It is Henry Tilney, whose many admirable qualities do not include much respect for feminine pretensions. The only point, I think, on which this Mr Knightley resembles Henry more closely than usual is his tendency, never more marked than here, to 'talk down' to Emma. As I conceded in Chapter 1, I now accept that, in an earlier study, I laid undue weight on the condescending side of Mr Knightley. That may have been an over-reaction against the consensus of unqualified admiration in the criticism then current. The crux remains: as Graphs 29 and 30 testify, Mr Knightley does not represent an immutable 'norm' to which Emma must humbly aspire. He is a fellow-member of the dance, a dramatic character created by a novelist who declared that 'pictures of perfection as you know make me sick & wicked' (*Letters*, pp. 486–7).

In the bottom section of Graph 30, each successive rolling phase of Emma's idiolect is correlated with the corresponding phase of Mr Knightley's. The upshot is best summed up by him. They are not, Emma suggests, too much brother and sister to dance together. He answers 'Brother and sister! no, indeed' (p. 331). The changing shape of their relationship and their eventual convergence is even more clearly shown in Graph 31, which confines itself to two sub-idiolects: the 5234 words that Emma addresses to Mr Knightley and the 7565 that he addresses to her. Each is separated, as before, into eight rolling phases: but, on this occasion, the frequency-pattern for every phase is correlated with that of every other to produce an eigen-map. To follow the path of each of them is to see how far each changes and how the speed of change diminishes as their idiolects converge towards the end of the novel. To compare their relative positions point by point — 1 vs. 1, 2 vs. 2, and so forth — is not merely to celebrate the metaphor of dancing but also to recognize the enormous force of Vološinov's doctrine of 'dialogic relationships' and Richard Simpson's subtle anticipation of it.[2]

The natural interpretation of Graph 31 is that it represents a gradual 'meeting of true minds'. But we must entertain the possibility that 'dialogic relationships' operate *impersonally* in such a way as to make those who speak much with each other speak more and more like each other. My trials suggest that that is an important part-truth — but only a part-truth. Instead of grasping at obvious exceptions like Edmund's parting with Mary, Emma's divergence from Mrs Elton, and Elizabeth's divergence from Wickham, let us take a more difficult case. The overall correlation between Emma and Harriet Smith averages out at 0.814. For the sub-idiolect of 5716 words addressed by Emma specifically to Harriet, it is 0.667. When the rolling phases of that sub-idiolect are correlated with Harriet's

---

[2] On the scale employed for Graph 31, the relative weighting of Vectors A and B is shown, inaccurately, as 4:1. A scale of 3:1, which would better represent the truth, is an unemployable 'bastard scale'. The essential point is that both characters move further on the horizontal axis and less far on the vertical than Graph 31 suggests.

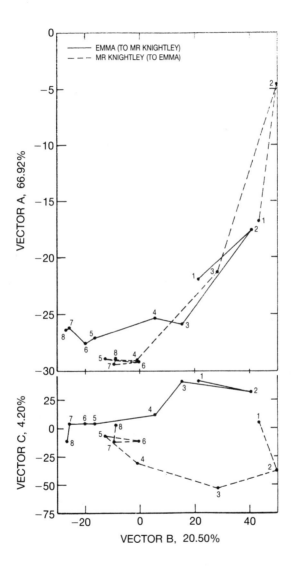

GRAPH 31. Changing Patterns of Conversation between Emma and Mr
Knightley
(Word-types 1-12 of Jane Austen's dialogue including their contracted forms)

idiolect as a whole, the results are as follows: 0.290, 0.309, 0.264, 0.338, 0.593, 0.693, 0.774, 0.732. While they never speak much like each other, that is to say, they clearly come to speak more like each other. This might be attributed to an increasing personal affinity; to the fact that, especially in their last meetings, Emma treats Harriet less condescendingly (and is obliged, perhaps, to do so); or to the impersonal functioning of the 'dialogic code'. To distinguish among those possibilities, even more sophisticated comparisons are necessary. If the eight rolling phases of Emma's address to Harriet are correlated, one by one, with the corresponding phases of her address to Mr Knightley, the resulting coefficients are 0.649, 0.372, 0.361, 0.480, 0.366, 0.489, 0.510 — and 0.811. On a question that warrants further investigation, the large disparity between the last coefficient and the rest shows the influence of something beyond the operation of impersonal forces in the language. It points rather to the achievement of a coherence in Emma's eventual idiolect, to the emergence of a compound self, of an individual character who — within the compass of the novel where she has her being — can meet her various fellows on firm ground. If only within the compass of the novel, the 'ceaseless action' is happily resolved.

Those conclusions are supported by the evidence of Emma's other 'dialogic relationships'. Instead of enlarging upon them, let us consider evidence of another kind. Both Emma and Mr Knightley change greatly in their use of the pronoun 'I'. The changes consist, in part, in striking changes of incidence. Beginning together a little below the general norm, they both turn away from the pronoun in the period of their disagreements only to take it up again, ever more strongly, in the latter part of the novel. They both end well above the general norm. The obvious implications about the changing condition of their relationship are confirmed by an inspection of examples, variously addressed. Along with their more straight-forward uses of the pronoun, both tend, at first, to use it in self-regarding ways, to take some note of precisely what self it is that speaks. On his side, for example: 'Emma knows I never flatter her' (p. 11); 'Perhaps you think I am come on purpose to quarrel with you' (p. 36); and, 'I . . . who have had no such charm thrown over my senses' (p. 37). On hers: 'as to my poor word "success", which you quarrel with, I do not know that I am so entirely without any claim to it' (p. 13); and, 'I could not have visited Mrs. Robert Martin, of Abbey-Mill Farm. Now I am secure of you for ever' (p. 53).

The point is not so much that they hold mistaken images of themselves as that an 'inner self' observes its image as it speaks. Emma turns from the pronoun in those parts of the novel where, puzzled by Mr Knightley's behaviour, she occupies herself with the affairs of others. Jealous of Frank Churchill and uncertain of his own standing with Emma, Mr Knightley almost forsakes the use of 'I'. Besides casting frequent aspersions upon 'him', he turns to moral generalities that give him access to an ostensibly impersonal voice of authority. As he appeals to duty, good sense, and filial affection and speaks, Johnson-like, of what 'a man' should do, he tells some austere truths and deflates some of Emma's idle fancies: but the impersonal idiom does little to conceal the private animus; and Emma is quick to find the gaps between the two.

In the period of his deepest unhappiness, Mr Knightley's selfhood is more nakedly exposed. His use of 'I' curves upward for two hundred pages and is marked by a recourse to plain forms of appeal, some of which he has seldom used before and none so tentatively as now: 'I think', 'I suppose', and versions of 'I imagine' are among the obvious examples. On several occasions, he even turns to 'I am sure' and 'I assure you' whose frequent use, in Jane Austen's portrayal of her characters, tends to reflect either the strident ignorance of Mesdames Elton and Norris or—as in the present case—a more genuine uncertainty of mind.

Towards the end of the novel, with the telling exception of the short period of unhappiness after the expedition to Box Hill, both Emma and Mr Knightley use 'I' far more freely than either did at first. At this time their incidences run almost side by side. As the two of them find new and joyful aspects of their relationship, partly by looking with fresh and often amused eyes at matters about which they had disagreed, the links between 'I' and 'you' take on a simple reciprocity not evident before. A breach remains, in each of them, between two distinct ideas of self: but the breach is now between present and past selves. Mr Knightley puts it in a manner that gives too much weight to his failures of tact, too little to his underlying motives: 'I do not believe I did you any good. The good was all to myself' (p. 462). And, when he comments on a change in her opinions, she replies, more bluntly but no less generously than he, 'I hope so—for at that time I was a fool' (p. 474).

It remains possible, no doubt, to argue that the 'new selves' of the closing phases of *Emma* are only new (and transient) roles, the roles of 'bourgeois' lovers, best content when they are most deceived. Yet, given that those roles do not consist in empty gestures but pervade the plainest stuff of the language, Jane Austen has earned the right to bestow the doubts on Mrs Elton and to give 'the small band of true friends' the last words of the novel.

II

Although Emma and Mr Knightley change more and show a more exactly sustained development than many other characters, other graphs like those lately offered are no less revealing. To avoid multiplying them endlessly, we need a more concise way of summing up the evidence of variation. A statistic known as the 'coefficient of variation' does much to meet the case.

As a simple — and extreme — example, take the set of correlation-coefficients for eight rolling phases in the idiolects of Marianne Dashwood and Georgette Heyer's hero, Alverstoke. When the frequency-pattern for each of Marianne's phases is correlated with her own overall pattern and Alverstoke's with his, the results are:

Marianne   0.663 0.591 0.869 0.805 0.889 0.884 0.959 0.977
Alverstoke 0.997 0.998 0.992 0.983 0.988 0.991 0.985 0.991

It is obvious that she changes far more than he. For more exact comparisons than loose statements of that kind (but without recourse to a graph), mean-values offer a beginning: the means for these two rows of coefficients are 0.825 and 0.991 respectively. But mean-values conceal the important difference between Marianne's 0.825 and the 0.825 of a hypothetical character whose coefficients all lay between 0.80 and 0.85. With Marianne and Alverstoke, a comparison of standard deviations from the mean — 0.127 and 0.005 respectively — also shows that she varies far more than he. Yet while that measure shows the degree of variation, *tout court*, it says nothing of the level at which it occurs: if every one of Marianne's coefficients were reduced by 0.5, the mean would fall to 0.325 but the unit of standard deviation would remain unchanged at 0.127. What is called for is a measure that relates the standard deviation to the mean.

The 'coefficient of variation' is derived by dividing the standard deviation by the mean and converting the result to a percentage. Thus:

$$\text{Marianne } (0.127/0.825) \times (100/1) = 15.39\%$$

$$\text{Alverstoke } (0.005/0.991) \times (100/1) = 0.50\%$$

TABLE 14. Coefficients of Variation for Leading Characters of Eleven Novels
(All idiolects of more than 6000 words: correlation of each segment with whole idiolect, taking the twelve most common words of Jane Austen's dialogue as base.)

Ten successive segments			Eight rolling phases		
38.35%	FANNY		15.39%	Marianne Dashwood	
34.48	Marianne Dashwood		13.43	MR KNIGHTLEY	
29.91	MR KNIGHTLEY		9.45	FANNY	
26.00	EMMA		6.47	EMMA	
20.71	Miss Bates		6.10	Crawford	
19.79	Mrs Bennet		5.74	Mrs Norris	
19.65	Crawford		5.59	Mrs Bennet	
18.87	Mrs Norris		5.40	DARCY	
17.98	ELIZABETH		4.75	ELINOR	
17.03	HENRY TILNEY		3.83	Mary Crawford	
			3.72	EDMUND	
	16.06	FREDERICA	3.44	Miss Bates	
13.52	ELINOR		3.35	HENRY TILNEY	
12.59	DARCY		3.05	ELIZABETH	
	12.30	MR WILCOX		3.04	MARGARET SCHLEGEL
12.23	Mary Crawford		2.54	Mrs Elton	
10.24	EDMUND			2.00	'SIDNEY PARKER'
10.17	CATHERINE			1.91	The Duchess
			1.85	Churchill	
	9.58	'SIDNEY PARKER'			
9.48	Churchill			1.81	Mitchy
9.10	Mrs Elton			1.76	Rhoda
				1.57	FREDERICA
	7.93	Jinny		1.55	Mrs Brookenham
	7.69	The Duchess		1.42	Helen Schlegel
	7.01	Mitchy		1.37	NANDA
	6.50	Helen Schlegel		1.34	MR WILCOX
	5.84	MARGARET SCHLEGEL		1.33	Jinny
	4.59	NANDA		1.30	Mr Longdon
	4.34	Neville		1.04	Neville
	3.94	VANDERBANK			
	3.93	Rhoda	0.95	CATHERINE	
	3.49	Bernard			
	3.21	Susan		0.68	Bernard
	3.20	Mr Longdon		0.65	Susan
	2.45	ALVERSTOKE		0.61	VANDERBANK
	1.85	Louis		0.50	ALVERSTOKE
	1.74	Mrs Brookenham		0.29	Louis

The characters included from the 'other' novels are: 'Sanditon': — *Sanditon 2*: 'SIDNEY PARKER'

Frederica: ALVERSTOKE, FREDERICA

The Waves: Bernard, Neville, Louis, Rhoda, Jinny, Susan

The Awkward Age: Mrs Brookenham, VANDERBANK, NANDA, Mitchy, The Duchess, Mr Longdon

Howards End: MARGARET SCHLEGEL, Helen Schlegel, MR WILCOX

Note. With Susan (5960) included, no characters from any novel lie close beneath the entry-level. Mrs Jennings (5659) and Isabella Thorpe (5657) are the nearest.

When the idiolects of all those characters who speak more than six thousand words apiece are treated in this way and when a corresponding set of coefficients for the ten successive segments of each idiolect is established, the results are as set out in Table 14.

In both columns of the table, Jane Austen's characters show far more evidence of variation than do those of the other novelists. Those of her characters who vary most (whether through changes of 'mode' or 'aspect' or through development in time) tend to be those who have figured most prominently in critical debate. (This suggests that we are most likely to disagree when we try to find a 'real' Marianne or a 'real' Fanny Price in a chameleon.)

While the table does not lend itself to simple value-judgements, a comparison between the two columns is revealing. For those, like Catherine Morland, who lie decidedly higher in the first column than in the second, it is likely that the degree of variation represented in the ten successive segments but smoothed away by the rolling phases is mere fluctuation, the mark of a stylistic fuzziness, the 'noise' of the communication-theorists. For those, like Darcy, who lie decidedly lower in the first column than the second, a phase of difference — it is his letter — does not obliterate a more general line of development. To establish such inferences more firmly, it would be necessary, of course, to go back behind the coefficients of variation to the original rows of correlation-coefficients, to the frequency-patterns from which they are derived, and ultimately to the novels themselves. But, even when Table 14 is taken alone, the contrast between its columns says something of a difference between exactly focused energy and the more or less disordered energy of 'entropy'.

Whereas Alverstoke lies close to the bottom of both columns, his consort Frederica lies high in the first column and far from the bottom of the second. But the row of correlation-coefficients for her ten segments shows that she 'develops' no more than he: 0.944, 0.475, 0.977, 0.964, 0.984, 0.955, 0.905, 0.966, 0.910, 0.962. There is some difference of 'aspect' between her conversations with him and her conversations with her brothers and sister. Her variation, however, stems chiefly from the change of 'mode' in her second segment where she offers him a protracted history of her family. (If that segment is left out of account, her entry in the first column falls to 2.74 and she becomes his immediate neighbour.) The variation in the idiolect of the Other Lady's 'Sidney Parker', who lies near the middle of both columns, does represent a development — but of an unusual kind.

In Jane Austen's brief account of him, he bids fair to become a Frank Churchill or a Henry Crawford but with a hint that his charm may be better-founded than theirs. The Other Lady takes up the hint and shows that the ostensible frivolity masks an incipient industrialist and man of state—something like a French Lieutenant's Woman's Man. As his motives are unfolded, it emerges that the frivolity was assumed to disguise an altruistic scheme. His apparent development, that is to say, actually betrays the increasing influence of a different authorial hand. Considering the strenuousness of the comparisons to which I have exposed them, Georgette Heyer and the Other Lady are not discredited. To establish one or two distinct idiolects and to sustain them at some length is a useful part of the 'classic realist's' craft: mere aberration, descending into entropy, would yield merely average coefficients.

Yet the craft of a first-rate novelist has higher reaches. The posturing of Forster's Mr Wilcox makes for striking fluctuations in his idiolect: his resemblance is not to any single Forsyte-stereotype (though Soames comes most to mind) but to several members of that tribe. From the upper middle of the first column, he slides far down the second. In token of a genuine development, Margaret Schlegel moves in the opposite direction. Given the lack of change in Helen Schlegel—an unyieldingness that underlies the telegrams and anger?—*Howards End* presents a nicely balanced triptych supported by a set of cameos.

To the extent that Forster is working on Jane Austen's lines, he shows less versatility than she. At first sight, Table 14 sets him in a more favourable light than Virginia Woolf or James. But they, more than Forster, carry the novel in new directions: and Table 14 shows glimpses of that truth.

It is not the central characters of *The Awkward Age* but Mitchy and the Duchess who stand highest in both columns. And, though the difference between them and Mrs Brook or Vanderbank is small by Jane Austen's standards, it is by no means negligible. As I proposed much earlier, survival in Mrs Brook's salon depends upon the preservation of a façade. The weaker characters, like Mitchy and the Duchess, betray their real feelings more freely than the rest. Vanderbank gives himself away on only one or two occasions— and, accordingly, slides towards the bottom of the second column of the table. Mr Longdon and Mrs Brookenham show evidence of development: he as he collects himself and learns to live with his

TABLE 15. Coefficients of Variation for Internal Monologue

Ten successive segments		Eight rolling phases	
%		%	
7.93	Jinny	**1.79**	**emma**
7.49	**anne**	1.76	Rhoda
4.34	Neville	**1.33**	**Jinny**
4.03	**emma**	**1.31**	**anne**
3.93	Rhoda	1.04	Neville
3.49	Bernard	0.68	Bernard
3.21	Susan	0.65	Susan
2.43	**fanny**	**0.57**	**fanny**
1.85	Louis	0.29	Louis

Note. The 'Bernard' included here excludes the long monologue that makes up the latter part of the novel. That later 'Bernard' does not much depart from the final idiolect of his precursor.

disappointment, she as her dominance is undermined. And, like so many of James's formidable young women, Nanda gradually learns to hold her ground. For the proper analysis of his kind of *Bildungsroman*, in a study where Jane Austen was not the centre-piece, it would be desirable to reduce the emphasis on equal segments and rolling phases, on changes of mode and differences of aspect. The emphasis, for James, should fall on crucial episodes and on the delicate changes in the idiolects of the central characters that help to mark those episodes as crucial.

And what of Virginia Woolf? In both columns, to my mind, her characters are arranged in a convincing hierarchy from the flighty Jinny to the withdrawn Susan and poor frozen Louis. Yet Table 14 offers less overt sign of change than one experiences in reading a novel where time is so powerful a force.

The first step towards a better understanding is to disregard the second column. In a novel where change is only in time, rolling phases smooth the evidence away. The second step, the foundation of all statistical analysis, is to compare like with like. The characters of all our other novelists engage in overt 'dialogic relationships'. In *The Waves*, conventional dialogue is chiefly represented by brief passages in which one character postulates what another *would* say; and I have excluded these passages as no true part of either character's idiolect. Given, therefore, that we are dealing not with dialogue but with meditations, it is remarkable that most of these six idiolects change as much as they do.

That is not an exercise in special pleading. To compare like with like (or, at least, with not entirely unlike), Table 14 should now be modified in such a way as to set the meditations of Virginia Woolf's six characters beside the 'thought-idiolects' of Jane Austen's later heroines. The result is shown in Table 15.

The fact that these variations are so much fainter than those for dialogue once more confirms the validity of Vološinov's emphasis on relationships—though not necessarily class-struggle—as a major determinant of 'style' in fiction. The fact that significant and *appropriate* differences survive when 'dialogic relationships' are reduced to ghostly postulates shows that his analysis leaves something to be said. The figures cited above speak for their own significance. For their appropriateness, we must turn, at last, to a closer examination of variation within Jane Austen's thought-idiolects and to a comparison between them and the speech-idiolects of the last three heroines.

III

When the thought-idiolects of Fanny, Emma, and Anne are brought together and the eight rolling phases of each are correlated with each other and with the remaining sixteen, the result—in a graph not reproduced here—is so appropriate that it is easily summarized. Fanny and Anne lie on opposite wings while Emma moves from the centre towards Anne's wing and then across to Fanny's. The general pattern suggests a broad contrast between self-absorption and an attention to others; and the differences between different kinds of egotism and altruism are brought out by Vector C. The scale of change, however, is at least as interesting as its nature.

Fanny's essential manner of thinking scarcely changes over the course of a long novel. Emma has most need to change, and changes most of all. But, despite its comparatively small size and despite the difficulty of separating it from the pure narrative of *Persuasion*, Anne's thought-idiolect shows the most exact line of development.

The test can be made more stringent. Instead of comparing thought-idiolect with thought-idiolect, let us assess the ultimate integrity of Jane Austen's characterization by comparing thought-idiolect with speech-idiolect. To do so, it is necessary to turn once more to the most common non-deictic words. With Anne's speech-idiolect especially, this carries the word-frequencies below any 'reasonable' working limit: that being so, the results are an

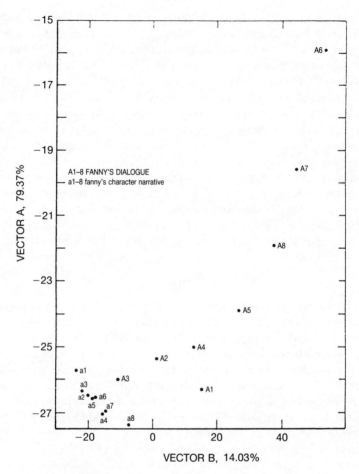

GRAPH 32. Fanny's Speech and Thought
(Non-deictic word-types 1-12 of Jane Austen's literary vocabulary)

astonishing testimony to the 'tensile strength' of the language itself—
or of the language as Jane Austen uses it in *Persuasion*, the
consummation of her art.

Emma's map bears out what has been said of her but adds little
to it. Her two idiolects stand apart from each other, as they should.
Both change vigorously and so much in unison that Vector A
accounts for 93.25 per cent of the pattern of her correlation-matrix.
(Vector B accounts for a further 4.01 per cent.) The essence of the

development is that both idiolects move, in their different degrees, towards the less formal and more 'personal' end of the spectrum as Emma's amiability increases and as she gives less attention to what is due to Miss Woodhouse of Hartfield. Her thought-idiolect, in short, follows the same path as her speech-idiolect.

As Graph 32 indicates, Fanny's case is otherwise. While the introduction of rolling phases gives a firmer shape to the development of her speech-idiolect, it does not disguise the force with which it changes. The childish idiolect of the early chapters (A1) gives way to a self-absorption so marked (A3) that her speech-idiolect moves almost into the territory of her thought-idiolect. But, as Miss Price begins to 'come out', her speech-idiolect moves in a rapid line of development to the crisis with Sir Thomas and the rest (A6). In the closing stages, it moves back to a less extreme position (A8). Her thought-idiolect, meanwhile, shows little change — less change, it will be recalled, than that of any character except Virginia Woolf's Louis.

Over and above the great change in Fanny's speech-idiolect, the extreme contrast between her two idiolects does much to account for her controversial reputation among Jane Austen's critics. The resolution I shall sketch is in keeping with the strange pattern of Graph 32. It makes it possible to accept the banishment of the Crawfords as a dramatic necessity without accepting that it is adequately managed. And, more important than either, it acknowledges the sombre power of Jane Austen's amplest novel.

Judged by the tenets of the English form of *Bildungsroman*, from *Tom Jones* onward, *Emma* is a superb achievement but not a unique departure. A heroine who has much to learn learns much. An imaginative rebel, shaking her finger at the constraints of life in Surrey, learns that true elegance is not the property of lace and pearls; that amiability is more than an easy friendliness and a connivance in clever gossip; that well-meaning interference is often damaging and almost always futile; and that she is not required to abandon but only to control the play of her imagination. But those who fulfil Jane Austen's prophecy that 'no one . . . will much like' her impose austere demands on one who has lived only twenty-one years in the world and also take a charitable view of life in Highbury and Hartfield.

Fanny's is a less familiar and more strenuous trial. To be last and least in a great household while being the most sensitive, the most

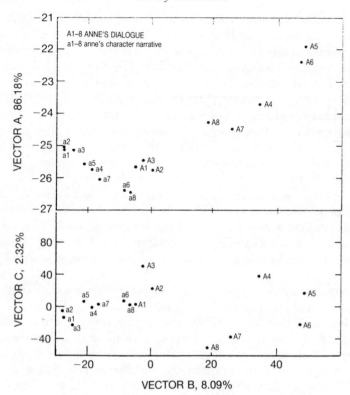

GRAPH 33. Anne's Speech and Thought
(Non-deictic word-types 1-12 of Jane Austen's literary vocabulary)

intelligent, and the most judicious of them all is an unhappy enough lot. To *know* that it is so, to doubt it, and always to be faced by further proof of it is worse. Fanny's essential task, I suggest, is to learn how to reconcile an ever-growing knowledge of her own strength and the weakness of her fellows with her need to live comfortably among them. Her early failures can be plainly seen in those moments of priggishness, censoriousness, and over-sensibility that figure prominently in much criticism of the novel. Her increasing maturity, to which less attention has been given, can be seen in her accepting that, once even Edmund has succumbed, nothing but her own pride will be served by a continued refusal to take part in the theatricals. It is manifested again in her silence about Maria's entanglement with Crawford at a time when a betrayal of Maria would have saved Fanny herself from her uncle's wrath. It is manifested in her stalwart resistance to successive attacks on her belief that Crawford is not a man of character and in her ability to stand alone at Portsmouth. And it is consummated, as I suggested much earlier, in her return to Mansfield. Fanny's thought-idiolect relaxes somewhat but does not *need* to change greatly. The real change is in her speech-idiolect and it gives evidence enough that she eventually learns to live at peace with those who are not her intellectual or moral peers.

From the 'mere reading' of the novel and quite without benefit of statistical analysis, Mary Lascelles described the story of *Persuasion* as, in part, 'the bursting open, for Anne, of the prison that Sir Walter and Elizabeth have made of Kellynch — the expansion of her world'.[3] That insight is borne out by Graph 33. In speech-idiolect and thought-idiolect alike, the first three rolling phases (A1–3, a1–3) show the narrow round Anne treads. As the gates of the prison begin to yield, the reader can see more room for hope than Anne has cause to do. But the movement from A4 to A6 shows that she becomes free, at least, to talk more freely. For her as for Fanny, the last two phases show a more settled speech-idiolect. But her thinking changes still. Notwithstanding small fluctuations as her hopes of Wentworth rise and fall, her thought-idiolect increasingly approximates to the rhythms of speech. In a6 and a8 especially, the accents of the inner voice are scarcely more stiff and formal than her speech-idiolect had been at the beginning. This is a mood of 'smiles reined in and spirits dancing in private rapture' (p. 240), a mood more exquisitely portrayed in its main lines and more fully realized in the very texture of Jane Austen's language than any of the moods that resemble it in the earlier novels.

Throughout this study, the strength and delicacy of Jane Austen's language has met increasingly severe demands. That is undoubtedly due, in part, to the capacities of the language itself, to the resilience of its 'force-field'. But only in the hands of a mature genius are those potentialities developed to the point where four thousand and six thousand words — the sizes of Anne's two idiolects — are enough not merely to establish and differentiate a character, not merely to show a sustained and appropriate line of development. Those few words are enough to unite the two idiolects as the two voices of a unique personality, the central body in the ever-changing firmament of her novel.

[3] Mary Lascelles, *Jane Austen and Her Art* (London, 1939), p. 181.

APPENDIX A

Sentence-length and Sentence-shape

In 1939 the eminent Cambridge statistician, G. Udney Yule, presented evidence that differences of sentence-length could be employed to distinguish between the styles of different prose-writers. His findings were corroborated and extended by C. B. Williams in 1940.[1] The column of mean sentence-lengths in Table 16 shows that, even in the dialogue of fiction, broad 'authorial' distinctions can be drawn. The mean sentence-length for each set of characters differs more or less sharply from the rest, ranging down from 15.7 for Jane Austen's dialogue to 9.6 for the dialogue of *Howards End*. (The mean for *Sanditon 2*, however, is the same as that for Jane Austen.) A closer inspection shows that Jane Austen's characters exhibit much the greatest diversity of mean sentence-length, ranging from Collins's 29.0 to Lady Catherine's 11.3 and Catherine Morland's 11.2. (Since the standard deviation for this set of forty-eight scores is 3.3, Collins's score lies four units of standard deviation above the mean.) The table also gives evidence of reduced overall differences between idiolect and idiolect in the later novels. But that is offset, on the basis of evidence not offered here, by the fact that, especially in the later novels, most of Jane Austen's major idiolects show a greater *internal* diversity of sentence-length than can be found in the idiolects of the 'other' novels. The evidence of narrative reveals that differences of 'mode', as well as differences of authorship, must be taken into account. The mean sentence-length for the 'thought-idiolects' of Jane Austen's six heroines is 23.3 and that for her pure narrative is 30.7. The 'other' novels show similar but less strongly marked differences of mode.

The extraordinary abundance of exclamation marks in Georgette Heyer's dialogue and of question marks in James's, as displayed in Table 16, affords further evidence of stylistic differences. It also

---

[1] See G. Udney Yule, 'On Sentence-Length as a Statistical Characteristic of Style in Prose: with Application to Two Cases of Disputed Authorship', *Biometrika*, xxx (1939), 363; and C. B. Williams, 'Sentence-Length as a Criterion of Literary Style', *Biometrika*, xxxi (1940), 356–61.

TABLE 16. Distribution of the Major Punctuation Marks in Dialogue

	.	!	?	Tot.	Av. S-L		.	!	?	Tot.	Av. S-L
CATHERINE 7040	379	113	138	630	11.2	Mr Parker 3536	140	21	13	174	20.3
HENRY TILNEY 6149	247	30	72	349	17.6	Diana 2604	108	10	6	124	21.0
Isabella Thorpe 5657	289	95	40	424	13.3	Lady Denham 1562	80	10	9	99	15.8
John Thorpe 2928	143	52	40	235	12.5						
Eleanor Tilney 1938	91	25	13	129	15.0	'SIDNEY' 8491	376	26	95	497	17.1
						'CHARLOTTE' 4108	175	9	88	272	15.1
ELINOR 9039	413	44	102	559	16.2	'Mr Parker' 2785	133	22	44	199	14.0
Marianne 6580	310	120	84	514	12.8	'Catton' 2700	139	15	32	186	14.5
Mrs Jennings 5659	224	120	42	386	14.7	'Lady Denham' 2090	92	17	7	116	18.0
Willoughby 5278	206	40	29	275	19.2						
John Dashwood 4462	193	34	14	241	18.5	ALVERSTOKE 20598	640	770	383	1793	11.5
Lucy Steele 3977	131	26	18	175	22.7	FREDERICA 20479	456	961	207	1624	12.6
Col. Brandon 3700	133	12	19	164	22.6	Jessamy 3983	68	268	60	396	10.1
Mrs Dashwood 3560	141	23	49	213	16.7	Charles Trevor 3285	102	91	17	210	15.6
EDWARD FERRARS 2359	92	18	19	129	18.3	Harry 3037	39	201	46	286	10.6
Anne Steele 2066	76	33	13	122	16.9	Lady Elizabeth 2352	46	112	52	210	11.2
						Charis 2141	32	159	37	228	9.4
ELIZABETH 13597	717	120	149	986	13.8						
DARCY 6399	318	9	29	356	18.0	Bernard 30972	1759	37	101	1897	16.3
Mrs Bennet 6048	331	107	45	483	12.5	Neville 9713	661	6	52	719	13.5
Jane Bennet 5203	275	46	29	350	14.9	Louis 8437	505	5	9	519	16.3
Collins 4444	146	5	2	153	29.0	Rhoda 8227	525	15	25	565	14.6
Mr Bennet 3248	194	17	35	246	13.2	Jinny 6143	453	3	13	469	13.1
Mrs Gardiner 2865	140	6	12	158	18.1	Susan 5960	370	0	2	372	16.0
Lady Catherine 2342	140	23	44	207	11.3						
Lydia Bennet 2214	103	46	14	163	13.6	Mrs Brookenham 17448	994	164	412	1570	11.1
Miss Bingley 2127	87	29	17	133	16.0	VANDERBANK 15375	887	178	420	1485	10.4
Wickham 2040	103	7	13	123	16.6	NANDA 10835	792	80	231	1103	9.8
						Mitchy 10778	559	152	342	1053	10.2
EDMUND 14300	747	55	87	889	16.1	The Duchess 8440	404	76	113	593	14.2
Mary Crawford 13030	596	110	92	798	16.3	Mr Longdon 7980	653	173	324	1150	6.9
Henry Crawford 6735	338	21	54	413	16.3						
Mrs Norris 6659	245	48	26	319	20.9	MARGARET 15563	1256	119	303	1678	9.3
FANNY 6117	324	87	40	451	13.6	Helen 9665	742	75	135	952	10.2
Sir Thomas 3953	173	9	21	203	19.5	MR WILCOX 8069	649	59	176	884	9.1
Tom Bertram 2995	156	24	7	187	16.0	Leonard 2489	197	15	34	246	10.1
Lady Bertram 2162	136	12	23	171	12.6	Mrs Munt 2396	167	24	37	228	10.5
						Charles Wilcox 2096	172	21	58	251	8.4
EMMA 21501	1120	237	167	1524	14.1						
MR KNIGHTLEY 10112	555	48	62	665	15.2						
Churchill 8225	470	69	68	607	13.6						
Miss Bates 7624	381	130	52	563	13.5						
Mrs Elton 6415	366	98	34	498	12.9						
Harriet Smith 5274	228	127	50	405	13.0						
Mr Woodhouse 4639	282	52	19	353	13.1						
Mrs Weston 4144	204	34	19	257	16.1						
Mr Weston 3197	184	23	25	232	13.8						
ANNE 4336	249	27	37	313	13.9						
Mrs Smith 3985	193	8	16	217	18.4						
Mary Musgrove 3733	177	68	24	269	13.9						
WENTWORTH 3386	175	39	20	234	14.5						
Admiral Croft 2034	123	20	13	156	13.0						

Note. The column headed 'S-L' represents the mean sentence-length for each character. It is derived by dividing the total of his or her words by the combined total of full stops, exclamation marks, and question marks.

gives a first glimpse of the intractable problems of definition that beset this line of inquiry. For all but one of Georgette Heyer's characters—the exception, appropriately, is the 'historian', Charles Trevor—exclamation marks occur more frequently than full stops. A traditional grammarian would hold that 'Oh!', 'Good heavens!', and 'So obliging of you!' are not true sentences and might set patiently about the task of distinguishing such exclamations from genuine exclamatory sentences. But modern grammarians recognize a profound difference between 'discourse syntax', the only correct syntax of the traditional grammarian, and the 'utterance syntax' of conversation. The exclamations, repetitions, half-formed phrases, and broken syntax of most 'utterance' are more directly registered in the dialogue of modern novels than in most novels of the eighteenth and early nineteenth centuries. They are also more directly registered in *Emma* and *Persuasion* than in *Northanger Abbey* and *Sense and Sensibility*. To attempt to distinguish between two different kinds of exclamation is to encounter a myriad of borderline cases and, worse still, to abide by the untenable doctrine that only 'correct' syntax has a proper place in literary dialogue. To ignore the exclamation marks entirely is to distort the sentence-lengths beyond recognition. To include them all is to be left with no good reason for excluding dashes, points of suspension, and the like: 'Oh! yes— Mr. Elton, I understood—certainly as to dancing—Mrs. Cole was telling me that dancing at the rooms at Bath was—Mrs. Cole was so kind as to sit some time with us, talking of Jane; for as soon as she came in, she began inquiring after her, Jane is so very great a favourite there' (*Emma*, pp. 156–7).

A more immediate reason for relegating the evidence of sentence-length to a brief Appendix is that it has not proved directly relevant to the methods of this study. When, for example, the mean sentence-lengths and the incidences of the major connectives in the idiolects of Jane Austen's characters are correlated, the coefficients tend to lie between 0.30 and 0.40—evidence of a positive relationship but not a strong one. Apart from the difficulties already cited, it is a weak relationship because sentence-length does not closely correspond to sentence-shape. The proliferation of adjectives and adverbs in *The Waves* is only one of many signs that, while Virginia Woolf's mean sentence-lengths are not far from Jane Austen's, her sentences are altogether plumper. Those of James are either short or loosely marshalled. Those of Georgette Heyer tend to be cast in a monotonously emphatic mould.

The table is presented, then, for its broad support of Udney Yule's findings; in the hope that other scholars may find a way of resolving the difficulties sketched above; and as an indication that, within a single novel, this form of evidence can complement that of the present study. To over-question, as Mrs Bennet and Lady Catherine do, is effrontery: to under-question, as Collins does, is to show scant interest in one's fellows. But, in another novel, similar evidence may point to different conclusions. Mr Longdon's over-questioning stands out, even in the highly interrogative idiom of *The Awkward Age*, as evidence of his puzzled response to a strangely altered generation.

APPENDIX B

A Sketch of Statistical Procedures and Associated Problems

I

In recent years, the methods of statistical analysis have become more accessible to the community at large than they have ever been. To calculate the standard deviation of a long column of figures, it is no longer necessary to undertake a laborious process of iterative calculation. It is enough to type the figures themselves on a computer keyboard, load a statistical package like 'MINITAB', and type the commands 'READ', 'STAN C1', and 'PRINT'. To transform a whole table of figures into a correlation-matrix, establish an eigen-matrix, and graph the principal eigen-vectors is scarcely more laborious.

This astonishing new facility in calculation can quickly carry a beginner out of his depth. Statistics, like other intellectual disciplines, raises complex problems of method and does not yield unassailable results. Academic debate is no less vigorous here than in other quarters and here, as elsewhere, analytical procedures are continually being refined. And yet the community would be the poorer if those who were not genuinely fluent in foreign languages were afraid to go abroad; if those who were not trained literary critics were persuaded that they should not read; and if those without thorough mathematical training were induced to avoid statistical analysis. It seems preferable to make the attempt, to take the obvious precautions, and to learn from the inevitable blunders.

The first precaution is to work with numbers large enough to reduce the likelihood of severe chance effects, leaving the analysis of small numbers to experts in that field. The best precautions against procedural errors are to employ reputable computer-packages like 'MINITAB' and 'MICROSTAT' and to repeat each set of calculations.

The analyses offered in this study scarcely venture into three areas where difficulties abound—the areas of field-definition, sampling, and prediction. Except for the distinction between pure narrative and character narrative, my fields are defined in advance by the conventions of direct speech. (Contrast this with the case where the association between cigarette-smoking and lung-cancer might reasonably have been attributed to factors as diverse as the tobacco leaf, the processes of curing, the use of certain additives, the cigarette-paper, the combustion-temperature, or various genetic or environmental dispositions among the smokers.) The difficulties of choosing representative samples and of establishing that they are representative are greatly alleviated by the policy—impracticable until recent years—of dealing in whole idiolects, of examining all the very common word-types, and of ranging across as many as a dozen novels, a million and a quarter words. The delicate assessments of probability and significance that arise when statistical prediction is undertaken are not required for the descriptive or 'reconstructive' analyses offered in this study. They would arise with great force if the method of analysing short passages, described at the end of Chapter 5, were employed in the identification of an anonymous author. To pursue the task effectively, it would be desirable to establish less narrow norms than those of a few major novelists, to analyse a number of specimen passages, and to test the result by a detailed analysis of peculiarities in the use of single words or phrases.

At times, perhaps, the reader may have given some thought to a possible circularity in the method of this study. The appropriateness of the results—of a close resemblance between two idiolects, for example—is upheld, in part, by appeal to the validity of the statistical procedures. The relevance of the procedures is upheld, in part, by appeal to the appropriateness of the results. Such an objection might be answered on theoretical grounds alone: the 'circularity' is actually a convergence of two mutually supportive lines of argument, each of which would generally stand in its own right. On the one side, a diversity of statistical procedures produces not isolated results but convincing patterns. On the other side, a diversity of literary examples, drawn from very well known novels, support each other. And on neither side are we left with inexplicable anomalies. But perhaps the objection is better met empirically by breaking the 'circle'—at any point at all—and returning to the novels and to the words as they are used there. (Chapter 1 is important from this point of view.) To turn back from the numbers to the novels is, sometimes, to find nothing more than a small but appropriate idiosyncrasy like Mrs Bennet's 'but however', or the 'my dear sir' and 'my fair cousin' which have extraordinary effects upon Collins's use of 'my'. It is, sometimes, to find syntax-shaping idiosyncrasies like Darcy's relative pronouns, Henry Tilney's 'or', and Mrs Jennings's use of 'so' and 'for' as anaphoric conjunctions. And it is sometimes to find phenomena as revealing as a changing use of 'I' or a changing 'I/me' ratio. The validity of any general pattern can thus be tested and is ultimately to be understood by recourse to the particulars from which it stems.

On the statistical side, continued trial and error, continued reading, expert advice, and the severe test of trying to describe the methods one is employing gradually dispel the clouds of ignorance. For some readers, perhaps, the following brief sketch of large and complex topics may offer a point of entry. For others, better acquainted with these matters, it will serve only to indicate that I do—or do not—appreciate something of what lies behind the command 'STAN C1', 'CORRELATION C1–C50', or 'EIGEN M1 C51 M2'.

By virtue of its rare lucidity and its emphasis on literary examples, Anthony Kenny's *The Computation of Style* (Oxford, 1982) makes an admirable introduction for students of the humanities. Among other introductory texts that explain—not merely define—the main procedures, David C. Howell's *Statistical Methods for Psychology* (Boston, 1982) is both clear and detailed. Two books by Paul G. Hoel, *Elementary Statistics* (New York, 2nd edn., 1960) and *Introduction to Mathematical Statistics* (New York, 4th edn., 1971) go rather further without becoming inaccessible. The *MINITAB Student Handbook* (Boston, 1976), by Thomas A. Ryan and others, bridges the gap between exposition and practice. These books, taken together, treat of all but one of the statistical methods employed in this study. The exception is eigen-analysis, which is treated, usually at an advanced level, in studies of 'Numerical Analysis'. For an understanding of that method, I have relied chiefly on Joseph Woelfel and Edward L. Fink, *The Measurement of Communication Processes* (New York, 1980) and on the close study of many eigen-matrices and 'maps'. And, finally, for sage counsel about the uses and limitations of statistical analysis, Ronald A. Fisher's *The Design of Experiments* (London, 6th edn., 1951) is invaluable.

II. THE CHI-SQUARED TEST

Without retracing the argument of Chapter 2, let us postulate, as a null hypothesis, that the 1654 instances of 'and' and the 652 instances of 'but' in the dialogue of *Mansfield Park* are distributed among the major characters in proportion to the size of their respective speaking-parts. Each character's percentage-share of the whole dialogue of the novel is taken, that is, to indicate his expected share of the 1654 and the 652. When these expected frequencies (as set out in the second and fourth rows of Table 17) are compared with the observed frequencies (as set out in the third and fifth rows), it is obvious that the distribution of 'but' conforms much more closely to the expectation than does the distribution of 'and'.

Example i

	ALL	Edmund	Mary	Henry	Mrs Norris	Fanny	Sir Thomas	Tom	Lady Btrm.	Others
%	100	22.57	20.57	10.63	10.51	9.66	6.24	4.73	3.41	11.68
and:E	[1654]	373.30	340.23	175.82	173.84	159.78	103.21	78.23	56.40	193.19
and:O	1654	335	389	146	202	118	103	108	53	200
but:E	[652]	147.16	134.12	69.31	68.53	62.98	40.68	30.84	22.23	76.15
but:O	652	161	137	46	69	62	42	27	26	82

With 'but', only Henry Crawford departs far from the expectation. With 'and', only Sir Thomas, Lady Bertram, and the residual set of minor speakers conform closely to it. Out of eighteen cases, there are ten conformities close enough to show that the expectation affords a tenable point of departure. There are seven discrepancies sharp enough to attract attention. But what of the eighteenth case, Edmund's 'surplus' of fourteen instances of 'but'? Let us take it as an illustration of the chi-squared test in which the squared difference between an observed frequency (O) and an expected frequency (E) is divided by the expected frequency to produce a ratio (χ^2).

The extraction of a ratio greatly reduces the absolute influence of the field-size and thus allows more sensible comparisons. The squaring of the differences removes the—sometimes—irrelevant distinction between positive and negative divergences, surpluses and deficits. Hence the formula itself and the calculation for Edmund's use of 'but':

$$\chi^2 = (O - E)^2/E = (161 - 147.16)^2/147.16 = 191.55/147.16 = 1.302$$

After rounding off the answer to 1.3, to avoid 'false accuracy', we compare it with the significance-levels set out in the relevant table of the statistical manuals.[1] Since it falls well below 3.84, the

---

[1] Tables 4 and 5, in Chapter 2, show slightly more conservative results than those derived by this straightforward application of the χ^2 formula. That is because Yates's correction-factor (which reduces the difference between 'O' and 'E' by 0.5) has been employed there. The object is to allow for the fact that, whereas the observed frequency must be a whole number, the expected frequency need not be.

threshold of the lowest generally accepted level of 'significance', Edmund's surplus of fourteen in a field of this size should not be given any statistical weight. (It might, nevertheless, bear some linguistic weight: that would be a question for empirical analysis without statistical support.)

When similar calculations are carried out for the other seventeen cases and the results are compared with the thresholds of 3.84, 6.63, and 10.83 — for 'significance', 'high significance', and 'very high significance' at the 5%, 1%, and 0.1% levels — it emerges that, in *Mansfield Park*, there is a much more energetic differentiation in the use of 'and' than in the use of 'but'. (See Example ii.)

Example ii

	Edmund	Mary	Henry	Mrs Norris	Fanny	Sir Thomas	Tom	Lady Btrm.	Others
χ^2 and	3.9^-	7.0^{++}	5.1^-	4.6^+	10.9^{---}	$0.0°$	11.3^{+++}	$0.2°$	$0.2°$
χ^2 but	$1.3°$	$0.1°$	7.8^{--}	$0.0°$	$0.0°$	$0.0°$	$0.5°$	$0.6°$	$0.4°$

Either, or both, of two courses can then be followed. The 'particularizing' course turns back to the novel and soon reveals that the different characters of *Mansfield Park* put 'and' to very different uses. The word can be used to connect quite different kinds of clauses, phrases, and single words. It can connect them in loose sequences or full-bodied accumulations. It can make the fulcrum of an 'Augustan' parallelism or carry a sentence off on a sudden tangent. And, as in Fanny's case, it can play comparatively little part in the structure of an idiolect. ('But' serves chiefly in antitheses and statements of objection, neither of which has much place in Henry Crawford's free-flowing yet deferential style.) The 'generalizing' course simply allows the words to take their place among the other very common words and exert their effects in the establishment of correlation-patterns.

III. STANDARD-DEVIATIONS AND Z-SCORES

Although nine cases are far too few to make up a normal curve, the distributions treated above will serve to illustrate the processes by which a mean, a standard deviation, and a set of z-scores are derived. When the raw frequencies first cited are transformed into incidences per thousand words, for each speaker the result is as in Example iii.

Example iii

	Edmund	Mary	Henry	Mrs Norris	Fanny	Sir Thomas	Tom	Lady Btrm.	Others
f:1000 and	23.43	29.85	21.68	30.33	19.29	26.06	36.06	24.51	27.04
f:1000 but	11.26	10.51	6.83	10.36	10.14	10.62	9.02	12.03	11.09

The mean-incidence (μ) for 'and' is 26.47 and that for 'but' is 10.21. The mean, as is well known, represents the sum (Σ) of all the scores (X) divided by the number of individual scores (N): $\mu = \Sigma X/N$. In extensive correlation-analyses, which usually depend upon sampled evidence, the sample-mean ($\overline{X}$) normally replaces μ. Thus: $\overline{X} = \Sigma X/(N-1)$.

With the appropriate mean established, the extent to which the scores diverge from it, overall, is expressed as a standard deviation. This value (σ) is calculated by squaring the difference between each successive score and the mean; summing these squared differences; dividing the result by the number of scores; and extracting the square root of that result. Thus, in the case of 'and':

$$\sigma = \sqrt{\Sigma(X-\mu)^2/N} \quad =$$

$$\sqrt{\{(23.43 - 26.47)^2 + (29.85 - 26.47)^2 + (21.68 - 26.47)^2 + \ldots \}/N}$$

$$= \sqrt{(9.24 + 11.42 + 22.94 + 14.90 + 51.55 + 0.17 + 91.97 + 3.84 + 0.32)/9}$$

$$= \sqrt{206.35/9} = \sqrt{22.93} = 4.79.$$

The original scores can now be transformed into z-scores, for a z-score is simply the difference between a given score and the mean, divided by the standard deviation. Thus, with Edmund's score for 'and':

$$z = (x - \mu)/\sigma = (23.43 - 26.47)/4.79 = -0.63.$$

When this calculation is carried out across the row of scores for 'and' (and, likewise, for 'but', where the standard deviation is 1.43), the z-scores are as set out in the first and second rows of Example iv. (The third row should be ignored for a moment.)

Example iv

	Edmund	Mary	Henry	Mrs Norris	Fanny	Sir Thomas	Tom	Lady Btrm.	Others
z_1 and	−0.63	0.71	−1.00	0.81	−1.50	−0.09	2.00	−0.41	0.12
z_1 but	0.73	0.21	−2.36	0.10	−0.05	0.29	−0.83	1.27	0.62
$z_1 z_1$	−0.46	0.15	2.36	0.08	0.08	−0.03	−1.66	−0.52	0.07

Given that, as the chi-squared values have independently testified, 'and' offers strongly divergent scores, the nine z-scores make a better-balanced array than might have been expected. The weakness of dealing with so few scores is better illustrated by the undue emphasis the z-scores attach to Henry Crawford's use of 'but', a single 'aberration' in a comparatively non-divergent set. With the proviso, then, that these small sets still serve only as manageable illustrations, we can turn to the manner in which z-scores may be employed in the statistics of correlation.

IV. PEARSON'S PRODUCT-MOMENT METHOD OF CORRELATION

There are numerous versions of Pearson's formula, distinguished from each other in conciseness; in their adaptation to raw scores, incidences, or z-scores; and in their suitability for use with computers, calculators, or pen and ink. But they all depend upon assessing the values within each pair of a set of pairs in terms of their relative divergences from the mean. Since z-scores are measures of that very divergence, it is evident that, when they have already been calculated, Pearson's coefficient (r) should be easy to derive. The following 'z-score version' of the formula is taken from Kenny's *The Computation of Style*, p. 82: $r = (\Sigma z_x z_y)/N$. With each successive pair of z-scores, that is to say, one member is multiplied by the other. (Particular care should be taken to preserve the positive and negative values on which many of the divergences depend.) The products of those multiplications are added (Σ) and the result divided by the number of pairs (N). Since the products for our example have already been listed, in the third row of the previous table, we need only write:

$$r = (-0.46 + 0.15 + 2.36 + 0.08 + 0.08 - 0.03 - 1.66 - 0.52 + 0.07)/9$$
$$= 0.07/9 = 0.008.$$

So very low a correlation-coefficient indicates that (within the limits of a nine-pair correlation) 'and' and 'but' vary independently of each other in the dialogue of *Mansfield Park* — much more independently than any of the pairs of words studied in Chapter 4. While 'and' is not differentiated with so obvious an energy in the dialogue of Jane Austen's other novels, that is partly because its several functions tend to 'average out'. It figures extremely prominently in the idiolect of Susan in *The Waves*. 'But' is most prominent in the idiolects of Catherine Morland and Harriet Smith.

So far as I am aware, the only important methodological problem of correlation-measures that bears on the analyses offered in this study is intrinsic to the argument of Parts Two and Three. The coefficients there are mostly very high precisely because, as I have tried to show, the different frequency-hierarchies do not rest upon *independent* variables but upon probabilistic configurations. Until more extensive and more expert work is undertaken, two kinds of comment can be used to 'hold the ground': the hypothesis that language functions as a probabilistic 'force-field' is in keeping with the broad thrust of communication-theory, a point sustained by the statistical patterns of Parts Two and Three; and, from a literary point of view, the resemblances and differences between idiolects and the signs of change within the larger idiolects are either in keeping with, or highlight the points of controversy in, the corpus of criticism of Jane Austen's novels. A future scholar may arrive at appropriate levels of 'significance' for results like these: in the meantime, the findings cannot — and do not — rest upon claims of 'significance' (in its technical sense) save in the first 'screening' of *separate* words described in Chapter 2.

No more need be said here of the more elaborate versions of Pearson's formula. In letting their servants do their living for them, the Decadents may have been ill-advised. It is not ill-advised to leave the lengthy iterative calculations on which worthwhile correlations rest to our servants, the computers, and to save our own time for living.

V EIGEN-ANALYSIS

The mathematical complexities of this method of analysis do not admit of a brief description or the working of a small example like those presented above. But some main points can be stated clearly.

As was indicated in Chapter 5, a low coefficient — as between Collins and Lydia Bennet — does not imply that either party resembles a third party (a Mrs Gardiner). But either may do so: though Collins differs sharply from Lydia and Mrs Bennet, they resemble each other closely. If the one trio are thought of as standing at the points of an almost equilateral triangle, the other trio would stand at the points of a triangle with long sides and a tiny base. As was indicated in Chapter 7, a high coefficient may stem either from a dearth of sharp differences or from the presence of unusual resemblances. It is 'easier' for others to stand close to those who are brought together in the first way than to those who are brought together in the second. Such uncertainties about the 'meaning' of a small set of coefficients can be relieved by recourse to the incidences of the words themselves, as was illustrated in Graphs 15 and 16. It is more to the present purpose that they can also be relieved by the construction of a correlation-matrix like those in Tables 7, 10, and 11. In any sizeable matrix, the whole configuration of interdependences serves to place each member — for our purposes, each character — in his only tenable position in relation to *all* the rest.

But large matrices are difficult to scan. The difficulty is met, once more, by the lengthy iterative processes to which computers are so well adapted. The method of 'multi-dimensional scaling' weighs all the coefficients of a matrix against each other and extracts a single 'map' in which a principal member — with our data, it would be Emma Woodhouse — is placed at the centre as a reference-point. The other members are then set in station not only relative to that point but relative to each other. Ideally the outcome would be represented in the form of a planetarium but the more usual two-dimensional projection is an acceptable substitute.

Having been unable to gain access to a satisfactory computer-programme of this kind at the time when it was needed, I was advised to employ eigen-analysis. Subsequent experience has shown that, in one important respect, eigen-analysis is preferable. Instead of offering a single 'final' location for each member, the several eigen-vectors highlight different kinds of interrelationship among the members and thus draw attention to subtle differentiae which would otherwise, almost certainly, have lain unnoticed. If the multi-dimensional map makes for simpler viewing, the eigen-map makes for better understanding.

In every eigen-matrix — every full set of eigen-vectors — that I have studied, the principal vector arranges the members according to their relative conformity to the whole. This seems to result from the fact that our coefficients show a striking mutual consistency: all of Jane Austen's vulgarians tend to resemble each other more closely than any of them resembles most of the other characters, and so on. The higher this degree of mutual consistency, the more powerful the principal vector. Thus the close harmony of Jane Austen's pure narratives, as illustrated in Graph 25, enables Vector A to account for 98.38 per cent of the whole configuration. In the changing relationship between Emma and Mr Knightley, as illustrated in Graph 31, overall conformity proves less important, the inter-relationship between phase and phase figures prominently—and Vector A accounts for only 66.92 per cent of the configuration. When Vector A falls to 50 per cent, 40 per cent, and lower—a phenomenon I have not encountered—it is likely that so many independent variables are at odds that it is desirable to redesign the experiment and make a fresh beginning. That would certainly be necessary if the residual percentage of the configuration were widely diffused among the lesser vectors. It is not necessary when the proportion 'lost' to Vector A is immediately taken up in Vectors B and C: to the extent that Graph 31 illustrates a low value for Vector A, it should be remarked that Vectors B and C take up 20.50 per cent and 4.20 per cent respectively. This pattern is not diffuse. It is complex and emphatic.

In walking about a neighbourhood, we pay more attention to the relative locations of landmarks than to considerations of latitude and longitude. It is in that spirit that I have placed the emphasis on patterns and relationships and given little attention to 'absolute' locations. But the reference-marks along the axes of each graph do have a meaning. The reader may have noticed, for example, that, in all the graphs presented, Vector A deals only in negative values: -15, -25, -35, and the like.[2] The missing positive values are reserved (paradoxically) for those negative coefficients which are conspicuously absent from our correlation-matrices. Although it would be unwise to make definite assertions on such a point, it seems unlikely that the probabilistic relationships among the very common words would allow two speakers of any 'normal' version of English to arrive at a coefficient of -0.5 or -0.8. The lowest to be found among the overall correlations of the thirty most common words

---

[2] In the eigen-matrix itself, the values are recorded as decimal fractions. They are usually converted to percentages for concise graphing.

of dialogue is between Nanda Brookenham and Virginia Woolf's Susan: the figure is 0.297.

In a full set of eigen-vectors, there are as many columns as in the original correlation-matrix. After Vector A has extracted the leading pattern, Vector B treats of the main residual interconnections, Vector C of those that next remain, and so on. In the many trials I have attempted, the first three vectors have almost always taken up over 90 per cent of the whole effect. The fourth has sometimes risen above 1 per cent but the remainder have been negligible.

As a comparison of Graphs 27 and 28 shows, it sometimes happens that the positive and negative 'poles' in Vector B (and also in Vector C) reverse themselves. That has to do with relativities of weighting. But, since the patterns of resemblance and difference are what matter, the mirror-image does not change the picture. The absolutes of oriental or occidental symbolism have no place here: the 'maps' serve their purpose when they show that Mrs Norris changes in 'aspect' far more than Emma and Elizabeth and that, with Mr and Mrs Bennet (unlike Emma and Mr Knightley), the twain will never meet.

It is unnecessary to enlarge on the interpretations I have attached to Vectors B and C in the various graphs. But it may be worth emphasizing, last of all, that—unlike Vector A—they are subject to interpretation. What is it, one asks, turning from map to matrix and back to the word-list and the text, that accounts for this particular ordering of the characters? The ordering itself is *there*, in these innermost recesses of the language. Its meaning must be excogitated and remains open to debate. With those possibilities in mind, Appendix C is designed to enable the reader to test my major findings and to make other trials than mine.

APPENDIX C

Distribution (as raw frequencies) of the Thirty Most Common Word-Types in Jane Austen's literary vocabulary.

Overall distribution in the dialogue of twelve novels:

	JA: ALL	NA	SS	PP	MP	E	P	S1	S2	F	TW	AA	HE
the	8130	712	1243	1452	1949	1929	845	425	862	1717	4411	2094	1511
to	9692	762	1720	1881	1970	2439	920	304	1008	2676	1412	2170	1193
and	7572	624	1309	1316	1654	1922	747	292	692	1367	2405	1268	1059
of	7281	599	1210	1459	1543	1780	690	301	601	1256	1818	1712	677
a	5698	574	905	845	1287	1531	556	256	485	1352	1545	1253	867
her	2491	130	483	435	524	740	179	58	178	395	218	828	215
I	11910	1264	1993	2054	2380	3104	1115	329	991	2947	2447	2650	1801
was	2206	160	484	376	392	549	245	50	163	508	206	251	277
in	4115	381	736	792	873	918	415	165	433	707	1247	941	518
it	5659	590	1062	907	1199	1448	453	153	433	1190	566	1483	879
she	2152	121	369	330	483	702	147	40	141	445	187	574	281
not	4960	553	709	908	1004	1343	443	124	298	619	445	427	348
be	4586	402	789	793	1035	1127	440	124	305	807	298	574	351
that	3901	339	678	820	755	953	356	97	263	1280	755	1433	684
you	7675	915	1190	1354	1633	1959	624	180	684	2587	312	2942	1297
had	1560	132	253	253	283	407	211	34	103	208	111	197	134
he	2727	220	494	553	375	736	349	64	261	843	403	718	264
as	2886	234	499	536	667	685	265	106	186	456	405	708	261
for	2905	305	581	500	644	627	248	115	323	701	352	910	360
his	1558	85	309	399	265	347	153	43	139	296	313	199	87
with	1913	186	325	360	378	464	200	71	200	384	838	518	227
but	3069	310	503	553	652	797	254	111	307	764	436	801	487
have	3749	329	648	661	783	970	358	132	363	638	413	546	464
at	1807	183	308	274	377	489	176	89	178	359	402	404	226
is	4563	479	743	833	941	1190	377	144	449	799	1044	588	595
all	1691	141	329	301	329	407	184	55	230	290	293	504	310
very	2170	217	301	298	401	743	210	80	167	379	41	147	146
him	1587	127	323	372	232	351	182	24	91	477	109	464	155
could	991	83	182	155	213	268	90	15	109	141	72	78	75
by	988	101	205	218	192	184	88	37	78	113	254	223	72

NB. In this table, the word-types are taken at face-value with no distinction between homographic forms.
The whole dialogue of Jane Austen's six novels amounts to 307360 words, distributed as follows:

Northanger Abbey	28930		Mansfield Park	63348
Sense and Sensibility	52334		Emma	78057
Pride and Prejudice	55976		Persuasion	28715

The whole dialogue of the other six novels is as follows:

'Sanditon'	10702		The Waves	72054
Sanditon 2	30023		The Awkward Age	75894
Frederica	69355		Howards End	45899

Distribution (as raw frequencies) of the Thirty Most Common Word-Types in Jane Austen's literary vocabulary.

Overall distribution in the 'pure narrative' of eleven novels:

	JA: ALL	NA	SS	PP	MP	E	P	S1	S2	F	AA	HE
the	15257	2150	2754	2671	3180	2359	2143	608	1760	2366	2533	3520
to	11320	1231	2267	2039	2416	1828	1539	348	1555	1884	1458	1345
and	12292	1465	2100	2066	2732	2177	1752	479	1367	1404	890	2028
of	11316	1535	2244	1968	2290	1702	1577	431	1181	1361	1505	1378
a	6043	815	1079	965	1269	1083	832	255	740	1249	1380	1180
her	8644	1224	1990	1645	1788	1155	842	187	1025	1066	974	1053
I	31	19	1	2		0	2	2	0	0	0	7
was	7224	796	1312	1341	1615	1276	884	202	712	976	813	1183
in	5693	747	1151	957	1180	868	790	177	717	797	846	765
it	3320	389	650	539	666	640	436	87	332	451	719	735
she	6243	824	1188	1255	1085	1037	854	122	997	1090	1153	1202
not	2651	323	509	452	512	479	376	83	213	350	194	477
be	2392	285	464	357	480	434	372	83	212	225	89	241
that	3187	379	674	676	514	536	408	89	380	734	600	730
you	2	2	0	0	0	0	0	0	0	1	4	17
had	4314	448	681	781	875	785	744	154	657	755	879	882
he	3277	242	572	649	721	657	436	112	453	1522	1252	969
as	3407	384	702	577	773	523	448	115	324	435	693	439
for	2926	368	619	485	626	454	374	108	379	364	472	444
his	3456	375	655	743	757	524	402	117	499	1414	1003	539
with	3425	431	644	643	739	586	382	127	439	574	781	462
but	2163	227	365	402	425	412	332	73	324	535	383	461
have	975	112	154	137	243	155	174	28	120	127	254	135
at	2470	290	507	467	506	396	304	88	336	409	563	377
is	128	42	14	11	28	16	17	3	1	1	11	217
all	1710	178	313	290	361	284	284	62	177	93	137	188
very	1237	139	187	169	252	306	184	81	175	91	45	53
him	1519	125	287	335	303	266	203	34	170	510	447	310
could	1933	196	366	307	414	362	288	56	228	111	114	187
by	2159	315	527	384	389	273	271	70	229	326	196	205

NB. In this table, the word-types are taken at face-value with no distinction between homographic forms.
The 'pure narrative' of Jane Austen's six novels amounts to 323817 words, distributed as follows:

Northanger Abbey	40606	**Mansfield Park**	66727
Sense and Sensibility	62299	**Emma**	63123
Pride and Prejudice	57560	**Persuasion**	43502

The 'pure narrative' of the other novels (excluding **The Waves**) is as follows:

'Sanditon'	10890	**The Awkward Age**	52028
Sanditon 2	42164	**Howards End**	55907
Frederica	53171		

Distribution (as raw frequencies) of the Thirty Most Common Word-Types in Jane Austen's literary vocabulary.

Overall distribution in the 'character narrative' of eleven novels:

	JA: ALL	NA	SS	PP	MP	E	P	S1	S2	F	AA	HE
the	2923	297	111	210	1070	904	331	66	140	314	74	299
to	2849	243	106	219	1044	914	323	29	188	410	26	169
and	2567	196	70	194	1047	777	283	44	160	203	27	179
of	2563	213	117	195	938	806	294	41	111	235	40	132
a	1549	140	55	122	533	499	200	26	109	235	31	142
I	2012	208	71	143	815	591	184	18	98	153		83
	111	2		14		83		5			6	22
was	1781	151	65	131	653	577	204	14	99	257	0	160
in	1327	132	61	118	452	390	174	31	115	118	22	69
it	1249	120	44	88	407	441	149	8	50	124	29	111
she	1807	152	55	124	708	623	145	11	98	145	29	123
not	957	96	31	69	317	329	115	11	35	106	9	54
be	1187	108	45	86	395	415	138	17	59	114	5	74
that	1043	80	32	93	411	311	116	17	44	145	14	80
you	50	1		5		39	3	7	9	12	25	4
had	1453	122	45	141	483	435	227	11	94	190	2	148
he	1319	81	48	134	461	418	177	17	89	279	26	107
as	752	65	23	74	263	229	98	7	41	70	31	52
for	706	50	25	62	249	248	72	7	61	116	13	62
his	972	65	61	129	333	280	104	15	101	192	12	56
with	578	45	23	49	220	169	72	5	43	71	19	34
but	639	50	20	49	209	233	78	3	42	88	11	52
have	543	48	17	48	179	196	55	2	30	49	7	26
at	468	40	23	41	164	146	54	10	25	45	14	40
is	53	5		12	0	34	1		12	0	10	25
all	488	28	16	37	184	156	67	6	38	40	5	39
very	363	23	12	20	106	163	39	2	24	28	3	7
him	536	29	32	58	182	154	81	19	30	108	0	
could	685	85	28	61	233	206	72	9	42	52	15	33
by	354	48	13	27	108	102	56	4	16	27	2	22

NB. In this table, the word-types are taken at face-value with no distinction between homographic forms.
The 'character narrative' of Jane Austen's six novels amounts to 78740 words, distributed as follows:

Northanger Abbey	6896	**Mansfield Park**	27566
Sense and Sensibility	3008	**Emma**	25549
Pride and Prejudice	6427	**Persuasion**	9294

The 'character narrative' of the other novels (excluding **The Waves**) is as follows:

Sanditon'	1211	**The Awkward Age**	1303
Sanditon 2	5215	**Howards End**	6321
Frederica	9168		

Distribution (as raw frequencies) of the Thirty Most Common Words in Jane Austen's Dialogue

	ALL	1all		Northanger Abbey				
			1A	1B	1D	1E	1C	1X
the	11910	1264	399	151	299	130	78	207
I	8130	712	115	217	146	80	43	111
you	7675	915	194	198	206	86	64	167
and	7572	624	135	153	108	64	41	123
of	7281	599	112	184	98	66	47	92
to (inf)	6252	519	133	132	94	39	42	79
a	5698	574	96	152	84	87	32	123
it	5659	590	185	152	95	68	54	105
not	4960	553	190	78	111	54	28	92
be	4586	402	104	93	67	27	31	80
is	4563	479	107	94	94	52	37	95
in	4115	381	75	111	74	31	28	62
have	3749	329	73	71	81	35	21	48
to (pr)	3440	243	54	53	63	21	21	31
my	3180	335	53	48	106	32	21	75
but	3069	310	103	44	65	25	19	54
as	2886	234	48	72	32	26	21	35
he	2727	220	54	24	56	26	17	43
her	2491	130	37	40	13	4	10	26
that (cj)	2335	174	48	55	27	6	15	23
for (pr)	2291	238	58	45	46	29	19	41
me	2279	215	81	21	56	18	15	24
was	2206	160	54	17	26	20	10	28
very	2170	217	88	36	26	7	4	50
she	2152	121	34	29	5	8	11	41
will (vb)	2097	198	41	51	32	19	11	44
do	2000	227	93	23	42	27	5	37
your	1944	212	35	62	43	10	22	40
with	1913	186	34	44	35	24	13	36
at	1807	183	41	38	32	24	16	32

Ancillary and contracted forms

	ALL	1all	1A	1B	1D	1E	1C	1X
I	16	0	14	18	13	13	10	15
you	2	0						1
an	763	83	3		1		3	1
it	19	5	32		12	2		12
not/cannot	680	65	3	4	2	3		1
is	75	9						
have	1	0						
he		0						
will	21	0						
do	70	3			2			1

Distribution (as raw frequencies) of the Thirty Most Common Words in Jane Austen's Dialogue

Sense and Sensibility

	2all	2A	2C	2K	2S	2F	2Q	2H	2D	2B	2P	2X
I	1999	283	264	230	242	114	185	164	93	129	80	209
the	1243	208	159	125	148	120	82	99	83	70	36	113
you	1190	287	148	119	82	69	129	37	90	44	32	153
and	1309	203	144	173	134	103	92	87	79	63	83	148
of	1210	235	167	99	148	113	76	93	91	57	32	99
to (inf)	1066	172	134	106	119	99	97	79	69	49	48	94
a	905	123	83	126	83	106	59	74	62	47	48	94
it	1062	161	125	129	96	111	75	80	67	39	29	150
not	709	148	92	62	55	57	58	34	53	36	34	80
be	789	148	105	71	50	85	72	43	69	35	20	91
is	743	130	113	98	35	71	35	41	55	21	21	123
in	736	124	86	66	99	64	50	57	54	46	20	70
have	648	156	101	56	58	51	57	42	40	30	20	39
to (pr)	654	135	73	48	78	63	55	44	52	23	23	60
my	626	73	90	79	105	28	47	47	35	41	19	62
but	503	78	72	52	37	39	51	42	31	22	23	56
as	499	75	41	50	55	51	41	40	36	32	23	55
he	494	97	51	62	18	31	40	25	38	3	41	88
her	483	71	25	58	83	56	13	80	34	14	16	33
that (cj)	391	93	42	28	43	31	23	30	39	23	6	33
for (pr)	412	54	41	46	34	31	45	39	43	22	22	35
me	444	61	82	29	101	10	53	25	16	29	11	27
was	484	36	31	48	98	26	44	58	16	33	20	74
very	301	54	29	43	16	44	23	15	12	9	11	45
she	369	64	21	56	35	48	16	33	19	13	25	39
will (vb)	343	59	42	43	24	33	26	15	34	9	7	51
do	277	59	25	54	17	21	17	11	12	9	10	39
your	384	101	35	35	38	22	39	28	30	12	9	35
with	325	49	50	34	33	22	27	24	30	8	7	41
at	308	48	36	30	28	21	27	23	25	19	12	39

Ancillary and contracted forms

	2all	2A	2C	2K	2S	2F	2Q	2H	2D	2B	2P	2X
I	6			2							3	1
you	120	18	10	9	24	11	10	7	15	7	3	6
an	0			5			2					
it	8			26								
not/cannot	146	18	30	6	7	6	12	8	2	3	1	24
is	10			1	1		1				10	
have	1										3	
he	1			1								
will	16			8			1				2	4
do	24		5	9			2				1	7

Distribution (as raw frequencies) of the Thirty Most Common Words in Jane Austen's Dialogue

Pride and Prejudice

	3all	3A	3B	3D	3E	3K	3C	3O	3L	3H	3J	3V	3X
I	2054	481	253	251	196	138	118	70	82	111	80	77	197
the	1452	360	203	114	80	164	77	57	64	52	68	69	144
you	1354	387	152	153	87	73	119	47	93	63	48	31	101
and	1316	308	128	159	111	106	70	63	47	83	51	67	123
of	1459	370	225	100	102	167	93	67	72	26	50	54	133
to (inf)	1223	308	141	110	113	101	69	73	57	40	46	44	121
a	845	198	94	92	58	59	59	37	34	29	49	34	89
it	907	208	96	114	93	50	59	55	47	39	27	40	92
not	908	251	94	112	97	48	38	55	34	36	30	27	86
be	793	210	74	77	78	66	51	37	43	25	20	29	83
is	833	202	73	77	82	47	53	28	33	25	30	30	105
in	792	208	110	125	66	70	34	33	29	24	41	28	87
have	661	175	64	62	53	49	47	31	36	30	17	30	61
to (pr)	658	144	100	68	58	61	32	32	40	21	21	35	60
my	709	144	90	54	72	102	38	10	22	35	22	18	57
but	553	145	64	99	72	27	29	39	16	17	14	23	48
as	536	130	47	57	47	51	37	36	12	19	20	13	67
he	553	126	36	59	76	9	26	65	7	19	14	32	66
her	435	88	28	77	37	46	23	36	16	3	35	21	29
that (cj)	563	138	62	73	74	69	21	23	20	10	24	25	47
for (pr)	397	92	43	50	36	41	23	18	19	15	14	12	42
me	442	121	67	42	53	39	16	12	19	12	11	26	39
was	376	64	77	27	33	15	2	54	11	28	6	22	33
very	298	68	24	39	29	24	14	18	13	7	6	17	40
she	330	67	17	47	33	31	13	18	17	9	16	14	34
will (vb)	393	87	26	74	34	10	43	8	17	18	15	8	42
do	312	85	15	64	32	64	15	8	13	20	15	4	37
your	453	109	81	56	10	45	38	28	39	5	25	4	25
with	360	76	38	48	34	45	11	6	11	10	12	13	36
at	274	63	30	39	27	20	16	13	10	13	12	8	23

Ancillary and contracted forms

	3all	3A	3B	3D	3E	3K	3C	3O	3L	3H	3J	3V	3X
I	1												
you	135	27	15	13	10	13	15	7	3	1	7	4	16
an	3				1		1			5			
it	117	29	17	10	19	6	7	2	4	5	3	4	11
not/cannot	5				1		1			1			
is	5												
have	0			2									
he	0												
will	1							1		1			
do	5												

Distribution (as raw frequencies) of the Thirty Most Common Words in Jane Austen's Dialogue

Mansfield Park

	4all	4B	4C	4D	4J	4A	4E	4G	4F	4X
I	2380	509	455	288	230	302	113	91	117	275
the	1949	445	417	222	190	147	94	101	47	286
you	1633	404	324	160	164	134	119	62	74	192
and	1654	335	389	146	202	118	103	108	53	200
of	1543	409	311	171	150	147	112	67	23	153
to (inf)	1306	288	272	151	146	131	93	50	46	129
a	1287	288	260	170	146	100	63	71	24	154
it	1199	299	243	117	123	138	44	66	36	142
not	1004	290	189	127	93	124	43	45	34	132
be	1035	217	185	123	108	98	78	59	33	113
is	941	238	220	101	90	81	61	36	19	127
in	873	206	202	99	77	74	59	43	21	105
have	783	193	174	71	66	57	61	27	25	118
to (pr)	664	184	148	58	74	70	52	26	22	55
my	578	159	122	56	79	55	41	29	21	57
but	652	118	137	46	69	62	42	27	26	82
as	667	161	118	62	77	74	44	51	16	69
he	375	156	114	26	28	55	32	10	17	36
her	524	57	76	64	84	34	22	23	22	49
that (cj)	420	150	91	36	27	57	37	11	11	43
for (pr)	525	107	113	57	70	37	45	32	10	46
me	427	115	86	54	44	85	17	19	13	27
was	392	82	68	38	47	49	7	16	23	61
very	401	83	76	23	53	56	20	16	40	46
she	483	71	64	48	56	33	15	15	33	62
will (vb)	490	157	85	72	38	44	33	33	27	52
do	460	106	102	54	50	52	18	24	23	57
your	414	80	92	52	46	24	48	12	10	28
with	378	102	81	45	36	26	24	20	9	41
at	377	64	94	39	46	41	19	17	11	46

Ancillary and contracted forms

	4all	4B	4C	4D	4J	4A	4E	4G	4F	4X
'I	7									2
you	1					1				
an	165	37	27	24	13	21	16	12	3	12
it	2					1				
not/cannot	153	25	23	9	14	34	10	7	13	18
is	22	4	1		1	6		1	3	6
have	0									
he	0									
will	4		1		2	2		2	1	
do	18		4		2	6		3	1	2

Distribution (as raw frequencies) of the Thirty Most Common Words in Jane Austen's Dialogue

Emma

	5all	5A	5B	5E	5D	5I	5M	5P	5O	5N	5X
I	3104	783	354	420	277	299	267	157	142	100	305
the	1929	521	237	249	169	171	95	104	102	81	200
you	1959	618	261	171	195	172	126	124	78	79	135
and	1922	526	264	180	211	144	159	130	84	62	162
of	1780	542	257	213	117	147	76	86	104	71	167
to (inf)	1544	464	210	172	124	121	110	86	73	54	130
a	1531	422	218	141	124	152	82	114	86	79	115
it	1448	391	161	146	137	88	134	89	83	79	135
not	1343	382	164	119	142	92	108	94	67	58	122
be	1127	366	143	109	70	87	59	73	60	53	107
is	1190	351	139	83	127	104	73	99	43	74	97
in	918	295	125	100	72	90	44	27	47	45	73
have	970	281	148	102	61	79	62	56	50	34	97
my	895	265	124	84	86	90	48	37	27	37	74
to (pr)	710	166	66	106	81	86	21	71	50	29	57
but	797	213	94	67	84	52	76	61	39	40	71
as	685	183	104	73	66	51	58	26	32	26	66
he	736	185	155	32	55	28	97	48	50	32	54
her	740	183	148	106	93	35	23	32	62	31	27
that (cj)	575	170	89	58	50	27	41	23	44	20	53
for (pr)	515	163	72	60	40	38	17	25	29	18	53
me	564	144	55	92	30	54	71	21	26	12	59
was	549	97	50	89	93	32	71	35	31	18	33
very	743	185	83	62	76	56	69	99	39	12	62
she	702	141	111	76	133	32	53	44	35	47	30
will (vb)	528	153	87	54	44	33	17	44	23	35	38
do	562	152	58	43	63	43	66	34	37	26	38
your	357	139	68	33	17	24	16	16	9	8	40
with	464	148	76	49	33	43	21	21	20	13	36
at	489	105	64	64	41	52	32	28	29	18	56

Ancillary and contracted forms

	5all	5A	5B	5E	5D	5I	5M	5P	5O	5N	5X
I	199	49	21	22	8	21	12	16	17	5	28
you	1							1			
an								8			1
it	154	42	21	11	21	8	9	8	14	10	10
not/cannot	22	4	1		6	3	2	4		1	1
is	0						1				
have	0										
he	0										
will	15	4		1	4	2	2		2	2	
do											

Distribution (as raw frequencies) of the Thirty Most Common Words in Jane Austen's Dialogue

			Persuasion				
	6all	6A	6V	6P	6B	6D	6X
I	1115	206	131	180	171	51	376
the	845	115	127	97	107	57	342
you	624	105	108	82	86	48	195
and	747	92	127	92	79	46	311
of	690	111	102	61	84	43	289
to (inf)	594	89	95	84	66	34	226
a	556	69	74	66	78	51	218
it	453	64	64	63	51	35	176
not	443	83	45	85	60	33	137
be	440	83	54	58	43	21	181
is	377	58	51	56	36	32	144
in	415	77	60	25	51	21	181
have	358	67	45	43	54	25	124
to (pr)	326	61	47	34	38	18	128
my	222	35	32	28	32	15	80
but	254	41	35	29	29	17	103
as	265	30	50	39	28	15	103
he	349	36	74	51	17	27	144
her	179	11	21	24	31	11	81
that (cj)	212	31	29	28	32	7	85
for (pr)	204	29	31	20	21	24	79
me	187	34	38	34	22	6	53
was	245	27	52	30	35	13	88
very	210	30	19	40	18	19	84
she	147	15	27	18	14	4	69
will (vb)	145	23	20	25	15	13	49
do	162	28	20	28	11	14	61
your	124	21	29	2	21	3	48
with	200	29	32	25	25	10	79
at	176	19	15	28	18	23	73

Ancillary and contracted forms

	6all	6A	6V	6P	6B	6D	6X
i	1						1
you	0						
an	61	11	11	7	6	3	23
it	0						
not/cannot	45	8	5	8	2	3	19
is	7		1	1		1	4
have	0						
he	0						
will	0						
do	5			2			3

Distribution (as raw frequencies) of the Thirty Most Common Words of Jane Austen's dialogue in the dialogue of 'other' novels

	'Sandlton'					Sandlton 2						
	7all	7P	7S	7H	7X	8all	8B	8A	8P	8G	8H	8X
I	329	79	82	60	108	993	297	182	64	61	83	306
the	425	148	111	38	128	862	242	90	78	70	59	323
you	180	60	40	17	63	685	234	122	47	50	32	200
and	292	98	74	54	66	692	174	67	70	61	56	264
of	301	108	61	25	107	601	180	77	67	45	42	190
to (Inf)	194	54	54	31	55	682	189	92	63	64	49	225
a	286	115	60	41	70	569	181	77	46	31	36	198
It	153	57	26	19	51	437	97	78	46	49	20	147
not	139	43	29	30	37	343	95	66	28	22	31	101
be	124	44	27	15	38	305	70	48	27	26	27	107
Is	150	65	30	15	40	461	116	70	40	38	29	168
In	165	68	34	14	49	433	138	65	45	40	29	116
have	132	49	31	29	23	365	102	52	40	30	21	120
to (pr)	110	37	37	11	25	326	96	53	29	30	28	90
my	115	42	24	28	21	248	84	17	19	14	26	88
but	111	26	29	21	35	307	80	41	20	35	22	109
as	106	30	29	19	28	186	51	21	19	15	14	66
he	64	25	12	14	13	261	42	26	48	57	22	66
her	58	11	32	9	6	178	59	12	9	25	18	55
that (c)	53	14	22	5	12	120	41	21	7	11	6	34
for (pr)	95	28	33	16	18	313	90	30	25	42	23	103
me	71	15	21	13	22	222	55	31	20	25	27	64
was	50	7	20	4	19	163	52	26	16	7	12	30
very	80	22	16	22	20	167	58	36	9	7	8	49
she	40	7	16	10	7	142	39	19	6	18	12	48
will (vb)	68	28	11	11	18	187	47	30	21	10	11	68
do	56	14	7	12	23	155	39	32	16	19	7	42
your	40	10	13	6	11	132	41	49	3	7	5	27
with	71	19	18	13	21	200	64	28	17	21	9	61
at	89	32	22	11	24	178	55	20	24	15	11	53

Distribution (as raw frequencies) of the Thirty Most Common Words of Jane Austen's dialogue in the dialogue of 'other' novels

	Frederica									The Waves							
	8all	8B	8A	8F	8C	8D	8K	8E	8X	10all	10A	10C	10B	10E	10D	10F	10X
I	3271	925	970	219	169	152	90	115	631	2447	927	306	293	312	260	264	85
the	1717	583	414	88	95	66	57	41	373	4411	1808	559	548	557	323	493	123
you	2683	955	749	140	67	141	81	74	476	312	112	58	38	38	25	19	22
and	1367	306	424	99	106	59	42	59	272	2405	938	321	323	308	199	268	48
of	1256	429	325	57	48	73	47	22	255	1817	877	212	214	197	139	128	50
to (Inf)	1862	571	567	105	85	57	53	48	376	808	397	130	87	87	46	40	21
a	1507	428	448	83	66	83	58	39	302	1713	794	199	208	192	147	105	68
It	1279	345	382	86	61	57	32	42	274	566	245	90	52	63	41	47	28
not	1918	469	628	133	84	114	60	62	368	533	230	99	42	53	42	37	30
be	807	259	268	36	21	23	33	16	151	298	131	44	40	22	26	20	15
Is	1163	309	367	79	19	70	40	36	243	1061	425	175	98	111	112	54	86
In	707	221	199	30	38	37	25	17	140	1247	528	165	150	112	122	138	32
have	808	286	230	43	10	45	22	21	151	413	153	57	61	57	40	26	19
to (pr)	814	259	228	32	45	41	30	20	159	606	265	69	80	76	50	42	24
my	687	241	154	30	16	29	20	17	180	957	334	101	140	91	130	123	38
but	764	192	262	55	34	32	26	24	139	436	205	63	41	51	34	31	11
as	456	132	124	25	27	22	15	13	98	405	193	54	46	35	41	29	7
he	914	172	293	95	73	52	26	43	160	403	165	140	20	12	32	10	24
her	395	98	121	9	59	9	17	4	78	218	99	12	32	36	10	29	0
that (cJ)	816	257	256	33	58	24	34	21	133	241	114	36	37	23	14	8	9
for (pr)	623	182	215	26	22	28	21	22	107	282	142	43	26	19	28	22	2
me	756	283	199	47	25	19	26	22	135	431	181	52	41	63	42	30	22
was	559	102	183	35	76	23	12	18	110	206	138	27	8	13	7	10	3
very	379	104	153	28	10	10	9	17	48	41	22	1	5	5	4	1	3
she	475	105	167	16	51	27	17	17	73	187	96	8	32	26	7	12	6
will (vb)	496	194	114	36	10	28	8	12	94	281	64	39	25	68	34	36	15
do	902	263	270	50	38	46	27	32	176	150	55	23	17	12	13	9	21
your	437	194	100	17	8	12	13	8	85	109	30	34	9	16	12	9	6
with	384	126	96	16	25	15	17	7	82	838	364	118	103	78	72	80	23
at	359	106	121	17	22	12	9	6	66	402	179	49	50	41	25	40	18

Distribution (as raw frequencies) of the Thirty Most Common Words of Jane Austen's dialogue in the dialogue of 'other' novels

	The Awkward Age								Howards End							
	11all	11D	11B	11A	11M	11I	11L	11X	12all	12A	12D	12B	12L	12G	12H	12X
I	3293	625	688	570	419	299	454	238	2033	636	438	336	200	95	111	217
the	2094	490	474	224	320	266	209	111	1511	476	329	276	71	76	82	201
you	3454	765	720	506	496	339	392	236	1415	487	230	281	81	90	66	180
and	1268	299	258	166	188	154	118	85	1059	340	314	163	55	71	29	87
of	1712	390	368	221	263	196	194	80	677	248	128	136	36	23	28	78
to (inf)	1375	355	258	182	199	159	143	79	804	284	169	142	41	43	29	96
a	1401	279	333	160	211	176	152	90	950	289	206	190	51	46	50	118
it	1893	452	406	288	252	166	199	130	1065	393	220	161	73	39	37	142
not	2072	478	387	380	256	206	212	153	1129	414	228	201	61	41	41	143
be	574	151	94	92	83	70	56	28	351	121	76	66	14	18	14	42
is	1792	413	362	296	261	171	166	123	1108	390	216	178	65	56	48	155
in	941	230	229	100	137	97	95	53	518	165	96	113	22	29	26	67
have	1079	246	242	153	140	115	128	55	598	227	101	126	39	19	13	73
to (pr)	795	199	154	103	112	89	94	44	389	124	76	74	25	23	14	53
my	579	106	114	61	111	71	71	45	337	97	47	86	28	16	22	41
but	801	174	165	123	126	77	78	58	487	171	111	80	29	30	14	52
as	708	167	122	107	123	99	67	23	261	95	53	54	17	9	10	23
he	863	284	115	197	102	59	47	59	314	106	103	31	8	8	25	33
her	828	214	138	69	111	150	86	60	215	73	33	58	6	11	10	24
that (cj)	749	174	150	120	98	91	71	45	303	107	76	59	11	14	8	28
for (pr)	854	193	143	139	120	116	88	55	328	109	67	55	18	21	20	38
me	804	152	194	129	104	55	112	58	324	117	69	48	22	16	11	41
was	287	62	72	43	24	15	50	21	298	91	71	49	25	10	15	37
very	147	31	21	23	15	21	26	10	146	50	27	22	4	19	6	18
she	770	191	142	100	72	112	79	74	312	100	51	76	7	17	17	44
will (vb)	494	157	73	72	76	45	25	46	279	102	56	51	8	20	15	27
do	1163	276	226	192	129	109	124	107	616	231	135	91	37	28	28	66
your	453	82	108	32	76	57	72	26	243	56	39	66	8	14	15	45
with	518	129	102	58	73	68	49	39	227	86	48	44	8	14	14	13
at	404	76	88	47	59	59	44	31	226	77	38	40	13	17	13	28

NB. For the six 'other' novels, the ancillary and contracted forms of word-types 1–30 are not listed separately but incorporated in the tables.

In the table for **The Waves,** the column headed '10X' is used not for minor speakers but for the words that the major characters attribute to others: e.g. Bernard: '"I have posted my letter," the green-grocer thinks, "to the Sunday newspaper. Suppose I win five hundred pounds ...."' (p.255). In the course of the novel, 2602 words are used in this way.

Distribution (as raw frequencies) of the Twelve Most Common Words in Jane Austen's dialogue: ten successive segments in idiolects of more than 6000 words.

Catherine Morland (7040)

word	total										
I	399	49	35	45	51	50	34	32	28	33	42
the	115	13	9	12	6	16	11	14	11	11	12
you	194	26	40	4	23	13	24	22	7	20	15
and	135	5	16	18	12	21	12	11	13	16	11
of	112	9	12	16	8	16	13	15	7	10	6
to (inf)	133	9	9	8	13	17	20	14	19	15	9
a	110	5	11	19	10	9	12	7	17	6	14
it	188	22	16	19	19	24	20	15	19	20	14
not	222	30	17	16	30	25	18	21	20	18	27
be	104	9	6	10	8	12	18	11	14	6	10
is	110	10	11	11	8	8	12	12	11	13	14
in	75	6	4	14	5	10	8	6	12	7	3

Henry Tilney (6149)

word	total										
I	151	22	17	20	14	20	7	0	15	18	18
the	217	20	32	16	17	31	14	27	23	21	16
you	198	21	11	29	15	10	22	30	24	12	24
and	153	15	15	20	18	10	14	18	16	11	16
of	184	19	25	19	20	24	13	21	18	15	10
to (inf)	132	13	14	19	15	13	10	11	13	9	15
a	170	18	14	9	13	15	22	25	24	15	15
it	83	7	9	15	5	12	6	9	13	5	2
not	82	6	10	8	6	6	10	6	10	9	11
be	93	9	7	8	8	13	16	3	7	8	14
is	94	9	11	4	8	15	14	3	13	8	9
in	111	13	11	8	13	12	6	11	13	11	13

Elinor Dashwood (9039)

word	total										
I	283	29	25	30	45	22	26	44	29	23	10
the	208	13	26	20	17	15	19	21	26	25	26
you	287	27	22	17	32	42	26	20	31	42	28
and	203	24	28	24	15	17	16	28	12	14	25
of	235	31	32	24	18	20	16	21	33	19	21
to (inf)	172	17	20	12	14	14	14	21	24	17	19
a	141	16	15	16	15	20	10	8	14	11	16
it	161	5	12	13	17	13	23	26	20	15	17
not	166	17	15	23	19	20	7	23	19	18	5
be	148	12	15	13	15	18	17	9	15	19	15
is	130	13	12	16	15	14	16	10	13	16	5
in	124	17	7	17	9	12	14	11	14	12	11

Marianne Dashwood (6580)

word	total										
I	264	25	11	24	22	25	32	25	22	39	39
the	159	15	27	19	12	15	9	17	13	18	14
you	148	12	8	12	13	18	34	7	24	1	19
and	144	15	23	20	15	8	8	15	10	13	17
of	167	14	26	20	17	14	12	16	19	17	12
to (inf)	134	11	11	12	15	12	19	11	16	14	13
a	93	9	16	14	12	7	12	3	6	8	6
it	125	11	9	15	18	21	11	12	9	10	9
not	122	14	11	9	12	16	14	14	19	7	6
be	105	8	14	8	11	8	12	12	13	9	10
is	113	10	20	14	17	16	3	9	16	5	3
in	86	10	12	13	7	9	9	4	11	6	5

Elizabeth Bennet (13597)

word	total										
I	481	46	59	51	52	38	50	45	27	52	61
the	360	28	33	40	25	49	46	31	37	34	37
you	387	49	23	59	15	33	46	13	29	45	75
and	308	30	23	26	36	31	34	38	39	25	26
of	370	31	41	44	39	40	44	34	36	27	34
to (inf)	308	34	33	28	28	39	29	22	24	40	31
a	225	37	31	15	23	29	20	23	23	11	13
it	208	21	16	18	18	18	20	26	23	27	21
not	280	27	29	32	30	34	24	31	24	25	24
be	210	17	28	13	26	18	19	27	23	23	16
is	202	29	22	26	19	20	14	20	23	17	12
in	208	21	22	26	26	21	21	20	11	22	18

Darcy (6399)

word	total										
I	253	23	17	30	24	25	17	18	22	34	43
the	203	23	27	12	31	19	25	19	17	14	16
you	152	17	21	26	12	6	4	1	23	26	15
and	128	7	15	10	17	13	10	20	14	9	13
of	225	21	22	21	36	24	27	18	23	21	12
to (inf)	141	11	17	10	10	15	15	15	11	16	21
a	109	19	14	13	5	8	8	17	8	7	10
it	96	16	9	10	5	9	14	8	3	15	7
not	111	11	13	17	4	12	12	6	14	14	8
be	74	4	13	8	11	8	3	9	7	7	4
is	73	16	12	12	6	4	7	1	9	4	2
in	110	18	7	10	12	12	10	14	10	6	11

Mrs Bennet (6048)

word	total										
I	251	15	22	23	31	28	26	26	29	24	27
the	114	8	16	20	9	2	12	9	15	15	8
you	153	27	13	17	11	23	4	4	10	29	15
and	159	12	17	13	14	15	16	17	18	19	18
of	100	14	6	14	9	5	19	9	8	7	9
to (inf)	110	13	8	11	14	11	14	10	10	13	6
a	105	16	10	15	9	7	8	6	10	12	12
it	115	13	8	10	8	8	19	7	14	15	13
not	122	15	11	17	16	15	12	11	9	9	7
be	77	9	6	7	7	7	7	8	10	7	9
is	127	10	5	12	16	13	19	10	15	11	16
in	62	8	3	9	7	9	7	5	4	6	4

Edmund Bertram (14300)

word	total										
I	509	38	39	43	51	45	55	48	59	77	54
the	445	49	73	36	48	38	47	41	29	34	50
you	404	59	31	31	38	50	46	52	50	25	22
and	335	41	31	32	29	36	33	38	32	37	26
of	409	31	52	37	38	34	34	34	45	50	54
to (inf)	288	29	27	27	39	22	25	26	27	34	32
a	336	42	37	52	21	27	33	25	27	35	37
it	291	32	23	34	42	21	40	77	22	21	29
not	242	21	32	25	28	24	22	20	22	27	21
be	238	27	26	28	35	24	27	26	15	21	9
is	210	25	21	19	22	31	20	25	12	27	8
in	193	22	22	27	19	17	12	21	20	13	20

NB. The ancillary and contracted forms have been incorporated in the table. Especially with the smaller of these idiolects, it is desirable to transform the ten segments into eight 'rolling phases'.

Distribution (as raw frequencies) of the Twelve Most Common Words in Jane Austen's dialogue: ten successive segments in idiolects of more than 6000 words.

Mary Crawford (13030)

	Total										
I	455	46	42	46	61	37	36	59	42	48	38
the	417	48	54	49	38	34	35	46	40	43	30
you	324	19	26	26	23	51	49	47	31	26	26
and	389	35	38	40	34	45	34	29	44	46	44
of	311	27	36	39	28	31	18	38	28	39	27
to (Inf)	272	23	30	26	26	31	18	29	31	32	26
a	287	25	33	39	35	34	20	24	24	35	18
It	243	36	22	26	27	24	26	19	17	18	28
not	212	23	16	21	24	24	24	16	22	18	24
be	185	19	22	18	20	19	12	19	18	18	25
Is	221	33	25	28	23	20	34	10	15	15	18
In	202	25	31	15	19	17	13	22	22	19	19

Henry Crawford (6735)

	Total										
I	288	37	25	21	34	13	30	29	30	33	36
the	222	23	21	20	14	48	14	26	17	19	20
you	160	10	21	11	13	16	11	9	12	31	26
and	146	12	19	15	17	10	15	17	13	10	18
of	171	21	14	12	16	21	13	21	18	19	16
to (Inf)	151	14	19	24	22	9	12	11	18	10	12
a	194	13	15	30	23	25	15	15	24	14	20
It	117	11	13	11	9	20	7	13	11	15	7
not	136	13	15	9	14	14	14	9	17	15	16
be	123	11	20	10	12	15	9	9	12	8	17
Is	101	9	5	10	10	14	11	11	12	9	10
In	99	7	16	7	15	8	9	10	8	13	6

Mrs Norris (6659)

	Total										
I	231	30	21	31	20	22	20	29	24	20	14
the	190	28	15	16	20	13	21	24	23	15	15
you	164	11	16	4	14	14	12	19	25	28	21
and	202	24	19	13	27	21	17	16	27	27	11
of	150	27	10	16	14	10	14	21	15	12	11
to (Inf)	146	13	13	24	11	12	11	12	13	19	18
a	159	23	14	20	22	13	18	17	9	16	7
It	123	6	12	9	19	16	19	6	12	9	15
not	107	7	12	12	10	19	8	9	12	12	6
be	108	10	15	15	11	9	12	8	8	13	7
Is	91	6	12	9	7	9	14	8	9	8	9
In	77	10	7	12	7	7	5	9	7	4	9

Fanny Price (6117)

	Total										
I	302	37	20	14	36	21	23	49	51	27	24
the	147	7	21	20	17	31	11	10	4	19	7
you	134	15	16	5	15	6	22	19	15	8	13
and	118	15	8	18	11	20	5	6	10	8	17
of	147	11	15	16	14	25	14	13	7	20	12
to (Inf)	131	27	8	11	14	10	11	12	13	15	10
a	121	6	19	19	13	11	13	7	4	15	14
It	139	19	11	10	13	13	19	14	12	12	16
not	158	14	15	11	15	10	25	24	15	14	15
be	98	8	11	11	12	7	8	5	11	10	15
Is	87	6	14	11	6	13	13	4	5	3	12
In	74	3	6	12	8	11	9	2	9	9	5

Emma Woodhouse (21501)

	Total										
I	783	65	77	39	84	77	77	81	93	73	117
the	521	46	55	73	49	53	42	53	45	55	50
you	618	58	64	54	28	58	67	43	85	71	90
and	526	61	47	62	71	50	52	51	57	42	33
of	542	52	63	46	57	62	55	45	57	60	45
to (Inf)	464	50	40	39	46	54	47	42	49	51	46
a	471	56	60	56	52	38	53	51	34	39	32
It	391	29	42	44	31	33	37	51	39	43	42
not	424	36	37	38	49	35	44	56	44	42	43
be	366	48	27	47	39	42	25	48	34	31	25
Is	355	35	34	49	40	32	31	42	35	34	23
In	295	38	25	30	26	29	25	31	29	28	34

Mr Knightley (10112)

	Total										
I	354	30	46	15	19	29	50	46	46	26	47
the	237	21	16	23	28	26	19	31	26	24	23
you	261	28	22	17	17	19	23	40	30	32	33
and	264	32	25	28	30	21	19	34	20	26	29
of	257	25	23	27	33	30	25	24	23	30	17
to (Inf)	210	28	24	25	17	23	12	19	20	24	18
a	239	29	30	26	29	25	19	14	30	23	14
It	161	16	10	15	26	15	15	13	22	16	13
not	185	16	19	20	21	21	25	13	17	17	16
be	143	17	9	17	18	16	17	12	21	8	8
Is	140	7	13	23	17	10	19	13	16	12	10
In	125	5	14	14	12	14	12	12	10	17	15

Frank Churchill (8225)

	Total										
I	420	42	43	41	29	42	56	40	47	40	40
the	249	30	26	29	38	9	11	25	26	34	21
you	171	10	16	21	19	18	29	15	13	7	23
and	180	14	20	19	22	9	14	22	22	21	17
of	213	25	25	15	23	19	19	27	19	21	20
to (Inf)	172	9	15	14	20	22	15	23	19	16	19
a	163	23	24	16	14	15	13	11	13	19	
It	146	15	19	18	18	27	11	7	10	11	10
not	130	10	11	11	17	17	12	13	10	12	17
be	109	10	10	16	14	15	14	10	5	9	6
Is	83	9	11	10	12	11	6	3	6	0	15
In	100	14	9	7	4	8	12	12	8	14	12

Miss Bates (7624)

	Total										
I	277	21	12	30	35	38	28	30	46	18	19
the	169	10	21	15	17	25	15	14	16	20	16
you	195	16	9	20	23	11	34	35	16	19	12
and	211	16	22	20	20	27	17	20	19	26	24
of	117	12	14	13	14	17	5	10	12	7	13
to (Inf)	124	15	18	13	12	7	18	6	9	13	13
a	132	9	13	20	12	16	6	16	14	11	15
It	142	23	11	17	6	8	16	6	17	18	20
not	158	12	14	15	15	13	19	13	20	19	18
be	70	7	4	8	9	8	9	4	8	6	7
Is	133	22	10	17	14	6	9	13	13	13	16
In	72	5	10	5	8	4	9	6	10	6	9

NB. The ancillary and contracted forms have been incorporated in the table. Especially with the smaller of these idiolects, it is desirable to transform the ten segments into eight 'rolling phases'.

Distribution (as raw frequencies) of the Twelve Most Common Words in Jane Austen's dialogue: ten successive segments in idiolects of more than 6000 words.

Mrs Elton (6415)

I	299	26	38	35	28	34	33	29	22	34	20
the	171	27	16	12	18	22	13	12	17	18	16
you	172	11	11	7	19	32	15	16	23	20	18
and	144	12	16	20	12	13	12	19	15	11	14
of	147	17	21	12	18	13	12	14	16	15	9
to (Inf)	121	5	8	18	13	11	13	11	17	12	13
a	173	16	20	16	17	19	14	20	17	14	20
It	88	14	14	11	6	6	7	5	9	7	9
not	100	5	12	11	14	6	11	4	6	17	14
be	87	7	10	9	9	7	9	6	14	6	10
Is	107	13	4	13	14	13	9	11	12	10	8
In	90	13	8	7	9	12	14	6	9	7	5

'Sidney Parker' (8491)

I	297	29	26	31	26	21	31	33	29	20	51
the	242	29	11	21	21	30	23	27	23	25	32
you	234	14	19	25	19	18	29	33	25	17	35
and	174	21	16	11	14	17	10	23	15	27	20
of	180	22	15	16	23	23	19	9	13	22	18
to (Inf)	189	12	18	21	20	16	21	19	19	20	23
a	181	15	18	22	22	20	24	17	15	13	15
It	97	4	6	11	9	16	6	13	12	10	10
not	95	7	10	15	8	12	10	11	8	8	6
be	70	9	6	10	12	14	3	5	5	3	3
Is	116	17	14	9	12	16	16	10	14	5	3
In	138	15	17	7	17	16	12	17	18	8	11

Alverstoke (20598)

I	925	100	93	108	91	88	91	88	89	87	90
the	583	68	56	61	56	44	60	64	36	64	74
you	955	109	102	98	102	91	103	78	116	82	74
and	306	27	33	25	28	22	40	27	41	32	31
of	429	42	52	46	37	45	52	33	36	48	38
to (Inf)	570	58	62	68	55	42	51	56	62	64	52
a	428	34	49	39	40	57	61	37	33	35	43
It	345	43	43	23	30	33	36	44	22	35	36
not	469	46	34	60	41	57	46	38	50	44	53
be	259	18	28	22	24	20	22	34	37	31	23
Is	309	35	35	30	19	28	34	30	24	43	31
In	221	21	23	18	17	24	24	23	24	24	23

Frederica Merriville (20479)

I	970	95	54	102	87	102	119	89	114	83	125
the	414	48	64	50	45	34	34	31	35	50	23
you	749	61	39	85	80	88	71	77	76	71	101
and	424	52	57	42	36	43	36	35	40	44	39
of	325	40	34	27	34	28	32	33	23	42	32
to (Inf)	567	54	67	52	52	57	53	52	58	61	61
a	448	37	59	46	41	44	47	66	27	49	32
It	382	35	40	28	47	43	25	38	37	47	42
not	628	57	57	66	66	75	75	55	56	44	77
be	268	19	24	24	27	26	23	36	31	29	29
Is	367	28	37	32	40	36	43	33	38	45	35
In	199	20	27	23	12	17	26	29	11	15	19

Bernard ('Part I' only: 15562)

I	524	20	44	68	64	45	49	58	75	59	42
the	872	121	92	75	84	66	71	81	87	97	98
you	80	10	2	6	27	0	3	17	6	5	4
and	403	41	35	31	40	42	46	46	40	46	36
of	413	43	32	31	40	44	52	43	41	42	45
to (Inf)	200	11	23	21	17	23	24	26	19	16	20
a	379	33	39	60	25	44	20	35	37	36	50
It	112	18	12	14	10	12	11	6	10	7	12
not	127	3	14	14	6	18	19	17	18	5	13
be	72	5	9	9	5	9	11	8	6	4	6
Is	280	37	29	39	14	20	39	43	15	16	28
In	274	32	23	36	20	28	26	25	21	32	31

Neville (9713)

I	306	26	25	35	37	35	39	28	33	26	22
the	559	74	66	50	47	40	47	65	57	58	55
you	58	0	0	0	6	19	5	10	11	0	7
and	321	30	30	26	31	16	37	34	48	42	27
of	212	18	23	25	16	24	20	13	27	25	21
to (Inf)	130	7	14	17	12	17	7	12	19	12	13
a	199	31	21	15	17	20	21	12	20	24	18
It	90	1	4	9	16	11	6	7	8	13	15
not	99	2	12	12	11	6	11	7	14	9	5
be	44	2	3	7	5	11	0	2	3	7	4
Is	173	17	24	13	16	24	24	17	9	10	19
In	165	22	10	18	17	18	18	22	12	18	10

Louis (8437)

I	293	31	29	28	29	34	28	27	39	30	18
the	548	66	49	43	61	62	46	54	63	54	50
you	38	0	0	2	0	16	9	0	0	3	8
and	323	27	24	26	31	41	24	34	35	39	42
of	215	22	20	23	25	32	25	17	21	17	13
to (Inf)	86	4	9	9	8	5	12	11	7	12	9
a	208	32	27	11	21	19	21	20	21	20	16
It	52	5	6	6	3	8	8	2	1	6	7
not	42	6	4	4	5	3	7	1	3	4	5
be	40	1	6	5	2	2	9	3	4	6	2
Is	98	13	18	7	9	13	9	7	10	4	8
In	150	17	11	17	16	18	17	18	16	8	12

Rhoda (8230)

I	312	40	39	42	50	24	25	9	41	33	9
the	557	71	34	55	62	42	54	53	52	72	62
you	38	0	0	0	2	14	0	0	11	6	5
and	308	26	22	30	16	30	42	38	25	32	47
of	197	20	11	12	25	26	22	19	13	28	21
to (Inf)	86	13	11	3	12	11	7	3	13	7	6
a	192	18	15	17	14	20	16	28	15	28	21
It	63	7	8	17	0	9	10	2	2	2	6
not	53	4	4	4	7	14	3	2	4	3	8
be	22	3	0	1	3	2	3	1	5	2	2
Is	111	12	14	15	6	10	14	17	6	8	9
In	112	12	12	12	10	13	13	8	12	13	7

NB. The ancillary and contracted forms have been incorporated in the table. Especially with the smaller of these idiolects, it is desirable to transform the ten segments into eight 'rolling phases'.

Distribution (as raw frequencies) of the Twelve Most Common Words in Jane Austen's dialogue: ten successive segments in idiolects of more than 6000 words.

Jinny (6143) / Susan (5960)

	Jinny (6143)											Susan (5960)									
I	260	30	31	30	34	29	20	3	37	27	19	264	35	25	33	18	33	18	25	30	26	21
the	323	27	38	38	36	24	29	31	36	31	33	494	34	47	42	49	57	76	39	51	60	39
you	25	6	1	0	0	2	7	6	1	1	1	19	8	0	0	0	0	0	0	7	0	4
and	199	18	19	17	10	23	24	23	20	26	19	267	31	26	32	33	17	25	25	25	31	22
of	139	9	7	14	14	13	13	11	17	22	19	128	3	14	15	8	11	16	15	10	19	17
to (Inf)	46	4	10	6	4	2	6	4	4	1	5	39	1	8	9	3	3	2	6	4	2	1
a	147	24	10	17	11	15	13	22	7	10	18	105	14	8	5	6	11	8	13	14	8	18
It	41	5	1	1	2	14	4	3	3	5	3	47	7	4	2	9	5	1	8	6	2	3
not	42	0	5	5	3	10	3	2	6	5	3	37	6	5	5	6	9	0	2	1	0	3
be	26	1	8	5	0	2	0	3	4	2	1	20	2	0	3	0	3	0	8	1	1	2
Is	112	12	7	8	22	15	17	9	12	6	4	54	8	6	2	13	5	3	10	3	2	2
In	122	12	12	13	13	9	9	15	13	12	14	138	17	15	12	14	14	18	8	10	18	12

Mrs Brookenham (17448) / Vanderbank (15375)

	Mrs Brookenham (17448)											Vanderbank (15375)									
I	625	66	73	59	66	57	48	44	64	73	75	688	73	50	66	73	78	56	76	69	74	73
the	490	48	46	48	47	68	51	52	60	36	34	474	47	50	61	52	36	48	46	45	53	36
you	765	82	80	77	77	74	62	76	67	72	98	720	49	94	63	82	75	71	64	77	82	63
and	299	26	41	37	20	35	33	32	28	21	26	258	34	26	27	21	19	24	21	26	35	25
of	390	39	33	44	36	52	44	42	29	46	25	368	32	38	48	48	36	40	33	31	34	28
to (Inf)	355	27	40	47	32	36	39	44	26	37	27	258	23	20	19	34	21	30	26	27	19	39
a	279	41	26	41	25	22	29	30	21	25	19	333	36	32	32	45	29	29	24	29	36	41
It	452	27	39	38	45	44	54	37	48	55	65	406	48	21	48	47	40	36	48	47	26	45
not	478	46	53	48	51	44	43	46	47	48	52	387	39	29	42	36	40	31	51	41	37	41
be	151	15	16	18	21	13	23	12	11	12	10	94	7	12	10	10	8	13	10	9	5	10
Is	413	43	34	43	48	43	40	38	46	33	45	362	41	35	41	29	31	38	34	39	25	49
In	230	16	33	23	28	26	19	17	33	19	16	229	25	24	21	15	18	31	21	25	26	23

Nanda Brookenham (10835) / Mitchy (10778)

	Nanda Brookenham (10835)											Mitchy (10778)									
I	570	65	58	41	65	52	46	56	74	51	62	419	29	37	35	36	45	41	59	49	47	41
the	224	14	28	25	29	25	33	19	20	21	10	320	37	35	28	54	41	31	18	19	24	33
you	506	53	58	32	30	48	63	51	52	54	65	496	44	33	49	40	52	55	57	47	60	59
and	166	12	15	22	17	23	15	22	11	15	14	188	18	15	18	18	15	20	16	13	25	30
of	221	16	26	27	19	19	32	21	19	26	16	263	22	28	26	29	29	35	14	25	27	28
to (Inf)	182	33	12	11	18	20	13	17	18	18	22	199	22	24	18	19	18	22	16	23	13	24
a	160	15	14	21	8	17	18	14	24	12	17	211	24	18	31	11	26	13	21	24	18	25
It	288	28	28	24	27	27	35	36	35	20	28	252	19	25	14	25	22	31	41	34	23	18
not	380	34	34	35	55	30	37	41	41	37	36	256	12	10	29	34	24	34	41	28	29	15
be	92	12	10	7	13	9	11	5	8	10	7	83	9	13	5	9	10	6	7	8	6	10
Is	296	36	32	31	32	27	35	27	34	22	20	261	25	20	33	25	26	21	23	36	28	24
In	100	5	8	12	10	13	12	12	9	10	9	137	11	17	17	10	18	15	13	7	12	17

The Duchess (8440) / Mr Longdon (7980)

	The Duchess (8440)											Mr Longdon (7980)									
I	299	32	32	21	19	54	26	25	46	23	21	454	48	37	45	48	42	37	60	43	47	47
the	266	23	29	32	29	20	30	34	20	28	21	209	17	19	25	37	25	22	16	15	14	19
you	339	29	29	34	27	53	41	24	41	26	35	392	43	28	34	35	34	46	39	53	34	46
and	154	14	20	15	20	15	19	14	13	9	15	118	9	16	11	15	15	12	6	9	13	12
of	196	16	19	32	19	12	27	13	19	21	18	194	21	14	10	27	29	19	20	24	22	8
to (Inf)	159	12	17	18	18	21	16	18	13	13	13	143	16	13	14	8	11	12	22	16	10	21
a	176	19	17	16	19	11	25	17	16	17	19	152	19	13	24	13	8	15	20	14	13	13
It	166	11	15	15	14	15	20	16	16	18	26	199	14	18	12	17	27	20	24	22	22	23
not	206	17	29	20	11	24	19	22	29	16	19	212	14	20	19	16	21	26	25	32	19	20
be	70	7	5	6	4	10	10	15	4	2	7	56	3	4	5	3	5	12	3	8	5	8
Is	171	21	10	16	18	10	19	20	15	18	24	166	17	9	15	22	18	15	17	28	14	11
In	97	12	7	13	10	7	9	15	8	7	9	95	6	7	11	14	9	8	10	10	9	11

NB. The ancillary and contracted forms have been incorporated in the table. Especially with the smaller of these idiolects, it is desirable to transform the ten segments into eight 'rolling phases'.

Distribution (as raw frequencies) of the Twelve Most Common Words in Jane Austen's dialogue: ten successive segments in idiolects of more than 6000 words.

Margaret Schlegel (15563)

	Total										
I	634	61	67	58	53	60	66	75	71	71	52
the	477	64	59	65	51	41	38	40	45	30	44
you	488	45	52	33	40	51	41	59	43	66	58
and	341	31	49	34	37	42	36	25	29	20	38
of	248	36	23	37	29	25	26	19	18	17	18
to (inf)	284	16	25	34	35	30	22	36	34	22	30
a	290	30	21	28	39	28	34	34	28	16	32
it	393	31	37	32	45	33	41	47	33	56	38
not	414	31	35	30	46	41	43	45	41	57	45
be	120	10	14	7	11	10	16	11	14	11	16
is	390	38	32	30	45	40	39	44	42	45	35
in	165	23	12	16	16	15	16	19	9	20	19

Helen Schlegel (9665)

	Total										
I	438	27	53	43	30	33	56	50	46	44	56
the	328	40	35	42	31	27	36	30	26	37	24
you	230	15	11	22	24	34	26	27	26	18	27
and	314	43	40	32	21	39	30	32	25	23	29
of	128	10	10	11	13	12	22	16	9	11	14
to (inf)	169	11	18	9	17	11	18	25	21	13	26
a	206	28	22	28	24	23	15	10	20	19	17
it	220	21	31	13	21	27	23	12	24	29	19
not	228	13	17	27	23	28	21	24	25	24	26
be	76	4	2	8	7	6	5	12	11	6	15
is	216	26	13	18	18	20	39	16	19	23	24
in	96	15	9	5	6	9	10	9	16	9	8

Mr Wilcox (8069)

	Total										
I	336	32	26	29	45	26	19	45	30	27	57
the	276	27	38	19	23	29	46	26	21	25	22
you	281	20	19	35	40	19	22	35	31	30	30
and	164	11	19	21	15	13	25	16	12	12	20
of	136	19	11	18	9	13	16	14	8	13	15
to (inf)	142	6	11	22	19	18	6	10	14	17	19
a	192	18	24	17	19	27	22	14	20	21	10
it	161	21	23	12	13	21	16	15	18	12	10
not	203	29	23	15	24	19	11	23	19	22	18
be	66	4	5	8	11	6	4	8	5	7	8
is	178	14	19	17	15	27	14	15	23	18	16
in	114	18	11	16	13	12	11	8	8	8	9

The same distribution in three major 'sub-idiolects'.

Emma (to Mr Knightley: 5243)

	Total										
I	211	24	10	17	9	20	23	21	34	30	23
the	107	8	13	9	12	8	16	11	7	11	12
you	166	19	9	5	17	18	17	21	13	27	20
and	121	18	12	16	14	13	11	11	13	6	7
of	129	8	19	6	15	18	16	11	10	14	12
to (inf)	113	12	9	14	19	12	11	8	16	8	4
a	110	15	23	8	13	10	6	11	13	7	4
it	84	8	6	5	6	10	3	14	8	12	12
not	106	12	11	9	10	7	13	13	8	8	15
be	69	11	10	7	11	6	8	3	6	3	4
is	84	11	15	9	5	13	3	18	1	5	4
in	78	6	9	5	8	5	11	9	11	8	6

Emma (to Harriet: 5716)

	Total										
I	192	16	12	20	15	11	18	33	17	28	22
the	165	11	13	14	18	23	18	15	18	16	19
you	162	11	12	29	23	18	14	1	7	15	32
and	144	14	15	9	10	18	18	25	15	16	4
of	153	16	17	12	19	14	12	18	14	13	18
to (inf)	120	18	12	12	8	7	11	13	9	19	11
a	139	13	15	19	13	23	6	18	12	15	5
it	112	7	7	10	15	15	14	5	15	17	7
not	107	9	11	11	7	5	18	13	10	13	10
be	117	17	17	7	9	12	14	16	10	7	8
is	109	13	12	9	7	17	5	12	15	13	6
in	80	11	12	6	7	10	6	12	3	8	5

Mr Knightley (to Emma: 7565)

	Total										
I	254	24	12	11	11	43	34	37	18	34	30
the	174	18	14	15	19	15	21	21	22	12	17
you	200	20	15	11	4	23	32	23	14	34	24
and	194	22	17	29	19	10	22	17	14	17	27
of	201	15	24	23	27	22	20	18	24	16	12
to (inf)	156	19	17	15	17	11	15	13	21	13	15
a	177	21	19	23	19	16	12	24	22	8	13
it	124	11	12	15	14	12	9	10	19	14	8
not	132	11	14	17	11	21	8	11	12	18	9
be	104	7	11	13	13	15	8	14	9	10	4
is	105	11	16	17	8	9	6	13	9	8	8
in	99	7	14	7	14	9	6	10	10	9	13

NB. The ancillary and contracted forms have been incorporated in the table. Especially with the smaller of these idiolects, it is desirable to transform the ten segments into eight 'rolling phases'.

Distribution (as raw frequencies) of the Twelve Most Common Non-Deictic Words in Jane Austen's literary vocabulary: ten successive segments in the 'speech' and 'thought' of three heroines.

	Fanny's 'speech-idiolect' (6117)											Fanny's 'thought-idiolect' (15418)										
the	**147**	7	21	20	17	31	11	10	4	19	7	**553**	76	56	58	61	60	42	53	57	43	47
to	**201**	35	14	15	22	11	17	27	21	21	18	**596**	55	53	61	70	54	56	59	51	75	62
and	**118**	15	8	18	11	20	5	6	10	8	17	**602**	74	63	74	59	65	55	58	66	45	43
of	**147**	11	15	16	14	25	14	13	7	20	12	**506**	51	50	46	54	44	36	60	54	54	57
a	**100**	5	18	18	9	10	10	7	4	8	11	**271**	21	23	25	40	28	22	34	20	28	30
in	**74**	3	6	12	8	11	9	2	9	9	5	**221**	16	24	28	19	31	16	21	20	20	26
it	**138**	19	11	10	13	13	19	14	12	12	15	**251**	26	30	13	35	26	21	16	20	23	41
not	**124**	12	13	8	8	8	23	15	10	14	13	**179**	26	19	14	19	16	19	14	18	15	19
that	**85**	4	9	13	7	5	8	8	17	10	4	**189**	26	14	19	10	28	29	14	14	19	16
as	**74**	8	4	8	3	5	9	6	9	17	5	**142**	15	15	15	12	12	21	14	19	3	16
for	**44**	4	4	4	5	4	6	3	8	3	3	**140**	13	15	16	16	12	15	9	15	12	17
with	**26**	2	6	2	2	1	3	2	2	4	2	**114**	15	12	16	13	15	9	12	7	5	10

	Emma's 'speech-idiolect' (21501)											Emma's 'thought-idiolect' (19730)										
the	**521**	46	55	73	49	53	42	53	45	55	50	**705**	63	77	67	72	86	84	69	67	61	59
to	**729**	72	68	73	77	89	72	62	69	80	67	**711**	64	73	82	57	78	68	68	57	84	80
and	**526**	61	47	62	71	50	52	51	57	42	33	**594**	77	56	69	48	60	62	72	43	51	56
of	**542**	52	63	46	57	62	55	45	57	60	45	**659**	56	61	72	94	75	62	66	54	60	59
a	**422**	53	56	49	48	32	44	45	30	37	28	**368**	47	28	29	46	29	45	39	26	28	51
in	**295**	38	25	30	26	29	25	31	29	28	34	**308**	27	31	41	28	31	27	30	27	32	34
it	**391**	29	42	44	31	33	37	51	39	43	42	**356**	29	43	31	30	44	32	40	34	32	41
not	**382**	32	35	32	45	32	38	53	39	40	36	**250**	27	18	21	23	32	42	24	18	20	25
that	**265**	32	17	27	22	25	22	27	21	36	36	**238**	24	22	21	21	23	25	17	31	27	27
as	**183**	20	20	21	27	24	15	13	9	11	23	**182**	19	18	23	20	14	16	20	17	16	19
for	**185**	18	22	19	12	17	16	25	22	14	20	**193**	22	23	21	13	21	16	14	19	25	19
with	**148**	26	15	13	19	10	12	7	17	19	10	**142**	14	18	13	10	11	16	12	17	13	18

	Anne's 'speech-idiolect' (4336)											Anne's 'thought-idiolect' (5667)										
the	**115**	17	13	17	11	13	6	7	10	12	9	**219**	22	22	27	19	23	23	23	10	27	23
to	**150**	13	18	12	8	14	19	19	17	14	16	**184**	22	11	21	19	22	20	14	19	14	22
and	**92**	13	10	8	8	5	7	4	13	13	11	**159**	17	16	20	22	17	12	16	15	11	13
of	**111**	10	7	15	9	13	14	11	10	12	10	**201**	13	22	23	23	19	27	19	17	21	17
a	**69**	10	9	5	11	6	7	6	3	6	6	**95**	8	8	9	14	11	15	8	6	7	9
in	**77**	8	6	8	6	7	7	7	8	7	13	**98**	9	7	11	7	13	12	8	13	8	10
it	**64**	2	8	8	8	5	6	3	8	7	9	**105**	10	16	9	13	5	12	5	12	14	9
not	**83**	4	11	5	7	11	14	7	9	6	9	**72**	3	12	4	8	3	8	7	12	6	9
that	**61**	4	4	8	6	7	8	2	6	5	11	**80**	5	9	8	12	7	9	8	10	5	7
as	**30**	2	4	1	3	5	3	1	3	3	5	**57**	5	1	8	8	10	5	6	6	4	4
for	**32**	5	4	3	3	7	0	4	2	1	3	**44**	5	7	5	4	3	7	2	4	3	4
with	**29**	4	5	2	2	2	3	4	3	2	2	**36**	5	6	5	2	5	2	3	1	2	5

NB. In this table, the word-types are taken at face-value without distinction between homographic forms. It will be apparent that, in the smaller sets, the numbers are too low to be used safely as they stand: 'rolling phases' are not merely desirable but necessary.

LIST OF REFERENCES

I. COPY-TEXTS

A full list is given in the Introduction.

II. SECONDARY REFERENCES

Akhmanova, O. S. *et al.*, *Exact Methods in Linguistic Research*, trans. D. G. Hays and D. V. Mohr (Berkeley and Los Angeles, 1963).

Amis, Kingsley, *What Became of Jane Austen? and Other Questions* (London, 1970).

Austen, Jane, *Jane Austen's Letters*, ed. R. W. Chapman (London, 2nd edn., 1952).

Austen-Leigh, James Edward, *A Memoir of Jane Austen* (London, 1870).

Babb, Howard, *Jane Austen's Novels: The Fabric of Dialogue* (Columbus, 1962).

Bateson, Gregory, *Steps to an Ecology of Mind* (London, 1972).

Bennett, Tony, *Formalism and Marxism* (London, 1979).

Bloch, Bernard, 'Linguistic Structure and Linguistic Analysis', in *Report of the Fourth Annual Round Table Meeting on Linguistics and Language Study*, ed. Archibald A. Hill, Monograph Series on Languages and Linguistics, vol. iv (Washington, 1953), pp. 40–4. (This series is now better known as the papers of the *'Georgetown University Round Table'* and is usually catalogued thereunder.)

Bradbrook, F. W., *Jane Austen and her Predecessors* (Cambridge, 1966).

Burrows, J. F., *Jane Austen's 'Emma'* (Sydney, 1968).

——, *'Persuasion* and its "Sets of People"', *Sydney Studies in English*, ii (1976–7), 3–23.

——, '"A Measure of Excellence": Modes of Comparison in *Pride and Prejudice*', *Sydney Studies in English*, v (1979–80), 38–59.

——, '"Nothing out of the Ordinary Way": Differentiation of Character in the Twelve Most Common Words of *Northanger Abbey, Mansfield Park*, and *Emma*', *British Journal for Eighteenth-Century Studies*, vi (1983), 17–41.

Butler, Marilyn, *Jane Austen and the War of Ideas* (Oxford, 1975).

Chapman, R. W., 'Miss Austen's English', *Sense and Sensibility*, Oxford Illustrated Edition (London, 3rd edn., 1933), pp. 388–424.

Chatman, Seymour (ed.), *Literary Style: A Symposium* (London, 1971).

——, and Samuel R. Levin (eds.), *Essays on the Language of Literature* (Boston, 1967).

Cherry, Colin, *On Human Communication* (Cambridge, Mass., 1957).

Chomsky, Noam, *Lectures on Government and Binding* (Dordrecht, 1981).

Coleridge, S. T., *Biographia Literaria*, ed. J. Shawcross (2 vols., London, 1907).

——, *Coleridge's Shakespearean Criticism*, ed. T. M. Raysor (2 vols., London, 1930).

Craik, W. A., *Jane Austen: The Six Novels* (London, 1965).

Croxton, Frederick E. *et al.*, *Applied General Statistics* (London, 3rd edn., 1968).

Culler, Jonathan, *Structuralist Poetics* (London, 1975).

Derrida, Jacques, *Of Grammatology*, trans. G. C. Spivak (Baltimore, 1974).

——, *Writing and Difference*, trans. Alan Bass (London, 1978).

Dillon, G. L., *Language Processing and the Language of Literature* (Bloomington, Ind., 1978).

Doležel, L. and R. W. Bailey (eds.), *Statistics and Style* (New York, 1968).

Empson, William, *Some Versions of Pastoral* (London, 1935).

Fish, Stanley E., 'Literature in the Reader: Affective Stylistics', in *Reader-Response Criticism*, ed. Jane P. Tompkins (Baltimore, 1980), pp. 70–100.

Fisher, Ronald A., *The Design of Experiments* (London, 6th edn., 1951).

Fowler, Roger, *The Languages of Literature* (London, 1971).

Harris, Roy, 'The History Men', *Times Literary Supplement*, No. 4144, 3 Sept. 1982, 935–6.

Hoel, Paul G., *Elementary Statistics* (New York, 2nd edn., 1966).

——, *Introduction to Mathematical Statistics* (New York, 4th edn., 1971).

Hofland, Knut and Stig Johansson, *Word Frequencies in British and American English* (Bergen, 1982).

Howell, David C., *Statistical Methods for Psychology* (Boston, 1982).

Jakobson, Roman, *Selected Writings*, vol ii (The Hague, 1971).

Jefferson, Ann and David Robey, *Modern Literary Theory: A Comparative Introduction* (London, 1982).

Kenny, Anthony, *The Computation of Style: An Introduction to Statistics for Students of Literature and Humanities* (Oxford, 1982).

Kroeber, Karl, 'Perils of Quantification: The Exemplary Case of Jane Austen's *Emma*', in *Statistics and Style*, ed. L. Doležel and R. W. Bailey (New York, 1968).

——, *Styles in Fictional Structure: The Art of Jane Austen, Charlotte Brontë, and George Eliot* (Princeton, 1971).

Lacan, Jacques, *Écrits: A Selection*, trans. A. Sheridan (London, 1977).

Lascelles, Mary, *Jane Austen and Her Art* (London, 1939).

Lewes, G. H., 'The Novels of Jane Austen', *Blackwood's Magazine*, lxxxvi (1859), 99–113; reprinted in *Jane Austen: The Critical Heritage*, ed. B. C. Southam (London, 1968), pp. 148–66.

Lodge, David, *The Modes of Modern Writing: Metaphor, Metonymy, and the Typology of Modern Literature* (Ithaca, NY, 1977).

Milic, Louis T., *A Quantitative Approach to the Style of Jonathan Swift* (The Hague, 1967).

——, 'Stylistics + computers = pattern stylistics', *Perspectives in Computing*, iv (1981), 4–11.

Miller, George A., *Language and Communication* (New York, 1951).

Mudrick, Marvin, *Jane Austen: Irony as Defense and Discovery* (Princeton, 1952).

Page, Norman, *The Language of Jane Austen* (Oxford, 1972).

Phillipps, K. C., *Jane Austen's English* (London, 1970).

Riesman, David, *The Lonely Crowd: A Study of the Changing American Character* (New Haven, 1950).

Ruthrof, Horst, *The Reader's Construction of Narrative* (London, 1981).

Ryan, Thomas A. *et al.*, *MINITAB Student Handbook* (Boston, 1976).

Shannon, C. E. and W. W. Weaver, *The Mathematical Theory of Communication* (Chicago, 1949).

[Simpson, Richard], 'Jane Austen', *North British Review*, ns xii (1870), 129–52.

Southam, B. C. (ed.), *Jane Austen: The Critical Heritage* (London, 1968).

——, '*Sanditon*: The Seventh Novel', in *Jane Austen's Achievement*, ed. Juliet McMaster (London, 1976).

Tave, Stuart M., *Some Words of Jane Austen* (Chicago, 1973).

Thorndike, Edward L. and Irving Lorge, *The Teacher's Word Book of 30,000 Words* (New York, 1944).

Tillotson, Kathleen, 'The Tale and the Teller', in Geoffrey and Kathleen Tillotson, *Mid-Victorian Studies* (London, 1965).

Wardhaugh, Ronald, *Reading: A Linguistic Perspective* (New York, 1969).

Wilden, Anthony, *System and Structure: Essays in Communication and Exchange* (London, 1972).

Williams, C. B., 'A Note on the Statistical Analysis of Sentence-Length as a Criterion of Literary Style', *Biometrika*, xxxi (1940), 356–61.

Woelfel, Joseph and Edward L. Fink, *The Measurement of Communication Processes* (New York, 1980).

Yule, G. Udney, 'On Sentence-Length as a Statistical Characteristic of Style in Prose: with Application to Two Cases of Disputed Authorship', *Biometrika*, xxx (1939), 363.

——, *The Statistical Study of Literary Vocabulary* (London, 1944).

Zipf, George K., *Human Behavior and the Principle of Least Effort* (Cambridge, Mass., 1949).

INDEX

Capitalized headwords indicate major literary characters studied in the text. Bold headwords indicate major works or authors discussed. Bold figures indicate important discussion of the headword.